Starting with AutoCAD LT

Robert McFarlane MSc, BSc, ARCST, C.Eng, MIMech E, MIEE, MILog

Senior Lecturer, Department of Integrated Engineering, Motherwell College

Edward Arnold
A member of the Hodder Headline Group
LONDON   SYDNEY   AUCKLAND

To Linda and Stephen
Good luck with your courses

First published in Great Britain 1995 by
Edward Arnold, a division of Hodder Headline PLC,
338 Euston Road, London NW1 3BH

British Library Cataloguing in Publication Data
A catalogue record for this book is available from the British Library

ISBN 0 340 62543 0

1 2 3 4 5   95 96 97 98 99

Produced by Gray Publishing, Tunbridge Wells
Printed and bound in Great Britain by The Bath Press, Avon

Contents

Preface

As an AutoCAD user I was very interested to read about AutoCAD LT (LT is an abbreviation for 'lite') prior to its release, and wondered if it would be as good as the literature claimed. It is only as a result of writing this book that I managed to 'delve into' the package – it is a pleasant surprise to find what it can do.

Traditional AutoCAD users will be able to convert over to AutoCAD LT quite easily (once they have mastered the simple Windows concepts); new users will find it very user-friendly and will be producing drawings after only a few hours of tuition.

The objective of this book is to introduce AutoCAD LT to anyone who wants to produce drawings using a commercial CAD package. AutoDESK have proved over the years that they are the market leaders in CAD software, and with AutoCAD LT they have produced another winner.

This book will prove a valuable aid for students studying for the City and Guilds AutoCAD schemes, as well as BTEC and SCOTEC students who take the draughting options in their courses. It will also prove useful to undergraduates and post-graduates at higher institutions who required draughting skills.

Industrial CAD users will be able to use this book as a reference source, and it will also prove useful to new CAD draughtspersons who are using AutoCAD LT for the first time.

As with all my previous books on AutoCAD, the reader will learn by example, backed up by tutorials. All the material has been produced using AutoCAD LT for Windows, and I have checked all the work to ensure that there are no errors. If an error does occur, then I apologise to you and can assure you that it is completely unintentional.

I hope that you enjoy learning about AutoCAD LT; if you have any suggestions which would make the learning process more interesting I would be grateful for your comments.

1. What is AutoCAD LT?

AutoCAD LT is a low-cost, high-performance professional CAD draughting package from AutoDESK with the following features:

2D draughting capability

Based on the very successful AutoCAD Release 12 draughting package, the user has access to basic entity creation tools, extensive editing facilities, block referencing, automatic dimensioning and access to powerful drawing aids.

3D draughting capability

Extruded 3D drawings, 3D wire-frame models using the user co-ordinate system (UCS), isometric and perspective drawings are all available to the user.

Drawing management

Unlimited number of layers can be created.

Customisation

The user can add linetypes and hatch patterns as required, and the toolbar and toolbox can be customised to suit the user's individual requirements.

Full AutoCAD compatibility

AutoCAD LT and AutoCAD both use the file extension **.DWG** for their drawing files. This allows full compatibility between the two different CAD packages.

Window features

Pull-down menus, cascading menus, dialogue boxes make the package more user-friendly.

Object linking and embedding (OLE)

AutoCAD LT drawings can be incorporated into other Windows application packages. The benefit of this is that if the original drawing is altered, the drawing in the application package is also altered.

On-line help

The user has access to a very extensive help facility simply by pressing the F1 key.

Other features

- Repetitive tasks can be 'programmed'.
- An aerial view is available for very large drawings.
- Copy other Windows applications into AutoCAD LT.
- Last four drawings are named, allowing quick opening.
- Ability to reset automatic save to a named file.
- Short or full menu availability.
- Support for digitisers, printers, plotters, displays.

It is not my intention to cover all of the topics mentioned above, but I would hope that when the reader has worked through the book that they will have the ability and *confidence* to try the other options which are available.

2. System requirements and installation

To use AutoCAD LT, the following hardware and software requirements are essential.

Hardware

You will need the following:

- a 386 or 486 Pentium-based PC or compatible
- a maths co-processor
- a minimum of 4 MB RAM
- at least 8 MB of free hard disk space for all AutoCAD LT files
- a permanent swap file, two to four times the RAM size
- a Windows-supported VGA monitor (or better)
- a Windows-compatible pointing device, e.g. a mouse
- a Windows-compatible printer/plotter.

Software

You will need the following:

- MS-DOS 3.31 or later (5.0 is recommended)
- Windows 3.1 running in enhanced mode.

Installation

The installation of AutoCAD LT is entirely dependent on your institution's policy, but the steps which are given in the *User's Guide* are very straightforward and it is recommend that these steps are followed. When the package has been installed and the user 'runs the Windows program' AutoCAD LT will have its own dialogue box with the following icons displayed for selection:

- AutoCAD LT – the actual program.
- Readme.doc – a document file which should be read by all users as it gives additional information which is not in the manual.
- LT Tutor – a useful addition which allows the user to browse through some interesting topics.

The author's system

The system the author uses is as follows:

- Elonex PC-433 with 8 MB RAM at 33 MHz and 80 MB hard drive.
- Elonex two-button mouse.
- MS-DOS 5.0 and Windows 3.1.
- Calcomp Designmate A1 plotter for all drawings.

The *User's Guide*

I have always found that the manuals produced by AutoDESK for the AutoCAD packages rather cumbersome and very difficult to use and understand. This seems to have been over-turned with AutoCAD LT, as the *User's Guide* is simple to use and can be understood. Users should refer to the *Guide* for any assistance which is not fully explained in this book, although I would hope that this would not be necessary.

3. Using the book

This book is intended to teach the reader how to use AutoCAD LT to increase their draughting skills and hence their productivity. This will be achieved by a series of interactive exercises, i.e. the reader will learn by worked examples. These examples will be 'backed up' by tutorials thus allowing the reader to practice the skills which have been discussed and used in the worked examples. While it is not essential, it would be advantageous if the reader knew how to use:

- the mouse (or the pointing device to be used)
- Windows applications, i.e. how to open and close packages.

There are several simple concepts, when using the book, with which the reader should become familiar. These are:

1. Menu selection will be highlighted in bold type, e.g. **Draw Line**.
2. User keyboard entry will also be highlighted in bold type, e.g.
   (a) coordinate input **@50,50; 125,230; @120<30**
   (b) command entry **ZOOM; ERASE; ELEV**.
3. Icon selection will be displayed as a small drawing of the icon.
4. The AutoCAD LT prompts will be in typewriter face, e.g.
   (a) Start point of a line: `from point`
   (b) End point of a line: `to point`
   (c) Move object: `Base point`
5. The symbol **<R>** or **<RETURN>** will be used to signify pressing the return or enter key.

Saving drawings

All drawings must be saved. This is essential as the drawing may be required for future work in a later chapter, or else the reader may not have finished an exercise, and can return to it later. Drawings can be saved either:

- on a floppy disk (formatted of course)
- in a directory on the hard drive.

It is the user's preference as to which method is used, but it will be assumed that a floppy disk is used. This means that when a drawing is being saved or opened, the symbol **A:** will be used, for example

- save drawing as **A:WORKDRG**
- open drawing **A:EXERC_1**

If a directory is to be used to save drawings this can be made within the AutoCAD LT directory, or simply on the C: drive. The directory name should be as simple as possible, e.g. **BOBLT**. The procedure for saving and opening from a directory is the same as from a floppy with the exception that the *directory* and the *drawing name* must be given, e.g. **BOBLT/WORKDRG**. Using Windows interface makes the directory method relatively simple.

All AutoCAD LT drawings have the extension **.DWG**.

4. The graphics screen and some terminology

Starting AutoCAD LT

AutoCAD LT is started from Windows with a *double click* on the AutoCAD LT icon using the left-button on the mouse – double left click. This opens the graphics screen which is divided into four distinct areas (see Fig. 4.1) as follows:

1. The toolbar.
2. The menubar.
3. The command prompt area.
4. The drawing area.

There is a fifth area (the toolbox) which will also be discussed later.

Let us now consider each of the areas above in turn.

1. Toolbar

The toolbar gives the user a large amount of information about layers, drawing aids, co-ordinates and also allows certain icons to be selected. Figure 4.2 gives a more detailed breakdown of the toolbar. The toolbar can be 'switched off', which will be discussed later, although I would recommend that it is always kept on.

Note that the actual display of the toolbar depends on the resolution of your monitor, and some users may have a toolbar which has more icons than I have shown. The toolbar display does not matter, as all items are available for selection in the menu items.

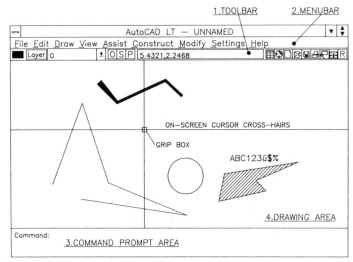

Fig. 4.1. The AutoCAD LT graphics screen.

2. Menu bar

The menu bar allows the user access to the following options:

File **Edit** **Draw** **View** **Assist** **Construct** **Modify** **Settings** **Help**

Moving the mouse into the menu bar area will result in the on-screen cursor being replaced by the **pick arrow**. By left-clicking on one of the named options, a pull-down menu will be obtained. Figure 4.3. gives the complete pull-down menu selection for the short menu option.

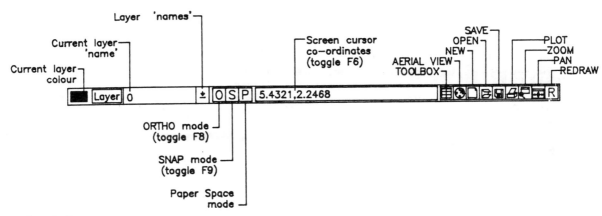

Fig. 4.2. Toolbar icon descriptions.

Notes

1. AutoCAD LT has two pull-down menu options:
   (a) short menu as detailed in Fig. 4.3
   (b) full menu which is the short menu with additions for 3D items, further drawing options and additional editing features.
   The user can 'toggle' between the short and full menus using the option from the menu bar.
2. The pull-down menus can be activated using the keyboard and the letter which is underlined, e.g. the Draw menu is activated with **ALT** and **D**. This is true for the other menu bar options.

3. Command prompt area

This is where the user 'communicates' with AutoCAD LT to enter:

(a) a command, e.g. LINE, ERASE, ZOOM, etc.
(b) co-ordinate data, e.g. 120,100; @50<30.
(c) other values, e.g. a radius of 50.

The command prompt area is also used by AutoCAD LT to give information to the user, and this could be:

(a) a prompt, e.g. enter the circle radius
(b) a message, e.g. entities do not intersect
(c) the command which has been selected, e.g. LINE.

4. Drawing area

This is the user's sheet of paper and is where the drawing is completed. It is normal to have the origin at the bottom left-hand corner of the drawing area and the co-ordinates are (0,0).

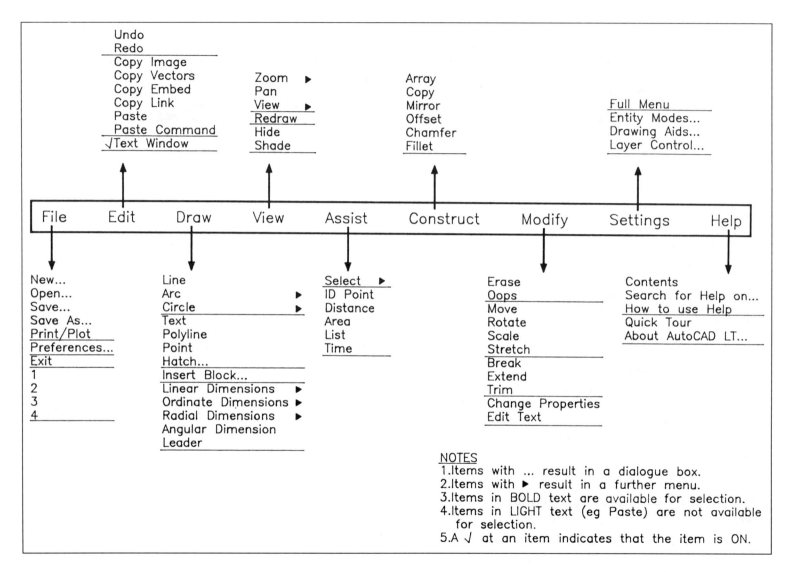

Fig. 4.3. Menu bar pull-down menus (short version).

The toolbox

The toolbox can be considered as being a fifth part of the graphics screen which allows the user access to a variety of options in icon form.

This toolbox can be 'toggled on/off' by different methods as follows:

(a) by selecting from the menu bar **File**

                         Preferences...

                         pick toolbox 'box' (X)

                         OK

(b) by picking the toolbox icon from the toolbar

The actual position of the toolbox on the graphics screen can vary, as is shown in Fig. 4.4, and this is obtained by picking the icon as follows:

(a) first pick of icon gives position 1
(b) second pick of icon gives position 2 – which can be moved to any part of the graphics screen
(c) third pick gives position 3
(d) fourth pick cancels the toolbox

I prefer to have the toolbox 'on' and in position 1, i.e. at the right hand of the graphics screen. I also prefer to activate the toolbox from the toolbar – first pick of the icon.

The toolbox icons are fully described in Fig. 4.5.

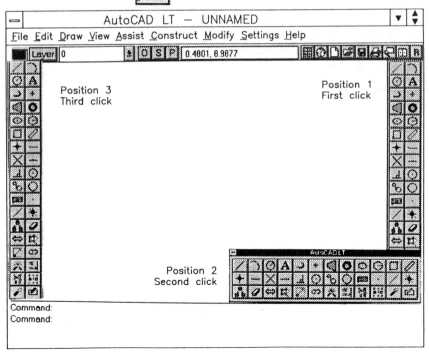

Fig. 4.4. Toolbox positions.

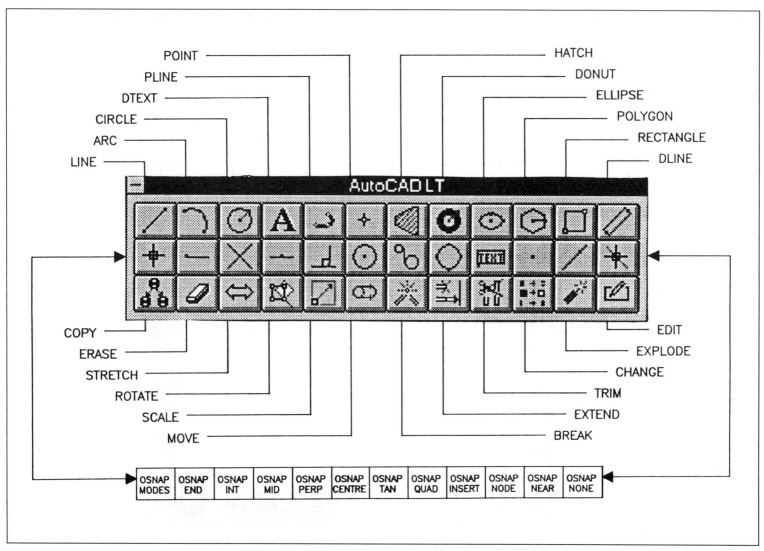

Fig. 4.5. Toolbox icons.

When the toolbox is in position 2, it can be moved to any place on the graphics screen using the following procedure:

1. Position toolbox in position 2.
2. Left-click on the blue toolbox name and *hold down* the left button.
3. Move to new position and lift your finger off the mouse button.

I prefer not use this option, as it can 'clutter-up' the drawing area.

Note

To become proficient at using AutoCAD LT it is essential that the user becomes familiar with both the pull-down menus from the menu bar and the icons in the toolbox. This can only be achieved through practice, and it is recommended that Figs 4.2, 4.3 and Fig. 4.5 are referred to constantly until their use becomes second nature.

Terminology

AutoCAD LT has its own terminology which may be confusing to new users. A brief description of some of the more commonly used words and phrases is given below.

Menu

A menu is a list of items from which the user selects the item required for a specific function. AutoCAD LT has different 'types' of menus: pull-down, pop-up, cascade, icon, for instance.

Command

A command is the name given to an AutoCAD LT function and can be activated by:

(a) selecting the command from a menu
(b) entering the command at the prompt line, e.g. LINE, ERASE, etc.
(c) entering the abbreviation for the command at the command line, e.g. L for LINE, E for ERASE, CP for COPY, etc.
(d) using ALT with E, D, M, etc., to activate the pull-down menu, then using the command letter underlined, for example:

ALT+D then L for the LINE command
ALT+M then M for the MOVE command

Options (b) and (c) require the user to know all the command names and abbreviations, while option (c) is really for users with no mouse (which is unusual).

Generally, commands are activated from the menus, and this will be the main selection method, although other methods will be used throughout the book.

Entities

Everything drawn in AutoCAD LT is called an **ENTITY**, e.g. lines, circles, text, hatching, blocks, etc. Entities are also referred to as 'objects', especially when using the construct and modify options, e.g. the prompt `Select objects` will be encountered, and this simply means that the user selects (or **picks**) entities that have been drawn on the screen.

Default settings

AutoCAD LT has certain values and settings which have been 'pre-set' by AutoDESK. These are essential for certain operations (such as dimensioning) and are called the 'default settings'. Defaults are shown at the prompt line inside special < > brackets.

Defaults can be altered by the user at any time; consider the following two examples:

enter	**LTSCALE\<R\>** at the command line
prompt	New scale factor <1.0000>
enter	**0.5\<R\>**
enter	**LTSCALE\<R\>**
prompt	New scale factor <0.5000>
enter	**\<RETURN\>**

The default value for LTSCALE was <1.0000> and we altered it to 0.5

enter	**CIRCLE\<R\>** at the command line
prompt	3P/TTR/<Center point>
enter	**CTRL+C**, i.e. hold down the CTRL key and press the C key.

The default for circles is set to the centre point (watch out for the American spelling!).

Cascade menu

Cascade menus are obtained from the menu bar when items that have a '>' after their name are selected. For example selecting from the menu bar:

(a) **Draw** then **Line**, will immediately activate the **LINE** command
(b) **Draw** then **Circle**, will give the cascade effect as shown in Fig. 4.6.

Cascade menus can be 'cancelled' by moving the pick arrow to a 'clear' part of the screen and left-clicking.

Icon

Is a menu selection item in the form of a picture. The toolbar and the toolbox have several icon menu items. Icons are also used to display hatch patterns and text fonts to the user.

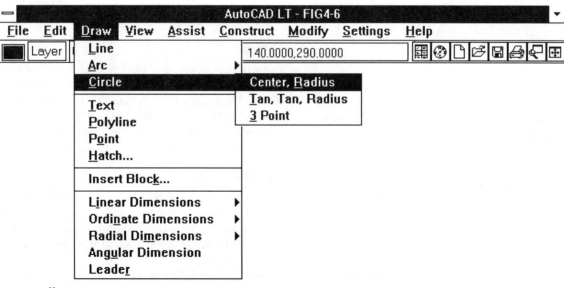

Fig. 4.6. Cascade menu effect.

Dialogue boxes

Dialogue boxes (often referred to as pop-up menus) are used extensively in AutoCAD LT, and the user should become confident in their use. By selecting from the menu bar:

Settings
Drawing Aids...

the drawing aids dialogue box (Fig. 4.7) will appear on the screen. This is a very useful dialogue box, as it allows the user to control the grid, snap and ortho modes (more on these in a later chapter) as well as other aids, such as BLIPS. In this type of dialogue box, the user 'activates' the required aid by 'clicking' a box as follows:

(a)   an X in a box means that the aid is *on*.
(b)   a blank box means that the aid is *not on:* it is off.

The **X-click-ON** concept is common in many of the dialogue boxes. Note the OK, Cancel and Help boxes at the bottom of the dialogue box. These are used as follows:

OK   accepts the values set in the dialogue box
Cancel cancels the dialogue box, without altering the 'set' values.
Help   gives information about the dialogue box being used, usually in the form of another dialogue box. This is cancelled by selecting **File-Exit**.

CTRL+C

Sometimes an AutoCAD user will become 'lost' when trying some command, and they may not be able to exit that command. If this ever happens then the **CTRL+C** effect should work. As described above, CTRL+C means hold down the CTRL key and press the C key. I have never known this method to fail.

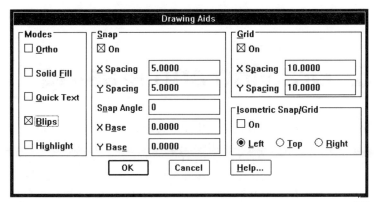

Fig. 4.7. Drawing aids dialogue box. This indicates that the aid is *on* ☒ and this indicates that the aid is *off* ☐. This dialogue box indicates that the GRID is on with spacings of 10, the SNAP is on with spacings of 5 and that BLIPS are on. All other aids are off.

Drawing files

AutoCAD LT refers to all drawings as files, and they are given the three letter extension **.DWG**. When a drawing is to be saved, the user enters the drawing name, but not the extension letters: AutoCAD LT adds these automatically. When naming a drawing a maximum of eight characters is allowed, but certain characters are not permitted, the two most common being the full stop (.) and a space. Drawing names should be kept as short as possible, and all users should keep a record of their drawings with a brief description of each. This saves a great deal of wasted time trying to find a drawing whose name has been forgotten. Typical drawing file names could be:

DRG_1	acceptable
DRG.1	unacceptable
DRG 1	unacceptable
DRAWING1	acceptable
DRAWING_1	unacceptable.

5. Drawing and erasing

In this chapter we will investigate how to draw some lines on the screen, and how these lines can be erased. The chapter will also introduce the reader to **BLIPS** and the **SELECTION SET**, which is a powerful aid when editing existing entities. An exercise will be given as a sequence of steps which the user can execute, and new topics will be described as they occur. We will also use different methods to activate the commands. Some readers might find this chapter rather laborious, but it forms the basis of all future work in AutoCAD LT.

Drawing

1. Open AutoCAD LT with a double left-click on the icon.
2. Pick the toolbox icon from the toolbar, and position the toolbox at the right-hand of the screen.
3. Activate the LINE icon from the toolbox and observe the command line.

    The prompt is: LINE From point. You now have to pick a **start** point for the line to be drawn, so move the mouse and pick (left-click) any point on the screen. Four things should happen:

    (a) the grip box on the cursor disappears
    (b) a small cross (BLIP) will appear at the start point of the line (if it does not don't panic)
    (c) as you move the mouse away from the start point a line is **dragged** from the start point to the cursor position. This drag effect is called the **RUBBERBAND**
    (d) the prompt is To point.

4. Move the mouse to another point on the screen and pick (left-click) an **endpoint** for the line.
5. You are still in the **LINE** command with the rubberband effect, and still being asked for the endpoint of the line.
6. Continue moving the mouse and picking points on the screen to give a series on 'joined lines'.
7. Finish the **LINE** command with a right-click after you have drawn several lines, and the prompt will return: Command:. The cursor now has the grip box back.
8. At the command line enter **LINE<R>** and you will again have the From point prompt. Now draw some more lines then right-click.
9. Use the line icon/direct entry methods and draw a series of lines on the screen, to give an effect similar to Fig. 5.1(a).

BLIPS

BLIPS are small crosses used by AutoCAD LT to identify the start and end points of lines, circle centres and so on. They are not entities, but aids, and will not be plotted on the final drawing. They can be 'turned off' by

(a) selecting from the menu bar **View** and **Redraw**
(b) entering **REDRAW<R>** at the command line
(c) picking the Redraw icon
(d) selecting from the menu bar **Settings**
    Drawing Aids...
    Blips box no cross, i.e. OFF
    OK

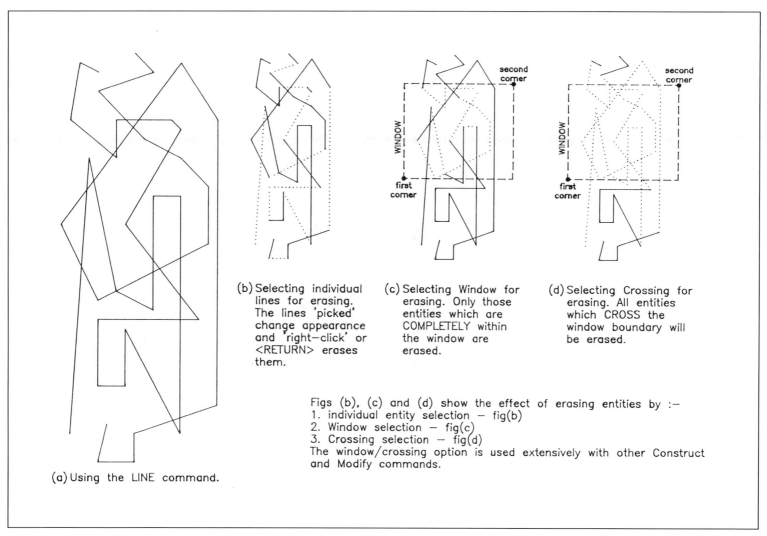

(a) Using the LINE command.

(b) Selecting individual lines for erasing. The lines 'picked' change appearance and 'right-click' or <RETURN> erases them.

(c) Selecting Window for erasing. Only those entities which are COMPLETELY within the window are erased.

(d) Selecting Crossing for erasing. All entities which CROSS the window boundary will be erased.

Figs (b), (c) and (d) show the effect of erasing entities by :—
1. individual entity selection — fig(b)
2. Window selection — fig(c)
3. Crossing selection — fig(d)
The window/crossing option is used extensively with other Construct and Modify commands.

Fig. 5.1. Drawing and erasing entities.

I find that BLIPS are a nuisance in drawings and always have them turned off – option (d). Options (a)–(c) are perfectly valid but have to be used regularly when new entities are drawn on the screen. The user must decide for themselves whether to turn the BLIPS off completely, or use the redraw option.

Erasing

Now that we have drawn some lines on the screen, we will investigate how they can be erased (seems daft!). The erase command is used extensively in AutoCAD LT and we will use it to demonstrate different options which are available to us. The actual command can be activated by different methods

(a) by picking the Erase icon from the toolbox
(b) by entering **ERASE<R>** at the command line
(c) from the menu bar with **Modify**
    Erase

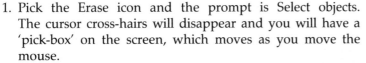

1. Pick the Erase icon and the prompt is Select objects. The cursor cross-hairs will disappear and you will have a 'pick-box' on the screen, which moves as you move the mouse.
2. Position the pick-box over one of the lines and left-click. The selected line will change appearance and the prompt is

```
Select objects: 1 found
Select objects
```

3. Continue moving the pick-box and pick other lines (about 8–10). Each line that is picked will change appearance.
4. When you have picked enough lines right-click or press **<RETURN>**.
5. The selected lines will be erased and the Command prompt is returned – Fig. 5.1(b).

OOPS

Suppose you had erased the wrong set of lines. Before you do anything else, select from the menu bar **Modify**
    Oops

The erased lines will be returned to the screen. Consider this in relation to a traditional draughtsperson who has rubbed out the lines. They would have to be redrawn.

Note that OOPS can be entered directly at the command line to give the same effect. It only works if it is used immediately after the erase command (or any other editing type command) was used.

Erasing – window and crossing

Individual selection of entities for erasing is satisfactory if only a few lines have to be removed. When a large number of entities require to be edited, the individual selection method is very tedious, and AutoCAD LT overcomes this by allowing the user to position a 'window' over an area of the screen which will allow several entities to be selected at 'one pick'.

We will demonstrate using the window effect with the erase command, so make sure that you have drawn about 20 lines on the screen then

1. From the menu bar select **Modify**
                    Erase

prompt	Select objects
enter	**w<R>** – for window
prompt	First corner
respond	**position cursor at any point and left-click**
prompt	Other corner
respond	**move cursor to drag out a window (rectangle) and left-click**

prompt	??? found and certain lines will be 'highlighted'
and	Select objects
enter	<RETURN>

The highlighted lines will be erased, see Fig. 5.1(c).

2. Enter **OOPS<R>** at the command line and the erased lines will be redrawn. Now enter **ERASE<R>** at the command line

prompt	Select objects
enter	**c<R>** for crossing
prompt	First corner
respond	**pick a point as before**
prompt	Other corner
respond	**drag out a window and pick the other point**
prompt	??? found and highlighted lines
and	Select objects
respond	**right-click**

The highlighted entities will be erased, see Fig. 5.1(d).

The window/crossing concept of selecting a large number of entities will be used frequently with editing type commands e.g. erase, copy, move, etc. The entities selected depend on the option used

window – all **COMPLETE** entities within the window are selected

crossing – all entities which **CROSS THE WINDOW BOUNDARY** are selected.

The window/crossing effect has been demonstrated in Figs 5.1(c) and (d).

Selection set

Window and Crossing are two options contained within the selection set of editing options. The complete selection set can be obtained from the menu bar with **Assist-Select** which gives the cascade menu as shown in Fig. 5.2.

At this stage we are not going to investigate all of the selection set options, but several are worth consideration.

1. Erase all of the lines on the screen and refer to Fig. 5.3(a). Draw a series of lines in a similar pattern to those shown, the actual layout and lengths of lines being of no real importance.

2. From the menu bar select **Modify**
Erase

prompt	Select objects
respond	from the menu bar select **Assist** **Select** **Last**
prompt	1 found (and last line drawn will be highlighted)
enter	**<RETURN>** to erase this line.

3. Now enter **OOPS<R>**.

4. Refer to Fig. 5.3(b) and enter **ERASE<R>** at the command line

prompt	Select objects
respond	select **Assist** **Select** **Fence**
prompt	First fence point
respond	**pick a point on screen** (point 1)
prompt	Undo/<Endpoint of line>
respond	**pick a suitable point** (point 2)
prompt	Undo/<Endpoint of line>
respond	**pick points 3,4,5 then<R>**

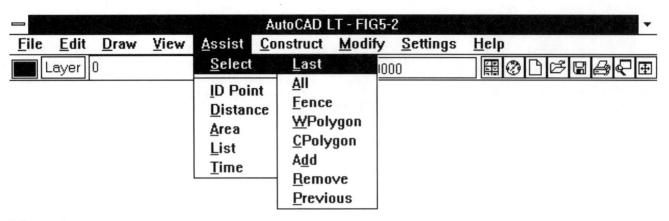

Fig. 5.2. Pull-down select options.

prompt	`??? found and certain lines will` `be highlighted`
and	Select objects
respond	**right click** and highlighted lines will be erased.

5. OOPS again, refer to Fig. 5.3(c) and select the **ERASE** icon then **Assist-Select-WPolygon**

prompt	`First polygon point`
respond	**pick point 1**
prompt	`Undo/<Endpoint of line>`
respond	**pick points 2,3,4,5 then <R>**
prompt	`??? found and highlighted lines`
and	Select objects
respond	**<RETURN>** and highlighted entities will be erased.

6. OOPS once more, use ERASE with the CPolygon option and repeat the procedure in step 5, picking points similar as before which will give the effect as Fig. 5.3(d).

The Fence/WPolygon/CPolygon options are very useful when the 'shape' to be edited does not permit the use of the normal rectangular window. WPolygon and CPolygon allow the user to 'make their own shape' for editing.

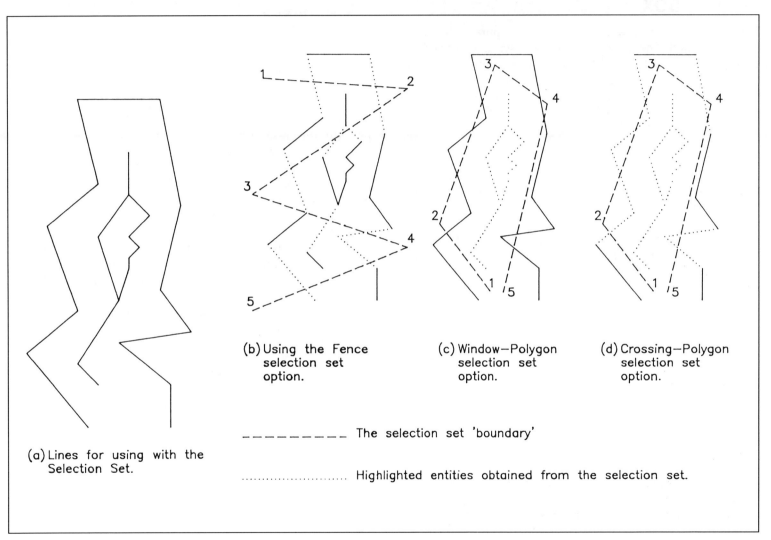

(a) Lines for using with the Selection Set.

(b) Using the Fence selection set option.

(c) Window—Polygon selection set option.

(d) Crossing—Polygon selection set option.

— — — — — — — — The selection set 'boundary'

.... Highlighted entities obtained from the selection set.

Fig. 5.3. Drawing and erasing entities.

The PICKBOX

When we used the ERASE command, the phrase PICKBOX was mentioned. The pickbox allows the user to select entities, and will be encountered with other editing commands. It may be that when you used the erase command, the 'size' of the pickbox was 'too big' and it proved difficult to select individual entities. The size of the pickbox can be altered by entering at the command line **PICKBOX<R>**

```
prompt      New value of PICKBOX<?>
enter       3<R>
```

The command prompt will be returned, and the size of the pickbox will be a 3 mm square. Figure 5.4. shows three different pickbox sizes.

The pickbox size can also be altered using the Selection Set option from the Full Menu using the Settings option from the menu bar. It is the user's preference as to the pickbox size, but I personally prefer to set it to 3.

Fig. 5.4. PICKBOX sizes.

❑ *Summary*

1. The line command can be activated from:
   (a) menu bar with **Draw-Line**
   (b) the line icon
   (c) entering **LINE<R>** at the command line.
2. The erase command can be activated from:
   (a) menu bar with **Modify-Erase**
   (b) the erase icon
   (c) entering **ERASE<R>** at the command line.
3. The erase command has a selection set which allows the user access to fence, window, crossing, wpolygon, cpolygon, etc.
4. Window includes all entities completely within the window.
5. Crossing includes all entities which cross the window boundary and are also completely within the window.
6. The selection set options are available with all editing type commands.
7. **OOPS** is a useful command which restores the last editing command.
8. **BLIPS** are aids to the user which can be turned off.
9. **REDRAW** is a command which will 'refresh' the screen and remove any **BLIPS** and 'ghost images' which are on the screen.
10. The pickbox size can be altered by the user.

Activity

Spend some time using the LINE and ERASE commands, and become proficient with the various selection set options for erasing. It is in your own interest to be able to use these options, as they will be used extensively in later chapters.

6. Limits and drawing aids

In this chapter we will investigate how to set drawing limits as well as how drawing aids can be set to assist the user. Hopefully you are still in AutoCAD LT, but if you are not, then start it as described before using the double click on the icon from your windows menu.

Limits

Erase all entities (easy by now!) and move the mouse from the lower left-hand corner of the screen to the upper right-hand corner. As you do this observe the screen co-ordinates displayed in the toolbar. They should change from 0,0 (lower left) to about 15,8 (upper right), but if you have different values from these don't worry. This is quite a small drawing area, so we will 'reset the drawing limits' using the following method. At the command line

enter	**LIMITS\<R>**
prompt	ON/OFF/\<Lower left corner> <0.0000,0.0000>
enter	**0,0\<R>**
prompt	Upper right corner<12.0000, 9.0000> or similar
enter	**420,297\<R>**
prompt	Command line
enter	**ZOOM\<R>**
prompt	All/Center/Extents.........
enter	**A\<R>**

Now move the mouse from the lower left to the upper right and observe the co-ordinates displayed in the toolbar. They should change from 0,0 to about 510,290. What we have achieved is to set an A3 sized sheet of paper. Your screen setting may already be set for A3, but it will do you no harm to follow the sequence described. We will investigate other methods of setting drawing limits in a later chapter.

Drawing aids

AutoCAD LT has three useful drawing aids which will be used continuously when drawing. These aids are

Grid	allows the user to put a series of imaginary dots over the drawing area. The grid spacing can be altered by the user at any time while a drawing is being created and as the grid is imaginary, it does not appear on the final plot.
Snap	allows the user to set the on-screen cursor to a pre-determined point on the screen, this usually being one of the grid points. The snap spacing can also be altered by the user.
Ortho	when this aid is used, only horizontal and vertical movement is permissible.

The grid and snap spacing can be set by two methods

1. Using the Drawing Aids dialogue box from the Settings option in the menu bar.
2. Using direct keyboard entry.

The keyboard entry method will be demonstrated for setting the grid and snap spacing, and then the user can investigate the dialogue box method for themselves — it is quite simple to use. I also find that the direct entry method is faster.

Grid spacing

At the command line

enter	**GRID<R>**
prompt	Grid spacing (X) or ON/OFF/Snap/Aspect<?>
enter	**10<R>**

A series of dots will appear on the screen, these dots being 10 mm apart and covering the 420×297 area set earlier.

Snap spacing

At the command line:

enter	**SNAP<R>**
prompt	Snap spacing or On/Off/Aspect/Rotate/Style<?>
enter	**5<R>**

Now move the cursor and you will find that it 'snaps' to:

(a) a grid point
(b) a point midway between two grid points

Grid/Snap/Ortho – ON/OFF

The three drawing aids can be turned on/off by different methods:

1. Using the drawing aids dialogue box with an X in the required box for the aid to be on. If the box is blank, the aid is off.
2. Using the toolbar by picking the O and S icons and:
   (a) icon white – aid is on
   (b) icon grey – aid is off.

3. Using the function keys to 'toggle' the aid:
$$F7 - \text{grid on/off}$$
$$F8 - \text{ortho on/off}$$
$$F9 - \text{snap on/off}$$
The first press of the function key puts the aid on, the second press puts the aid off.

Note

1. My preference when using aids is
   (a) GRID and SNAP from the keyboard and enter required values.
   (b) use the function keys to toggle aid on/off.
2. Take care with the ortho aid. As it only permits horizontal and vertical 'movement', the user can become confused when a command does not give the expected result. I tend to work with ortho off.

Activity

You are now going to try a drawing for yourself. Erase any entities from the screen and refer to the drawing in Tutorial 1. With a grid spacing of 10 and a snap spacing of 5 produce a layout similar to that shown. The actual size of each part of the drawing does not matter, the object of the exercise being to give you some time to practice with the drawing aids.

When you have completed the drawing **proceed to Chapter 7**.

❏ *Summary*

1. Drawing limits are set with the **LIMITS** command.
2. The drawing aids – grid, snap, ortho – can be set from the Drawing Aids dialogue box or from the keyboard.
3. The aids can be toggled on/off:
   (a) using the toolbar icons
   (b) using the function keys.

7. Saving, exiting, loading

It is essential that all users know how to save and open a drawing and how to exit AutoCAD LT. In my experience, in both colleges and industry, these functions cause new users to CAD draughting a great deal of concern, and it is my intention in this chapter to explain how they can be achieved without worry.

Make sure that you have a formatted floppy disk in the A: drive of your computer.

Leaving AutoCAD LT

In the previous chapter we created our first simple drawing, and we now want to leave AutoCAD LT, so from the menu bar select **File**
     Exit

In response to this selection, AutoCAD LT displays the Message dialogue box as shown in Fig. 7.1. This dialogue box will be encountered frequently, and it is important that the user understands the replies that are possible

  (a) Yes – if this option is clicked then the current drawing will be saved, but this may affect the drawing name.
  (b) No – clicking on this option will allow you to leave AutoCAD LT, but the current drawing will not be saved, and several hours work may be lost.
  (c) Cancel – returns to the drawing screen.
At this instant **click on cancel**.

Saving a drawing

All drawings should be saved before exiting AutoCAD LT

This statement is very important and all CAD users should be aware of it, and practice what it says.

At this stage we have not saved the tutorial drawing, so from the menu bar select **File**
     Save As...

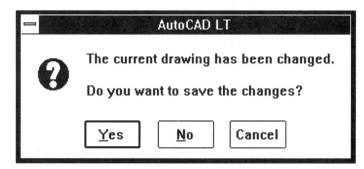

Fig. 7.1. The message dialogue box.

AutoCAD LT will display the Save Drawing As dialogue box (Fig. 7.2) which has the following important 'areas':

1. the file name to be saved box
2. the previously saved file name column
3. the directories – current and available
4. the drives
5. the file types available
6. the Type It box.

There are different methods of saving a drawing available to us, but for the present we will only consider one – the Type It option, so from the dialogue box:

respond   **pick the Type It box**
prompt   `dialogue box disappears`

and   Save current drawing as <?>
enter   **A:TUT-1<R>**
prompt   `Current drawing name set to A:TUT-1`
and   Command prompt returned.

Note: if you are using a directory instead of a floppy, you should enter the directory name before the drawing name, e.g. **C:\BOBLT\TUT-1**.

Now select from the menu bar **File-Exit** and you should leave AutoCAD LT and be returned to your Windows screen menu. Now take a break before proceeding.

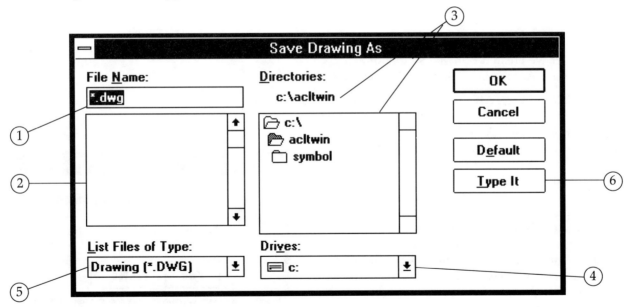

Fig. 7.2. Save As dialogue box.

Loading a drawing

To load a previously saved drawing into AutoCAD LT it is necessary to 'Open a drawing file', so

1. Load AutoCAD LT from Windows.
2. Ensure floppy in drive A: and from the menu bar select

> **File**
> **Open...**

3. AutoCAD LT displays the Open Drawing dialogue box which is identical in appearance and layout to the Save Drawing dialogue box we have discussed.
4. Pick the Type it box.
5. The prompt is   `Enter name of drawing`
   enter   **A:TUT-1<R>**   (**C:\BOBLT\TUT-1**   for
                  directory use).
6. The dialogue box will disappear and you drawing of Tutorial 1 will be displayed on the screen. You can now edit this drawing as required.

The yes/no message options

If you do edit your TUT-1 drawing and then select **File-Exit** from the menu bar, you will again be faced with the Message Dialogue box, but his time if you pick

(a) Yes – the edited drawing will be saved with the name A:TUT-1 and the original drawing of TUT-1 will be 'overwritten'.

(b) No – the edited drawing will not be saved and the original TUT-1 will still be 'available'.

❏ *Summary*

1. The proper procedure for exiting is
   (a) Complete the drawing
   (b) Save the drawing
   (c) Exit AutoCAD LT.
2. The save procedure is
   (a) select File-Save As...
   (b) pick Type It
   (c) enter drawing name A:********.
3. To open a drawing
   (a) select File-Open...
   (b) pick Type It
   (c) enter drawing name A:********.
4. Other save/open methods will be discussed later.

8. Standard sheet 1

Traditionally the first thing that a draughtsperson does when starting a new drawing is to get the correct size sheet of drawing paper. This paper will probably have borders, company logo and other details already printed on it. The drawing is then completed to fit around the pre-printed material. CAD draughting is no different from this, with the exception that the user does not 'get a sheet of paper'. Companies who use AutoCAD LT will want their drawings to conform to their standards in terms of name box, text size, linetypes, etc. Parameters which govern these factors can be set every time a drawing is started, but this is tedious and time wasting and is against CAD philosophy. It is desirable to have all standard requirements set automatically, and this is achieved by making a drawing called a **standard sheet** or **prototype drawing** (you may have other names for this). Standard sheets can be made to suit all sizes of paper, e.g. A3, A2, A1, A0 and any other size required, and will contain the company/individual draughting settings. This means that it is the standard sheet which is used for all drawings i.e. it is now equivalent to the 'sheet of paper'.

We will make a standard sheet based on A3 paper (all work in the book is for A3 drawings), save it, and use it for all future work. At this stage, the standard sheet will not have many 'settings', but we will continue to refine and add to it as we progress through the book.

The procedure will introduce the user to some new dialogue boxes, and is as follows:

1. Load AutoCAD LT or clear the screen of all entities.
2. Set the Full Menu from the menu bar with **Settings**
   Full Menu

3. Pick the toolbox icon, and position the toolbox at the right side of the screen.

4. Set drawing limits by selecting **Settings**
   Drawing
   Limits

prompt	Reset Model space limits ON/OFF/<Lower left corner><???>
enter	**0,0<R>**
prompt	Upper right corner<???>
enter	**420,297<R>**, i.e. A3 size paper

5. From the menu bar select **View**
   Zoom
   All

6. Using the Drawing Aids dialogue box, set the following:
   Blips: off
   Ortho: off
   Snap: 5 and on
   Grid: 10 and on

7. At the command line enter **PICKBOX** and set to **3**.

8. From the menu bar select **File**
    Preferences...

The Preferences dialogue box will be displayed, which allows us to set some useful features (Fig. 8.1)
(a) Settings – toolbar and toolbox on, i.e. cross.
(b) Measurement – pick the arrow and set to **Metric**.
(c) Automatic save – very useful as it allows you to set a time for an automatic update of the drawing being created. This means that if you have a 'disaster' you will only have lost about 15 minutes work. You can reset the figure, but 15 minutes is reasonable.

(d) Save file name – allows the user to set the drawing file name for the automatic save. It must have the extension .SV$. I usually leave it as it is.
(e) Pick OK when you are satisfied with the settings.

9. From the menu bar select **Settings**
    Units Style...

which will display the Units Control dialogue box (Fig. 8.2). Set the unit styles for
(a) Decimal to 0.00 precision, i.e. 2 decimal places.
(b) Decimal angles to 0 precision, i.e. 0 decimal places.
(c) Pick OK.

Fig. 8.1. Preferences dialogue box..

Fig. 8.2. Units control dialogue box.

10. At the command line enter **GRIPS\<R>**

prompt	New value for GRIPS\<1>
enter	**0\<R>**
Now enter	**PICKFIRST\<R>**
prompt	New value for PICKFIRST\<1>
enter	**0\<R>**

Nothing seems to have happened, but the box which was attached to the screen cross-hairs has disappeared. What we have done is to 'disable the grips', but at present you will be unaware of what this is all about. Grips will be considered on their own in a later chapter.

11. Now enter **LINE\<R>**

prompt	From point and enter **0,0\<R>**
prompt	To point and enter **380,0\<R>**
prompt	To point and enter **380,270\<R>**
prompt	To point and enter **0,270\<R>**
prompt	To point and enter **0,0\<R>**
prompt	To point and enter **\<RETURN>**

This gives a 'drawing border' on an A3 sheet of paper and all drawings will be created within this border. The border is not drawn to the 'limits' due to plotting considerations.

12. Now select from the menu bar **File**

  Save As...
  Type It

prompt	Save current changes as
enter	**A:STDA3\<R>**
prompt	Current drawing name set to A:STDA3.

We have now set a standard A3 sheet of paper with units, grid, snap, etc. set to our own values. This standard sheet will now be used for all future drawing work, although it will be modified as we progress through the book.

Exit AutoCAD LT before proceeding to the next chapter.

9. Lines and co-ordinate input

The lines created in Chapter 6 were drawn at random with no attempt being made to specify exact lengths. To draw lines (and any other entity) accurately, co-ordinate input is used and there are three 'types' available:

1. Absolute input.
2. Relative (incremental) input.
3. Polar (incremental) input.

In this chapter we will use our standard sheet and create several squares using the different co-ordinate input methods which are available, as well as some other interesting line creation methods. To start the exercise

1. Load AutoCAD LT.
2. From the menu bar select **File**
                              Open...

which will display the Open Drawing dialogue box. Using the mouse pick **Type It** and

prompt   Enter name of drawing
enter   **A:STDA3<R>**

This will load our previously created standard sheet.
3. Now refer to Fig. 9.1.

Absolute co-ordinate input

This takes co-ordinates from an origin. The origin has co-ordinates of (0,0) and is positioned at the lower left-hand corner of the screen. The origin point can be moved by the user, but this will be investigated in a later chapter. The normal X–Y axis system is used to specify points, i.e.

(a) positive X to the right, positive Y upwards
(b) negative X to the left, negative Y downwards.

From the menu bar select **Draw-Line** and in response to each prompt, enter the following X–Y co-ordinate pairs, pressing **<RETURN>** after each entry

From point	20,30	the line start point
To point	70,30	
To point	70,80	
To point	20,80	
To point	20,30	to complete the square
To point	**<RETURN>**	to end the line sequence

Relative co-ordinate input

This option takes co-ordinates from the **LAST POINT** entered, and uses the @ symbol. Enter **LINE<R>** at the command prompt and then the following X–Y co-ordinate pairs in response to the prompts (remember **<RETURN>**)

From point	**105,35**	the line start point
To point	**@50,0**	
To point	**@0,50**	
To point	**@–50,0**	
To point	**@0,–50**	to complete the square
To point	**right click**	to end the line sequence

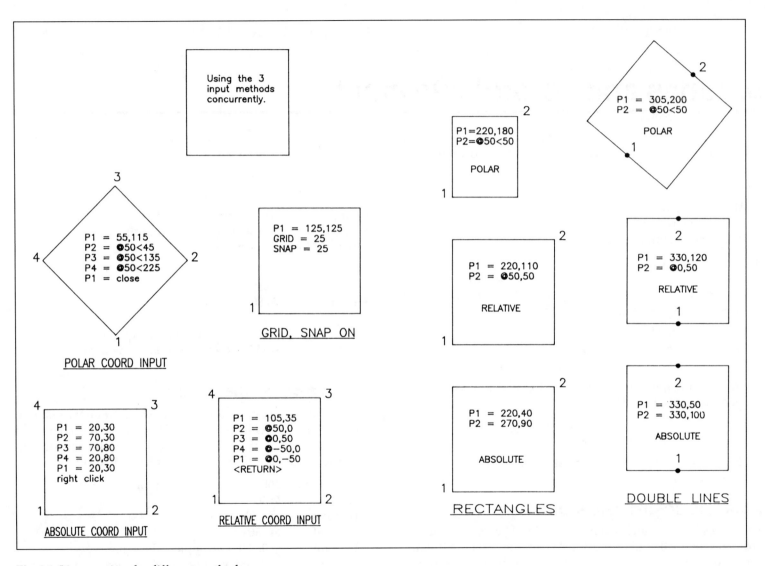

Fig. 9.1. Line creations by different methods.

The @ symbol has the following effect:

(a) @50,0 is 50 units in the positive X direction and 0 units in the Y direction from the last point, which is 105,35
(b) @0,–50 is 0 units in the X direction and –50 units in the negative Y direction, i.e. downwards from the last point on the screen.

Polar co-ordinate input

Also allows co-ordinates to be specified relative to the last point and uses the @ symbol as before, but also introduces angular input using the < symbol.

Left click on the line icon in the toolbox, and enter the following co-ordinates

From point	**55,115**	the line start point
To point	**@50<45**	**(note: no comma)**
To point	**@50<135**	
To point	**@50<225**	
To point	enter **C<R>**	closes the square and completes the line sequence.

The entries can be read as follows:

(a) @50<45 is 50 units at an angle of 45° from the last point which is 55,115
(b) @50<225 is 50 units at an angle of 225° from the last point on the screen.

Note

The entry **C<R>** is for **CLOSE** and will close a shape, i.e. a line will be drawn from the current screen position to the start point of the shape. This will work for all straight sided shapes.

Using the three input methods

The three co-ordinate input methods (absolute, relative, polar) can be used in the one sequence. Select the line command by any method, then enter the following

From point	**90,200**	The line start point
To point	**@50,0**	Relative input
To point	**140,250**	Absolute input
To point	**@50<180**	Polar input
To point	**C<R>**	

Grid-snap method

The grid and snap are drawing aids, and we will now use them to draw a 50 unit square, so

(a) set the grid to 25
(b) set the snap to 25
(c) using LINE with a start point of 125,125 draw a 50 unit square.
(d) set the grid back to 10, and the snap back to 5.

We now have five squares on the screen, which have been created with the LINE command. AutoCAD LT has two other line entity commands which allow line shapes to be created. These commands are

(a) rectangle
(b) double lines.

Rectangle

This is a very useful command which allows the user to create rectangular shapes by specifying two points on the rectangles' diagonal. It can be used with absolute, relative or polar input.

Absolute input

From the menu bar (Full Menu) select **Draw**
                                    Rectangle

prompt	First corner
enter	**220,40<R>**
prompt	Other corner
enter	**270,90<R>** to give a 50 unit square.

Relative input

Repeat the rectangle selection and enter **220,110** as the first corner and **@50,50** in response to the other corner prompt. A 50 unit square will be created.

Polar input

Pick the rectangle icon icon from the toolbox and enter the first corner as **220,180**. For the other corner, enter **@50<50**. This gives a rectangular shape which is not quite a square due to the co-ordinates of the second point. Can you work out the correct polar entry for a perfect 50 unit square using 220,180 as the first point? – some trig needed!

Double lines

This command allows the user to draw parallel lines, the user specifying the distance between the lines. It can be used to draw rectangular shapes, although this is not its prime function. It is another option available to the user. Like the other commands it can be used with absolute, relative or polar input.

Absolute input

From the menu bar select **Draw**
                        Double Line

prompt	Break/Caps/Dragline?Offset ...<start point>
enter	**W<R>** for width between lines
prompt	New DLINE width<?>
enter	**50<R>**
prompt	Break/Caps/Dragline/Offset ...<start point>
enter	**330,50<R>**
prompt	Arc/Break/CAps...
enter	**330,100<R>**
prompt	Arc/Break/CAps...
enter	**<RETURN>**

Relative input

At the command line enter **DLINE<R>** and a start point of **330,120** the width still being 50. For the next point enter **@0,50<R>** and then right click to complete the command. A 50 unit square will be drawn.

Polar input

Activate the DLINE icon and enter **305,200** as the start point and **@50<50** as the next point and then **<RETURN>** to complete the command. The resultant shape is a 50 unit square. Compare this with the rectangular polar entry.

Saving your drawing

Your drawing should now have 11 shapes as Fig. 9.1 (but with no text). This drawing has to be saved as it will be used in other chapters and it must now be changed, and we will give it the name **DEMODRG**, so from the menu bar select **File**

>**Save As...**

which will display the Save Drawing As dialogue box. From the dialogue box pick Type It and

prompt	Save current drawing as <A:STDA3>
enter	**A:DEMODRG<R>**
prompt	Current drawing name set to <A:DEMODRG>

The above is only one method of saving a drawing and others will be discussed as we progress through the book, but the following points are worth noting

1. We opened a drawing as **A:STDA3**, our standard sheet.
2. We created several entities.
3. The SaveAs.. entry displayed the dialogue box with the default name as <A:STDA3>, i.e. the name of the 'opened drawing'.
4. The A:DEMODRG entry as the name to be saved, means that the created entities are saved with this as the drawing name, and the original A:STDA3 standard sheet has remained 'untouched'.

The co-ordinate system

The terms 'co-ordinates' and 'angles' have been used without any explanation of what they are. The X–Y axis convention used in AutoCAD LT is shown in Fig. 9.2 and displays four plotted points with their co-ordinate values.

As an added exercise, erase all entities from the screen (making sure you have saved your squares) and then use the LINE command with:

From point	20,30
To point	–40,50
To point	–60,–70
To point	50,–60
To point	c

This will result in two line segments being drawn near the origin point (lower left of screen). By selecting **View-Zoom-All** from the menu bar the four lines drawn will be 'seen'. These lines use the (0,0) point as their origin.

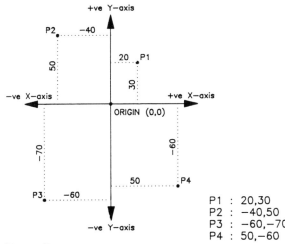

Fig. 9.2. X–Y co-ordinate system.

Angle convention

When using polar co-ordinates, the < symbol is used to signify angular input and (a)   positive angles are anti-clockwise
(b)   negative angles are clockwise.

Figure 9.3 shows four lines drawn from the origin using polar entry. Using the LINE command enter the following:

1. From point 0,0   To point 40<40
2. From point 0,0   To point 50<130
3. From point 0,0   To point 60<−110
4. From point 0,0   To point 30<−15

Note that these four lines are drawn from the 'zoomed all' origin point from the previous work.

Leaving AutoCAD LT

Before continuing to the activity for this chapter use the **File-Exit** sequence to exit AutoCAD LT, picking **No** in the message dialogue box which will appear. Why pick **No** and not **Yes**?

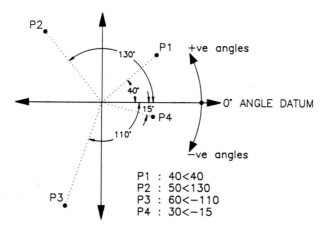

Fig. 9.3. Angle convention.

❏ *Summary*

1. Co-ordinate input can be **absolute**, **relative** or **polar**.
2. ABSOLUTE entry is from the origin – the point (0,0). Positive directions are UP and to the RIGHT, negative directions are DOWN and to the LEFT. The entry format is always **x,y**, e.g. 30,–40, i.e. 30 units in the positive x direction and –40 units in the negative y direction.
3. RELATIVE entry refers co-ordinates to the **LAST POINT ENTERED** and uses the @ symbol to achieve this. The entry format is always **@x,y**, e.g. @–50,60, i.e. –50 units in the negative x direction and 60 units in the positive y direction from the last point entered.
4. POLAR also refers co-ordinates to the last point entered and uses the @ symbol as before, and the < symbol for angular input. The format is **@x<a**, e.g. 50<60, i.e. 50 units at an angle of 60 degrees from the angle datum.
   Note that there is **no comma** with polar entry.
5. An angle of –45 degrees is the same as an angle of +315 degrees.
6. All three co-ordinate input methods can be used in the same line sequence.
7. The line sequence was terminated by

   (a) using the **<RETURN>** key.
   (b) right clicking on the mouse.
   (c) 'closing' the shape

8. The rectangle command is useful, but care must be taken with polar entry.
9. Double lines accept the three co-ordinate input methods.
10. The line command can be activated by

    (a) menu bar selection, i.e. Draw-Line
    (b) command entry, i.e. **LINE<R>**
    (c) icon selection.

    It is the users preference as to which method is used.
11. The standard sheet was the drawing 'opened' for this exercise, but the drawing was saved as A:DEMODRG. This allows the standard sheet to 'keep its original settings'.

Activity

This activity will be completed using only the LINE command (and possibly ERASE if you make mistakes). You should

1. Load AutoCAD LT
2. Open your A:STDA3 standard sheet drawing.
3. Refer to Tutorial 2 and complete the three templates as shown using co-ordinate input. Any of the entry methods can be used, but you should practice the three methods.

4. When you have completed your drawing save it using

   (a) File-SaveAs.
   (b) Type It
   (c) A:TUT-2 as the drawing name.

5. Exit AutoCAD LT and proceed to the next chapter on circles/arcs.

10. Circle creation

In this chapter we will investigate how circles can be added to our drawing of the squares, so

1. Load AutoCAD LT.
2. Select from the menu bar **File-Open...** and from the dialogue box
   (a) pick Type It
   (b) enter **A:DEMODRG<R>** at the prompt.
3. Your drawing of the squares should be displayed, with the toolbox at the right of the screen.
4. Now refer to Fig. 10.1.

AutoCAD LT allows circles to be created by three different methods

(a) centre point and radius
(b) specifying any three points on the circle circumference
(c) by specifying two tangent specs and a radius.

The circle command can be activated from

(a) the menu bar using the Draw option
(b) the toolbox icon
(c) the command line, i.e. direct entry.

Generally absolute co-ordinates are used to specify the circle centre point, although the next chapter will introduce the user to the Object Snap modes, which allow greater flexibility in selecting existing entities on the screen.

Before starting the circle creations, erase the 'non-square' which was drawn using the rectangle command – it is the smallest rectangle on the screen – with the ERASE command and pick one of the lines then **<RETURN>**. The complete rectangle is erased with only one pick. This is because the rectangle is a single entity and not four separate lines as you may have thought.

Centre-radius

1. At the command prompt enter **CIRCLE<R>**

prompt	3P/TTR/<Center point>
enter	**45,55<R>**
prompt	Radius<?>
enter	**20<R>**

2. Select the circle icon from the toolbox

prompt	3P/TTR/<Center point>
enter	**150,150<R>**
prompt	Radius<20?>
enter	**35<R>**

3. From the menu bar select **Draw**
   Circle
   Center,Radius

and enter **105,235** as the centre point and **23** as the radius.

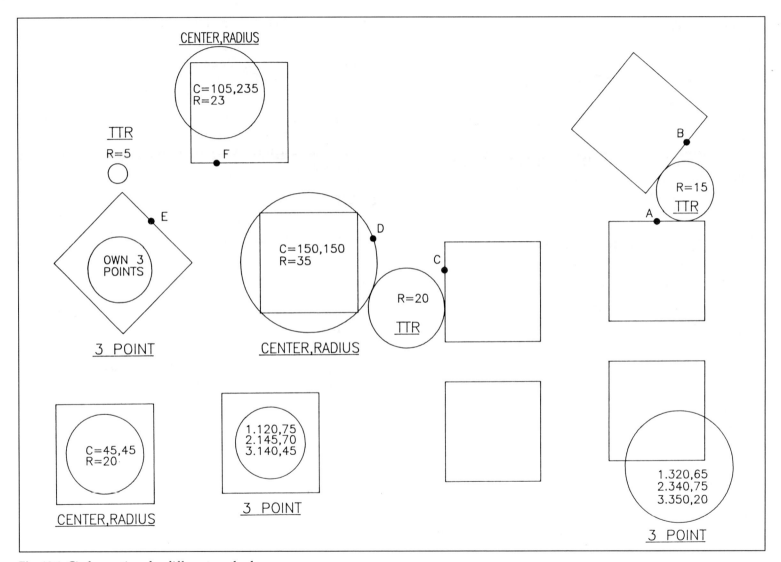

Fig. 10.1. Circle creations by different methods.

Three point

1. Select the circle icon and

prompt	3P/TTR/<Center point>
enter	**3P<R>**
prompt	First point and enter **120,75<R>**
prompt	Second point and enter **145,70<R>**
prompt	Third point and enter **140,45<R>**

2. Select from the menu bar **Draw-Circle-3 point** and enter **320,65; 340,75; 350,20** as the co-ordinates.
3. Repeat the 3 point circle method, and pick your own three points inside the left-hand 'tilted' square.

TTR: tangent–tangent–radius

This method allows the user to select two entities (lines, circles, arcs) which will be tangent to the circle to be created.

1. Select from the menu bar **Draw**
    Circle
    Tan,Tan,Radius

prompt	Enter Tangent spec
response	pick line A using the box on the cursor
prompt	Enter second Tangent spec
response	pick line B
prompt	Radius<?>
enter	**15<R>**

2. Select the circle icon and

prompt	3P/TTR/<Center point>
enter	**TTR<R>**
prompt	Enter Tangent spec and pick line C
prompt	Enter second Tangent spec **and pick** circle D
prompt	Radius and enter **20<R>**

3. Activate the circle TTR method again and:

prompt	Enter Tangent spec and pick line E
prompt	Enter second Tangent spec **and pick** line F
prompt	Radius and enter **5<R>**

This last circle is interesting. The circle has been drawn 'tangent to nothing'. AutoCAD LT assumes that the tangent spec lines are extended and thus draws the circle as tangent to these 'imaginary' lines.

Saving

At this stage we want to save our drawing for future work, so from the menu bar select **File**
    Save As...

(a) check the file name is **DEMODRG**
(b) pick **OK**
(c) the existing file warning dialogue box is displayed (Fig. 10.2)
(d) pick **Yes**.

This will now update the A:DEMODRG to include the circles. The original drawing of the squares has been 'overwritten'.

Fig. 10.2. Save As warning dialogue box.

❏ *Summary*

1. Circles can be drawn by specifying
   (a) a centre point and a radius
   (b) three points on the circle circumference
   (c) two tangent specs and a radius.
2. The TTR method can be used with any two entities, e.g.
   (a) two lines
   (b) two circles
   (c) a line and a circle
   (d) a line and an arc, etc.
3. The centre point can be obtained
   (a) by co-ordinate input
   (b) by picking any point on the screen
   (c) by using OSNAP to reference existing entities (next chapter).
4. The radius can also be obtained by the methods listed above.

Activity

Open your A:STDA3 standard sheet and attempt Tutorial 3. It uses the commands already used ie LINE, CIRCLE and ERASE. The co-ordinate entry method is at your discretion, although relative is probably the best. At this stage you may need to do some 'sums' for the circle centre points in exercise A. When the drawing is complete, save it as **A:TUT-3**.

11. Object snap

The lines and circles drawn so far have been created by co-ordinate input. While this is (and will be) the most common method of creating entities, it is often desirable to reference entities already drawn, e.g. we may want to draw a circle at the midpoint of an existing line, or draw a line from the centre of an existing circle and perpendicular to another line. This is achieved using the object snap modes (OSNAP), and is one of the most commonly used draughting aids. It is used continuously, and the user should become proficient in its applications. The object snap modes which are available to use are

- ENDpoint of a line or arc.
- INTersection of two entities.
- MIDpoint of a line or arc.
- CENtre of a circle or arc.
- QUAdrant of a circle or arc.
- NEArest point on an entity.
- PERpendicular to a line, circle or arc.
- TANgent to a circle or arc.
- NODe to a point entity.
- INSertion point to a block.

The object snap is usually activated **transparently**, i.e. while using a draw command, and this is achieved by
  (a) selecting the appropriate toolbox icon
  (b) entering the mode at the command line – the three capital letters above.

The icon selection method is quicker to use, but we will investigate both methods. The actual object snap icons are not listed by name, and the user must be familiar with them. They are detailed in Fig. 11.1.

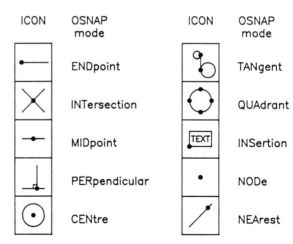

Fig. 11.1. Object snap icons and modes.

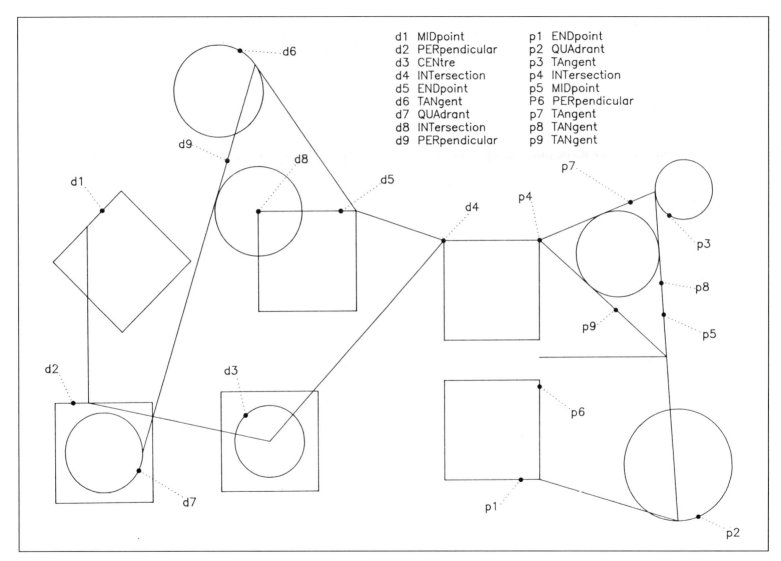

Fig. 11.2. Object snap using LINE and CIRCLE.

Loading the drawing

To demonstrate object snap modes, we will use our **A:DEMODRG** drawing of the squares and circles, so

1. Load AutoCAD LT.
2. At the command line enter **OPEN<R>** and
   (a)   select the drives box
   (b)   select **a:icon**
   (c)   select **demodrg.dwg file name** (turns blue)
   (d)   pick **OK**.
3. This will load the squares and circles drawing. If you have any problems using this new method of opening a drawing, pick **Type It** and enter **A:DEMODRG** at the prompt.
4. Refer to Fig. 11.2 and erase the entities not required – you may want to refer to Fig. 10.1. to see what I have erased.

Using object snap from the keyboard

Our first example of object snap modes will be to draw a line sequence using keyboard input. The sequence is given as a series of command entries, so at the command line

enter	**LINE<R>**
prompt	From point
enter	**MID<R>**
prompt	of
response	**pick line d1**
prompt	To point
enter	**PER<R>**
prompt	to
response	**pick line d2**
prompt	To point
enter	**CEN<R>**
prompt	of
response	**pick circle d3**

prompt	To point
enter	**INT<R>**
prompt	of
response	**pick point d4**
prompt	To point
enter	**END<R>**
prompt	of
response	**pick line d5**
prompt	To point
enter	**TAN<R>**
prompt	to
response	**pick circle d6**
prompt	To point
enter	**QUA<R>**
prompt	of
response	**pick circle d7**
prompt	To point
response	**right click to end sequence**.

Now enter **CIRCLE<R>** at the command line and

prompt	3P/TTR/<Center point>
enter	**INT<R>**
prompt	of
response	**pick point d8**
prompt	Radius
enter	**PER<R>**
prompt	to
response	**pick line d9**

Using object snap icons

As before the sequence is given as a series of entries, so select the line icon and

prompt	From point
response	**pick the ENDpoint icon**
prompt	ENDP of
response	**pick line p1**
prompt	To point
response	**pick the QUAdrant icon**
prompt	QUAD of
response	**pick circle p2**
prompt	To point
response	**pick TANgent icon**
prompt	TAN to
response	**pick circle p3**
prompt	To point
response	**pick INTersection icon**
prompt	INT of
response	**pick point p4**
prompt	To point
response	**pick MIDpoint icon**
prompt	MID of
response	**pick line p5**
prompt	To point
response	**pick PERpendicular icon**
prompt	PER to
response	**pick line p6**
prompt	To point
response	**right click** to end sequence

Now select the circle icon and

prompt	3P/TTR/<Centre point>
enter	**3P<R>**
prompt	First point

response	pick TANgent icon and then line p7
prompt	Second point
response	pick TANgent icon and then line p8
prompt	Third point
response	pick TANgent icon and then line p9

Your drawing should now resemble Fig. 11.2 but without the text. Now save your work as **A:DEMODRG** – we will refer to this drawing again.

Notes

1. The following points should be remembered
   (a) the ENDpoint snapped to depends on what point on the entity is 'picked'
   (b) a circle as four quadrants, and the quadrant snapped to depends the circle pick point.

   These are illustrated in Fig. 11.3.
2. My command entry has shown the OSNAP mode in capitals e.g. **END**, **MID**, etc. Capitals are not required and **end<R>**, **eND<R>**, **EnD<R>** are valid entries. This is also true for all keyboard entry.

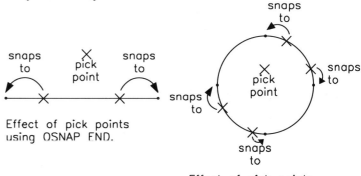

Fig. 11.3. Effect of pick points on OSNAP.

Running object snap

While the use of the object snap icons will greatly increase the draughting process, it is still 'inconvenient' to have to pick the icon every time an ENDpoint (for example) is required. AutoCAD LT allows the user to 'pre-set' the object snap mode to ENDpoint, INTersection, CENter, etc., and this is then called the **running object snap**. Pre-setting an object snap does not preclude the user from selecting another mode, i.e. if you have set an ENDpoint running mode, you can still pick the CENtre icon to snap to a circle/arc centre. The running snap mode can be set

1. By direct entry with **OSNAP<R>**

    prompt   Object snap mode
    enter   **END<R>** or **INT, CEN, QUA**, etc.

    This will now snap any entity being drawn to the endpoint of the line picked, without having to select the ENDpoint icon.

2. From the menu bar with **Assist**
                Object Snap...

    This gives the running mode dialogue box (Fig. 11.4), and by picking the desired box (gives a X) that mode will be pre-set.

3. By picking the running mode icon from the toolbox which gives the running mode dialogue box as before.

Cancelling running object snap mode

A running mode can be left 'active' once it has been pre-set, but this can lead to problems when you do not want to snap to **ENDpoint**, **CENter**, etc. The running mode can be cancelled by

1. Entering **OSNAP<R>** then **<RETURN>** in response to the prompt. This cancels the pre-set object snap.
2. Activating the dialogue box, and removing the × from the mode. This also cancels the pre-set mode.

3. Picking the NONE icon from the toolbox.

This allows the user to select an entity without the pre-set mode being used, but still leaves the running mode 'active'.

❏ *Summary*

1. Object snap (OSNAP) is used to reference existing entities, and aids the creation of new entities.
2. The user can pre-set a running object snap.

Activity

Using your A:STDA3 sheet attempt tutorial 4. It consists only of lines and circles, and OSNAP should be used as indicated. Save this drawing as **A:TUT4**.

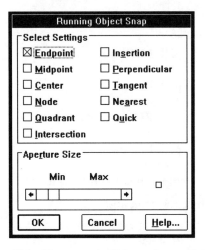

Fig. 11.4. Running Object Snap mode dialogue box with ENDpoint set.

12. User exercise 1

By now you should have the ability and confidence to create line and circle entities by various methods. For example:

(a) freehand
(b) co-ordinate input
(c) referencing existing entities.

Before proceeding with other draw and edit commands, we will create a working drawing which will be used to introduce several new concepts as well as reinforcing your existing skills. The exercise will also be used to demonstrate how a 'new' drawing is created using our **A:STDA3** standard sheet.

1. Load AutoCAD LT and ensure your floppy is in the drive.
2. Either (a)   select from the menu bar **File-New...**
       or   (b)   pick the New drawing icon from the toolbar.
3. The Create new drawing dialogue box will be displayed.
4. Note that the existing name in the Prototype box is **acltiso.dwg**. This is AutoCAD LT's default drawing name.
5. Using your pointing device
   (a) click to the left of the dot, acltiso|.dwg
   (b) use the backspace key to erase the acltiso name, |.dwg
   (c) enter **A:STDA3**, i.e. **A:STAD3|.dwg**.
6. Now left click the pointing device at the New drawing name box and enter **A:WORKDRG** to give Fig. 12.1.
7. Pick OK.
8. Your A:STDA3 standard sheet will be loaded onto the screen.

9. Refer to Fig. 12.2 and draw full size the given shape.
   (a) do not attempt dimensioning
   (b) the start point is given for you – use it!
   (c) use your discretion for absolute or relative input
   (d) the only commands are LINE and CIRCLE (CEN,RAD option)
   (e) hopefully you will not need to use ERASE
   (f) you may need some simple calculations for the circle centres.
10. When the drawing is complete, pick the **SAVE icon**.
11. The command prompt will display SAVE then be returned 'blank'.
12. Quit AutoCAD LT.

What we did

1. We created a new drawing and entered A:STDA3 as the prototype drawing name ie our standard sheet.
2. The new drawing name was entered as A:WORKDRG.
3. The drawing was completed and the SAVE icon picked.

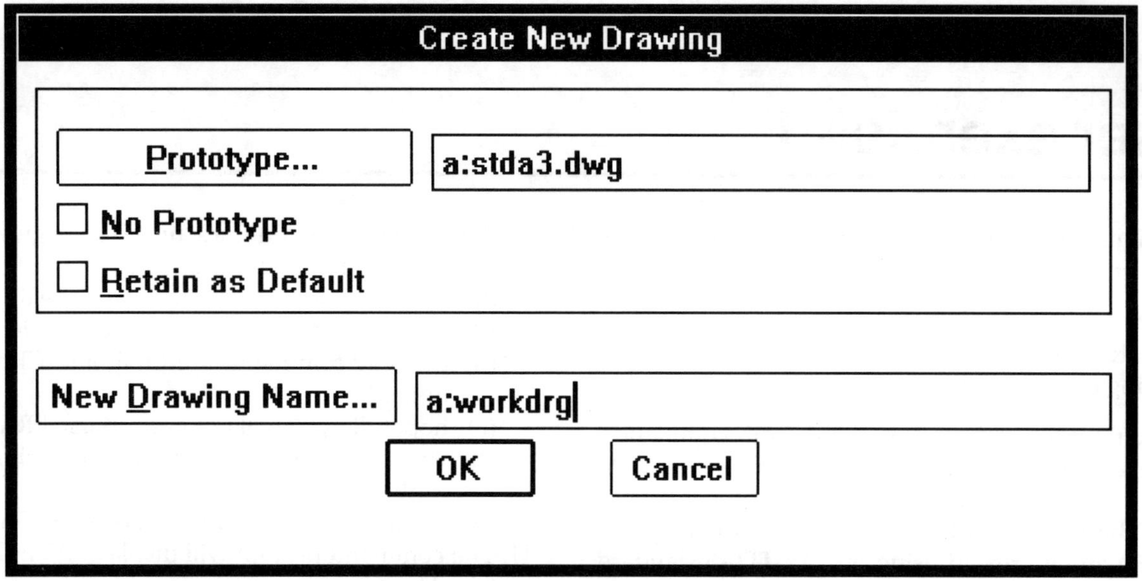

Fig. 12.1. Create New Drawing dialogue box.

What actually happened

Using the **New...** option allows the user to enter their own prototype drawing name in the required name box. For us, this was A:STDA3. The name of the actual drawing to be saved is then entered in the New Drawing name box, i.e. A:WORKDRG. When OK is picked, AutoCAD LT loads the prototype drawing with all the default settings and the user can then complete the required drawing without having to reset parameters. Selecting the SAVE icon (or File-Save from the menu bar) **automatically** saves the drawing on the screen with the new drawing name ie A:WORKDRG. This drawing also has the standard sheet defaults.

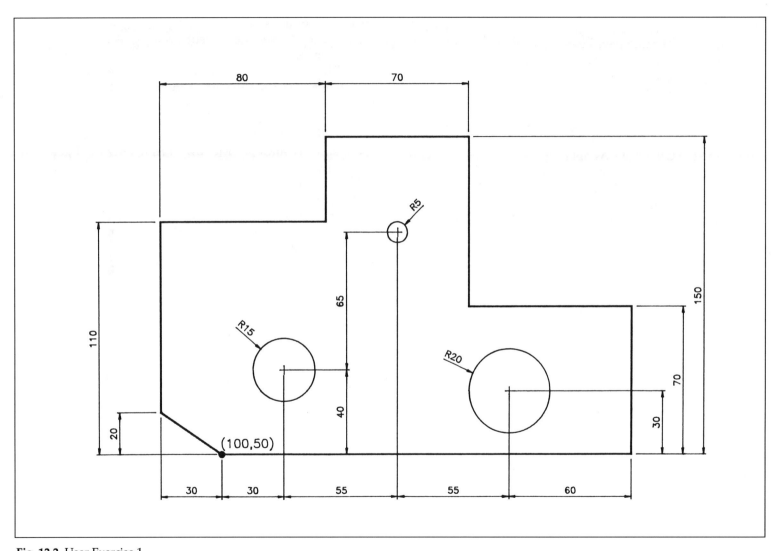

Fig. 12.2. User Exercise 1.
1. Draw the shape to the size given. 2. Do not dimension. 3. Use the **SAVE** icon.

Note

1. The same effect could have been obtained by
   (a) opening the A:STDA3 standard sheet
   (b) completing the drawing
   (c) using Save As... and entering A:WORKDRG as the drawing name.
2. The user now has two methods of starting a new drawing
   (a) using the New/Save option
   (b) using the Open/Save As option
3. Both methods make use of the A:STDA3 standard sheet.
4. The method used is at the user's discretion, but the New option is 'theoretically' more correct.
5. Take a note of AutoCAD LT's prototype drawing **ACLTISO** – you may need it some time.

6. The save options are
   (a) SAVE – saves the current drawing using the drawing name that was 'started' – the user has no control over it. This options will 'overwrite' the named drawing if it already exists. Use with **caution**.
   (b) SAVE AS – allows the user to enter a different drawing name if required.
7. I would recommend that the SAVE AS option is used until the user becomes proficient with AutoCAD LT. I generally use this option.
8. The 'start a drawing' options are
   (a) NEW – begins a drawing, the user specifying the prototype name and the new drawing name.
   (b) OPEN – usually used to display a previously saved drawing.

13. Arc, donut and ellipse creation

These three drawing commands will be discussed in turn. Each can be activated from the menu bar, the toolbox icon or by entering the command at the prompt line. Co-ordinate input or referencing existing entities are both available. To demonstrate the commands, we will use our drawing of the squares and circles, so

1. Load AutoCAD LT.
2. Open drawing **A:DEMODRG**.
3. Refer to Fig. 13.1 and erase all entities not required. You may want to refer back to Fig. 11.2 for this.

Arcs

AutoCAD LT allows arcs to be created by six different methods. All methods are basically the same, and use combinations of arc centre, start point, end point and included angle. We will investigate four of the methods, and you can try the others at your discretion.

1. CSE: Centre, Start, End by co-ordinate input.
   From the menu bar select **Draw**

   Arc

   Center,Start,End

prompt	Center/<Start point>:_cCenter
enter	**30,40<R>**
prompt	Start point
enter	**60,40<R>**

| prompt | Angle/<End point> |
| enter | **30,70<R>** |

2. CSE: Centre, Start, End by referencing existing entities. Repeat the CSE arc selection and

prompt	_cCenter
respond	**INTersection icon and pick point d1**
prompt	Start point
respond	**MIDpoint icon and pick line d2**
prompt	Angle/<End point>
respond	**MIDpoint icon and pick line d3**

3. SCA: Start, Centre, Angle.
   Select this arc option from the menu bar and

prompt	Center/<Start point>
respond	**INTersection icon and pick point d4**
prompt	Center
respond	**CENter icon and pick circle d5**
prompt	Included angle
enter	**120<R>**

4. CSA: Centre, Start, Angle.
   Use this option from the menu bar and
   (a) centre – **INTersection icon and pick point d6**
   (b) start – **END**point icon and pick arc d7
   (c) angle – enter **–120<R>**.

5. Three point.

This option allows the user to pick three points on the arc circumference, so select it then

(a) start point: ENDpoint of arc d8
(b) second point: INTersection of point d9
(c) end point: MIDpoint of line d10.

Donuts

A donut (the American spelling of 'doughnut') is a 'solid filled' circle or annulus, the user specifying both the inside and outside diameters. The command allows for repeated donuts to be created.

1. From the menu bar select **Draw-Donut**

prompt	Inside diameter<?>
enter	**0<R>**
prompt	Outside diameter
enter	**8<R>**
prompt	Center of doughnut
enter	**190,35<R>**
prompt	Center of doughnut
respond	**CENter icon and pick circle d11**
prompt	Center of doughnut
respond	**right click to end sequence.**

2. Pick the donut icon and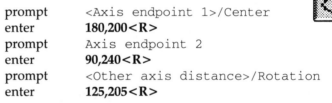
    (a) enter an inside diameter of 15
    (b) enter an outside diameter of 18
    (c) enter 245,135 as the doughnut centre
    (d) **MID**point icon and pick arc d12 as the doughnut centre
    (e) right click.
3. Enter **DONUT<R>** at the command line and
    (a) enter an inside diameter of 20
    (b) enter an outside diameter of 25
    (c) pick ENDpoint icon then line d13
    (d) right click.

Ellipse

To draw an ellipse, the user specifies

(a) three points on the axes endpoints
(b) the ellipse centre, then two points on the axes endpoints.

1. Select from the menu bar **Draw-Ellipse**

prompt	<Axis endpoint 1>/Center
respond	**MIDpoint icon then pick line d14**
prompt	Axis endpoint 2
respond	**MIDpoint icon then pick line d15**
prompt	<Other axis distance>/Rotation
respond	**INTersection icon and pick point d16**

2. Select the ellipse icon and

prompt	<Axis endpoint 1>/Center
enter	**180,200<R>**
prompt	Axis endpoint 2
enter	**90,240<R>**
prompt	<Other axis distance>/Rotation
enter	**125,205<R>**

3. Repeat the ellipse selection and

prompt	<Axis endpoint>/Center
enter	**C<R>**
prompt	Center of ellipse
enter	**80,220<R>**
prompt	Axis endpoint
respond	**ENDpoint icon and pick ellipse d17**
prompt	<Other axis distance>/ Rotation
respond	**ENDpoint icon and pick ellipse d18**

4. Enter **ELLIPSE<R>** at the command line and

    (a)   use the **C** option
    (b)   enter **220,200** as the ellipse centre
    (c)   enter **@30,0** as Axis endpoint
    (d)   enter the **R** option
    (e)   enter **60** as the rotation about the major axis.

Hopefully your drawing screen should be the same as Fig. 13.1 but without the text.

❏ *Summary*

Arcs, donuts and ellipse are entities. All can be created using co-ordinate input or by referencing existing entities.

Arcs

1. Different selection methods.
2. Normally drawn in an anti-clockwise direction.
3. Arcs may be drawn 'in the wrong sense' if the start points and end points are wrongly selected.
4. A negative included angle will draw the arc clockwise.

Donuts

1. The user specifies both inside and outside diameters.
2. An inside diameter of 0 will give a 'filled' circle.
3. The command stays 'active' until cancelled by the user with a right click or a **<RETURN>**.

Ellipses

1. Drawn by different methods which involve:
    (a)   the axes endpoints
    (b)   the ellipse centre and axes endpoints
    (c)   rotation about the major axis.
2. An ellipse is drawn as a series of arcs.

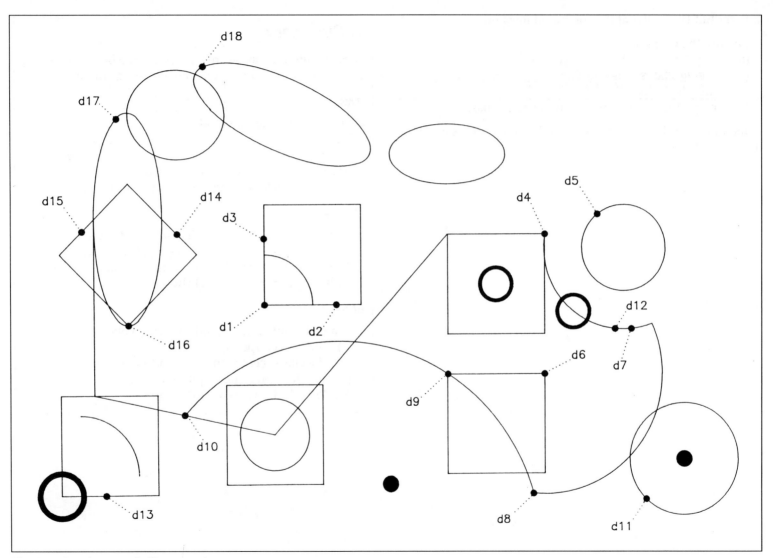

Fig. 13.1. Arc, donut and ellipse creation.

14. Fillet and chamfer

When a drawing has been completed, it may be necessary to alter/modify it to meet a customer requirement. AutoCAD LT is equipped with several commands to permit an existing drawing to be 'edited', and we will begin by investigating the fillet and chamfer commands.

Load AutoCAD LT and open your **A:WORKDRG** previously created and saved (hopefully) from Chapter 12.

Refer to Fig. 14.1.

Fillet

Before the fillet command can be used, the required radius must be 'set', so from the menu bar select **Construct**

Fillet

prompt	Polyline/Radius/<Select first object>
enter	**R<R>** to specify the radius option
prompt	Enter fillet radius <0.00>
enter	**20<R>**

Now repeat the **Construct-Fillet** selection and

prompt	Polyline/Radius/<Select first object>
respond	**pick line d1**
prompt	Select second object
respond	**pick line d2**

The corner of the drawing will be 'filleted' and the unwanted lines automatically removed.

Using the fillet command
(a) set the radius to 15 and pick lines d3 and d4
(b) set the radius to 30 and pick lines d5 and d6
(c) set the radius to 0 and pick lines d7 and d8 – interesting?

Chamfer

A chamfer requires the user to specify two distances (these can be the same or different) before it can be used, so from the menu bar select **Construct**

Chamfer

prompt	Polyline/Distance/<Select first line>
enter	**D<R>** to specify distance option
prompt	Enter first chamfer distance<?>
enter	**15<R>**
prompt	Enter second chamfer distance <15.00>
enter	**25<R>**

Now repeat the **Construct-Chamfer** selection and

prompt	Polyline/Distance/<Select first line>
respond	**pick line d9**
prompt	Select second line
respond	**pick line d10**

The corner will be chamfered and the unwanted lines removed. The 'pick' order is important

(a) the first line picked has the first chamfer distance, i.e. 15
(b) the second line picked has the second chamfer distance, i.e. 25.

Using the chamfer command

(a) set distances of 12 and 18 and pick lines d11 and d12
(b) set distances of 3 and 5 and pick lines d13 and d14.

The fillet and chamfer effect has been demonstrated with lines which are perpendicular to each other, but it also works with 'inclined' lines as shown in Fig. 14.1. Try it for yourself by drawing two sets of inclined lines (three or four) then use the fillet/chamfer commands on each set. You only have to watch the size of the radius/chamfer used. Why is this important?

The fillet command will also work with circles/arcs and if the entered radius is too small AutoCAD LT will display the message No valid fillet with radius of ...

Saving

Before proceeding to the next chapter, make sure that you save your drawing as **A:WORKDRG**

❏ *Summary*

1. **FILLET** and **CHAMFER** are construct commands.
2. Both commands can be entered from the keyboard.
3. Both commands require the radius/distances to be set before they can be used.
4. When values are entered, they stay as the default until altered by the user.
5. Lines, circles and arcs can be filleted.
6. Lines can be chamfered, the distances having the same or different values.
7. A fillet radius of 0 is useful in extending two inclined lines to a point.
8. Chamfer distances of 0 will also extend two lines to a point.
9. The second chamfer distance is assumed to be the same as the first distance, unless a different value is specified by the user.

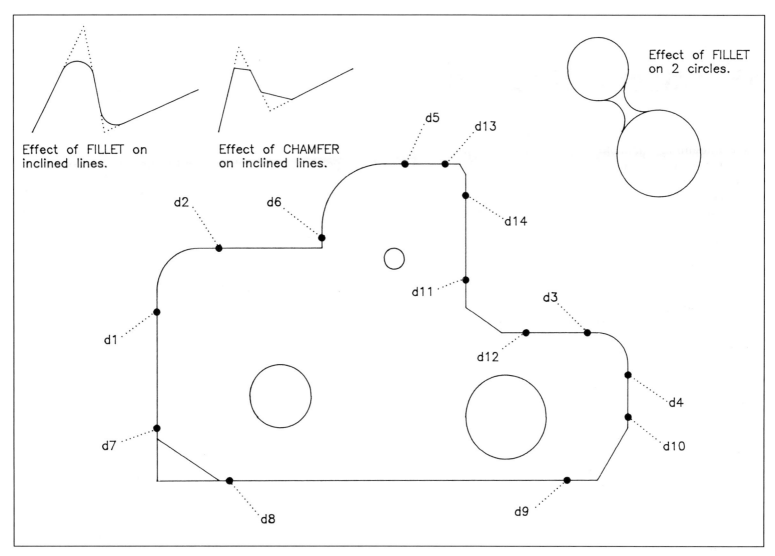

Fig. 14.1. A:WORKDRG after using the fillet and chamfer commands.

15. Offset, extend and trim

In this chapter we will investigate three of the most commonly used draughting commands, and will demonstrate them by adding centre lines (of a sort) to our drawing from the previous chapter. You may still have **A:WORKDRG** on the screen, in which case you can proceed with the exercise, otherwise you will have to open it – which should give you no problems now?

Offset

This commands allows the user to draw parallel entities, i.e. lines, circles and arcs. The user can specify

(a) the offset distance
(b) the point the entity to be offset has to pass through.

Refer to Fig. 15.1 and from the menu bar select **Construct**
Offset

prompt	Offset distance or Through <through>
enter	**60<R>** the offset distance
prompt	Select object to offset
respond	**pick line d1**
prompt	Side to offset
respond	**pick a point d2 to the right of selected line**
and	line d1 will be offset by 60 to the right
prompt	Select object to offset
	(i.e. any more 60 offsets)
respond	**pick line d3**
prompt	Side to offset
respond	**pick a point d4 to the left of selected line**

and line d3 will be offset by 60 to the left
prompt Select object to offset
respond **right click** to end sequence.

We have now offset two lines which should be through the centres of two of the circles. The second offset line is not a 'full centre line', but both offset lines are the same length as the original selected lines.

Using the same procedure, offset the bottom horizontal line of the component by 30 and 40 to give circle 'centre' lines through the two larger circles.

Now enter **OFFSET<R>** at the command line and

prompt	Offset distance or Through
enter	**T<R>** the through option
prompt	Select object to offset
respond	**pick line d5**
prompt	Through point
respond	**CENter icon and pick circle d6**
prompt	Select object to offset
respond	**pick line d7**
prompt	Through point
respond	**CENter icon and pick circle d6**
prompt	Select object to offset
respond	**right click**

Your A:WORKDRG should now resemble Fig. 15.1 and the three circles should have lines through the centre. These lines are not yet 'real' centre lines, and are of different sizes. We will now investigate how these centre lines can be 'tidied up'.

Extend

The extend command will extent an entity 'up to a boundary', the user specifying

(a) the actual boundary (an entity)
(b) the entity to be extended.

Refer to Fig. 15.2(a) and from the menu bar select **Modify**

Extend

prompt	`Select boundary edge(s)...`
	Select objects
respond	**pick line d1**
prompt	`1 found` and `Select object`
respond	**pick line d3**
prompt	`1 found` and `Select object`
respond	**right click** to end boundary selection

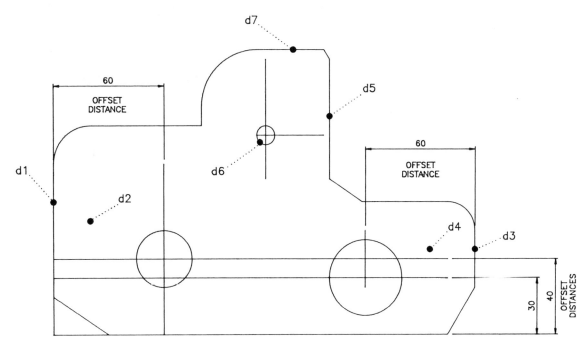

Fig. 15.1. A:WORKDRG after using the OFFSET command.

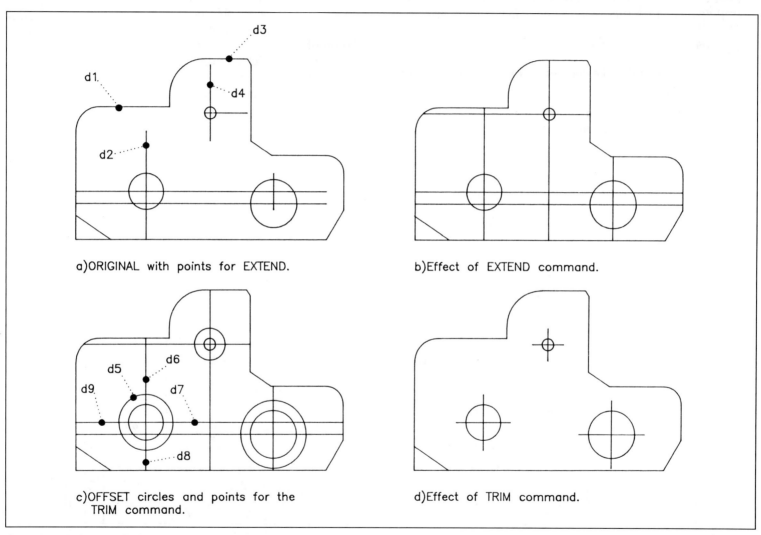

a)ORIGINAL with points for EXTEND.

b)Effect of EXTEND command.

c)OFFSET circles and points for the
TRIM command.

d)Effect of TRIM command.

Fig. 15.2. A:WORKDRG after using the EXTEND AND TRIM commands.

prompt	`<Select object to extend>/Undo`
respond	**pick line d2**
prompt	`<Select object to extend>/Undo`
respond	**pick line d4**
prompt	`<select object to extend>/Undo`
respond	**right click** to end sequence.

Can you now extend (using the icon) the remaining horizontal and vertical lines to give Fig. 15.2(b). Note that one of these lines extends to an arc!

Offset

Use the offset command again and offset the three circles a distance of 5 'outwards'. The procedure is the same as for the line offsets.

Trim

The trim command is used to 'erase' an entity at a boundary, the user specifying

(a) the boundary entity
(b) the entity to be trimmed.

Using Fig. 15.2(c), select from the menu bar **Modify**
Trim

prompt	`Select cutting edge(s)...`
	`Select objects`
respond	**pick circle d5 then right click**
prompt	`<select object to trim>/Undo`
respond	**pick lines d6,d7,d8,d9 then right click**

The four 'centre lines' will have been trimmed to the offset circle, which should now be erased. Using the other offset circles as the 'cutting edge', trim (using the icon) the remaining circle centre lines then erase the offset circles to icon leave Fig. 15.2(d). One of these trims may be rather difficult to pick at this stage, so just leave it for the present. You have now added 'neat centre lines' to the circles.

Saving

At this stage save your drawing as **A:WORKDRG** for future work.

Further exercise

Before leaving this chapter, we will investigate the offset, extend and trim commands with some other examples. I consider this to be useful, due to the importance of the three commands. Refer to Fig. 15.3 which illustrates the following

(a) A:WORKDRG with an offset of 15. Note that the arcs and lines 'blend' with the offset, but that straight line corners do not.
(b) Using trim with circles is useful as demonstrated. Lines, arcs and circles can all be trimmed.
(c) Extending a line and arc to a circle. Lines and arcs can also be extended to other line and arc entities.
(d) Trim using the fence option. This is achieved by
     1. selecting the TRIM command.
     2. pick the trim boundary then **<R>**
     3. pick Assist-Select-Fence from the menu bar
     4. pick the fence 'line' then **<R>**
(e) An interesting application of the TRIM command.

These examples (a)–(e) are only some applications of the three commands. I would recommend that the user spends some time with then by drawing different line, circle and arc entities and then trying TRIM, OFFSET and EXTEND.

Note

One of the most common questions I am asked by new users to CAD draughting is 'where do I start'. There is no 'right answer' to this, as different users will complete a drawing as 'they see it'. My advice to new users is

1. Have GRID and SNAP on (set to 10 and 5) and ORTHO off.
2. Begin at a corner and draw the outline using relative co-ordinate input if this is possible, or else position circles.
3. Use offset/trim as much as possible.
4. Complete the drawing using information given
5. Use drawing aids as required.

❏ *Summary*

1. OFFSET, TRIM and EXTEND are very useful commands.
2. Offset is a Construct command activated from the menu bar.
3. Lines, circles and arcs can be offset either by
   (a) entering and offset distance.
   (b) selecting an entity to be offset through.
4. Extend and Trim are Modify commands and complement one another.
5. Extent and Trim are activated from the menu bar or using the icon.
6. Extend and Trim have the same command 'format'
   (a) select the extend or trim boundary (cutting edge)
   (b) select the entity to be extended or trimmed.
7. Lines and arcs can be extended.
8. Lines, circles and arcs can be trimmed.

Activity

I have included two activities for this chapter to give the user some practice in using the commands.

1. Tutorial 5 which should be attempted using the procedure
   (a) Load AutoCAD LT
   (b) Pick the New icon
   (c) Enter A:STDA3 as the Prototype name
   (d) Enter A:TUT-5 as the New Drawing Name then OK
   (e) Complete the drawing
   (f) Pick the SAVE icon
   (g) Exit AutoCAD LT

   The above procedure will open your A:STDA3 standard sheet, allow you to complete the drawing with your default variables set, and save the drawing as A:TUT-5.

2. Tutorial 6 has three exercises which use the LINE and CIRCLE commands as well as trim, offset etc. The procedure for starting a New drawing as in activity 1 should be used, but remember to enter the New Drawing Name as A:TUT-6.

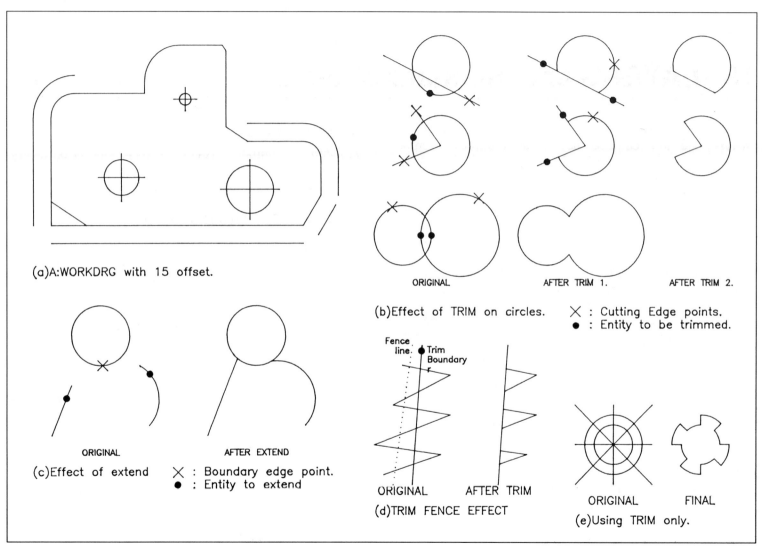

(a)A:WORKDRG with 15 offset.

ORIGINAL   AFTER TRIM 1.   AFTER TRIM 2.

(b)Effect of TRIM on circles.   ✕ : Cutting Edge points.
                                  ● : Entity to be trimmed.

ORIGINAL   AFTER EXTEND

(c)Effect of extend   ✕ : Boundary edge point.
                        ● : Entity to extend

Fence line. ● Trim Boundary

ORIGINAL   AFTER TRIM

(d)TRIM FENCE EFFECT

ORIGINAL   FINAL

(e)Using TRIM only.

Fig. 15.3. OFFSET, EXTEND and TRIM.

16. LAYERS and standard sheet 2

All entities that have been created so far have had a continuous linetype, and no attempt has been made to introduce centre or hidden linetypes. AutoCAD LT has a facility called **LAYERS** which allows the user to assign different linetypes and colours to named layers. For example, a layer may be for red continuous lines, another may be for green hidden lines, and yet another layer could be for blue centre lines. As well as linetypes and colours, layers can be used for specific drawing purposes, e.g. there may be a layer for dimensions, one for hatching, one for construction lines, etc. Individual layers can be switched on/off as required by the user to mask out drawing entities which are not required.

The concept of layers can be imagined as a series of transparent overlays, each having its own linetype and colour. The overlay used for dimensioning could be removed without affecting the rest of the drawing.

The following points are important when considering layers

1. All entities are drawn on layers.
2. Layers must be 'created' by the user before they can be used.
3. New layers are created using the Layer Control dialogue box.
4. Layers are perhaps the most important concept in AutoCAD LT. They are essential for good and efficient draughting, and the user must become proficient with them.

Getting started

We will discuss different aspects of layers, and create several new layers using our standard sheet, so open your **A:STDA3** drawing. Draw a line and circle anywhere on the screen.

The Layer Control dialogue box

The 'original' layer control dialogue box is shown in Fig. 16.1, and is activated from the menu bar with **Settings**
                    Layer Control...

1. The format of the layers is:

Layer Name	State	Color	Linetype
0	On ..	white	CONTINUOUS

2. Layer 0 is the layer on which all entities have been drawn, and is 'supplied' with AutoCAD LT. It is the **CURRENT** layer which appears in the menu bar i.e. Layer 0 with a black colour. This is a anomaly which the user may find strange. The 0 layer colour is white, but the colour in the menu bar is black. This is normal – white is black with AutoCAD LT.
3. Certain boxes in the dialogue box are in bold type (e.g. New) and others are in light type (e.g. SetLtype). Bold type boxes can be selected (i.e. picked), light type boxes cannot.

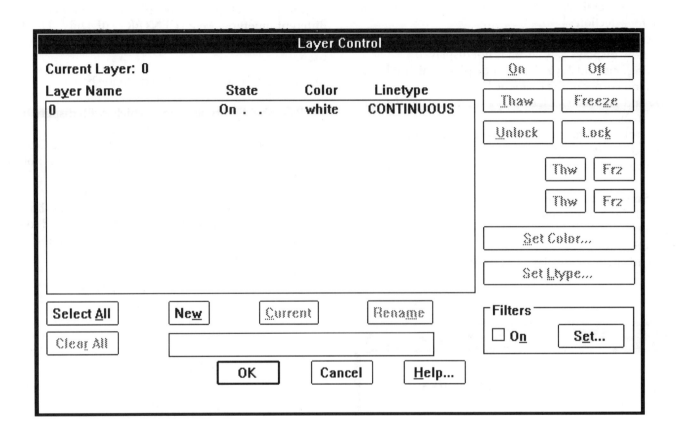

Fig. 16.1. Layer Control dialogue box.

4. Move the pointing device anywhere on the '0,On,white, CONTINUOUS' line, pick it (left click) and it will turn blue. Immediately several boxes change to bold, i.e. they are now available for selection.
5. Pick the off box and note:
   (a) state now displays . . . , i.e. on is not displayed
   (b) **warning: current layer is off** is displayed at the lower left-hand corner of the dialogue box.
6. Pick OK and AutoCAD LT displays the Message dialogue box (Fig. 16.2).
7. Pick OK from the message dialogue box and you will be returned to the drawing screen. Your line and circle will have disappeared because the layer they are drawn on (0) is off.
8. Activate **Settings-Layer Control...** and
   (a) pick 0 layer line – turns blue
   (b) pick **On** box
   (c) pick OK
   (d) line and circle are displayed as layer 0 is now on.

Fig. 16.2. Message box.

Linetypes

Before we can proceed with creating layers, it is necessary to consider linetypes. AutoCAD LT is equipped with several different linetypes, e.g. CENTER, HIDDEN, DASHED, etc. and these must be 'loaded' into the system before they can be used.

1. Activate the Layer Control dialogue box.
2. Pick the 0 layer 'line' which will turn blue.
3. Pick the SetLtype... box which will display the Select Linetype dialogue box as Fig. 16.3.
4. This dialogue box only displays a CONTINUOUS linetype, which means that the other linetypes have not yet been loaded.
   Note that your Linetype dialogue box may show several linetype names indicating that the other linetypes are loaded into your system and you can proceed to step 9.
5. Cancel the Select Linetype dialogue box, and cancel the layer control dialogue box.
6. From the menu bar select **Settings**
   Linetype Style
   Load

prompt	Linetype(s) to load
enter	***<R>**
prompt	Select Linetype File dialogue box
respond	**pick OK**
prompt	several names scroll at the prompt line
then	?/Create/Load/Set
respond	**<RETURN>**

7. Now activate the layer control dialogue box the pick the 0 line then SetLtype.
8. The Select Linetype dialogue box will now display several names indicating that the different linetypes are now loaded. Pick next/Previous to 'see' the different linetypes which are available.

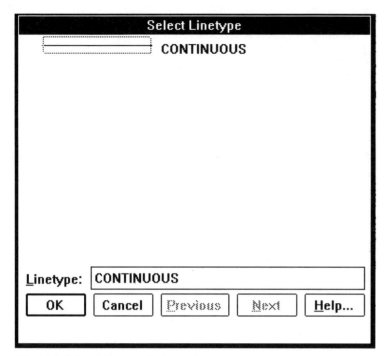

Fig. 16.3. Select Linetype dialogue box.

9. Move the pointing device to the CENTER picture, pick it and
   (a) CENTER picture turns 'white'
   (b) CENTER name appears in the Linetype name box.
10. Pick OK and note that CENTER is the linetype name in the 0 layer line.
11. Pick OK from the layer control dialogue box and you will be returned to the drawing screen.
12. Your line and circle should now be displayed as centre lines.

LTSCALE

This is a variable which controls the appearance of lines e.g. centre lines, hidden lines, etc. It is short for **LINETYPE SCALE** and can be activated from the command line. At the prompt line enter **LTSCALE<R>**

    prompt   `New scale factor<1.0000>`
    enter   **0.5<R>**

Your centre lines should now be better defined?

Using LTSCALE, enter different scale factors and note the effect on your two entities. Decide on the value which gives the 'best appearance'. For the A3-sized paper we are using I would recommend that the LTSCALE value is set between 0.4–0.6.

Colour

Layers can be used to add colour to a drawing by assigning a specific colour to a named layer. Activate the layer control dialogue box and

1. Pick the 0 layer line.
2. Pick the SetColor... box which will display the Select Color dialogue box
3. Using the Standard Colors pick RED and note that red appears in the Color: box.
4. Pick OK to return to the layer control dialogue box, and red will be the layer 0 colour.
5. Pick OK from the layer control box to return to the drawing screen and your line and circle entity will be red centre lines (I hope).
6. Note that the menu bar displays a red box at the left end, i.e. the current layer (0) has colour red.

Exercise

Using the layer control dialogue box, set the linetype and colour of layer 0 back to CONTINUOUS and WHITE, respectively. The colour white means that you pick the black colour from the Standard Color line.

Note on Select Colour dialogue box

When the SetColor... option is selected from the layer control dialogue box, the Set Colour dialogue box will be displayed. The appearance of this dialogue box will depend on the type of monitor you have. Many users will have a full colour palette of 255 colours available for selection, while others will only have about 14. This does not matter, as we will only consider the standard colours.

AutoCAD LT designates colours by numbers, and the following are the assigned numbers for the standard colours:

1 red	2 yellow	3 green	4 cyan
5 blue	6 magenta	7 black(white)	8 grey?
9 rust?			

These numbers are used to assign colour pens in a plotter, thus allowing multi-coloured drawings to be obtained.

Creating new layers

Erase the line and circle entities from the screen, and ensure that layer 0 has been returned to colour white and continuous linetype. The layers that have to be created are

Usage	Layer name	Layer colour	Layer linetype
General	0	white	CONTINUOUS
Outlines	OUT	red	CONTINUOUS
Centre lines	CL	green	CENTER
Hidden lines	HID	yellow	HIDDEN
Dimensions	DIMEN	blue	CONTINUOUS
Text	TEXT	magenta	CONTINUOUS
Hatching	SECT	cyan	CONTINUOUS

1. Activate the layer control dialogue box, and note the flashing |. This is where we enter the layer name.
2. Enter OUT at the | then pick the New box.
3. The name OUT is transferred to the layer list and assigned a white colour and a CONTINUOUS linetype. These are the defaults.
4. Enter CL at the | then pick New.
5. Enter HID at the | and pick New.
6. Enter DIMEN, TEXT, SECT at the | picking New after each entry.
7. Select the OUT layer line (turns blue) then
   (a) pick the SetColor... box
   (b) pick RED from the standard colours
   (c) pick OK from the colour dialogue box
   (d) layer OUT should have colour red.
   (e) deselect the OUT layer by picking it – blue colour disappears.
8. Select the CL layer line and
   (a) pick the SetColor... box
   (b) pick GREEN from the standard colours
   (c) pick OK
   (d) layer CL colour is green and line still active (blue)
   (e) pick the SetLtype... box
   (f) pick CENTER picture then OK
   (g) layer CL should have a CENTER linetype
   (i) deselect the CL by picking the ClearAll box – blue disappears.
9. Using the above method, set the colour and linetype of the new layers we have created. The procedure is quite simple, and if you make a mistake it is easy to rectify by altering the color and linetype to the correct setting.
10. When all the colours and linetypes have been set, pick OK from the layer control dialogue box. The layers we have made are now available to use.

The current layer

The current layer is the one on which entities will be drawn. Its name and colour appear in the menu bar and can be set by

1. Activating the layer control dialogue box.
2. Pick the layer line to be current, e.g. OUT – turns blue.
3. Pick the Current box – Current Layer: OUT at top.
4. Pick OK.
5. Layer name OUT in menu bar with colour red.

I usually start a drawing with OUT as the current layer, but this is a personal preference. Other users may want CL or 0 as the current layer, but it does not really matter. The layer control dialogue box at this stage should appear as shown in Fig. 16.4 and is different from when the layers were created. This is because AutoCAD LT lists the layers in numeric layer number order then in alphabetical order and not in the order they were created.

There is another way in which the current layer can be changed which is quicker than using the layer control dialogue box. This is from the menu bar by left-clicking on the white layer name area. The created layers will be listed as pull-down items as shown in Fig. 16.5. By picking the required layer name (turns blue), that layer will be current. The layer control dialogue box can also be activated from the menu bar by picking the grey layer box.

Current Layer: OUT

Layer Name	State	Color	Linetype
0	On . .	white	CONTINUOUS
CL	On . .	green	CENTER
DIMEN	On . .	blue	CONTINUOUS
HID	On . .	yellow	HIDDEN
OUT	On . .	red	CONTINUOUS
SECT	On . .	cyan	CONTINUOUS
TEXT	On . .	magenta	CONTINUOUS

Fig. 16.4. Layer control dialogue box.

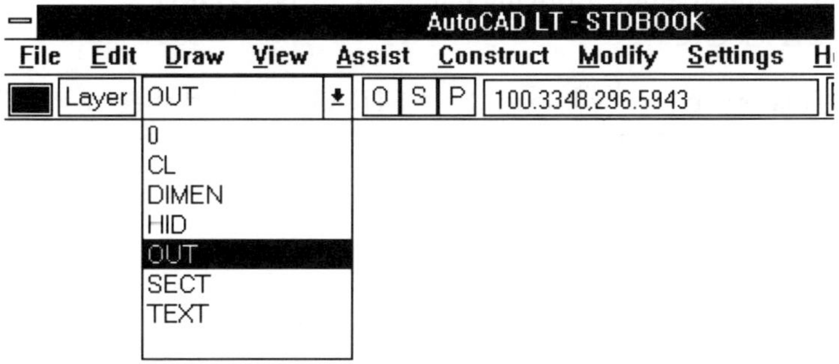

Fig. 16.5. Current layer selection from menu bar.

Saving the standard sheet

Now that the required layers have been created, and the current layer set to OUT, select the SAVE icon or pick File-Save from the menu bar. This will update the **A:STDA3** standard sheet drawing opened at the start of the chapter. The standard sheet has now been saved with

    (a) units set to decimal metric
    (b) limits set to A3 paper
    (c) several variables set, e.g. LTSCALE to 0.5, BLIPS off, etc.
    (d) several layers created.

With the layers now saved in the standard sheet, the layer creation process does not need to be undertaken every time layers are required to be used. New layers can be added to our standard sheet at any time.

It is possible to retain our A:STDA3 standard sheet as the prototype drawing for all future work, but at our level I would not recommend this. The standard sheet should always be used when starting a new drawing using the procedure previously discussed, i.e.

1. Select the New icon or File-New from menu bar.
2. Enter A:STDA3 as the Prototype drawing name.
3. Enter the new drawing name, e.g. **A:NEWDRG**.
4. Pick OK.

This procedure will load the A:STDA3 standard sheet with all the settings and layers.

Using layers

Having created new layers it is now possible to draw entities with hidden and centre linetypes simply by altering the current layer, either from the layer control dialogue box or from the menu bar (easier method). All future work should be completed with layers used properly, i.e. if text is to be added to a drawing, then the TEXT layer should be current, etc.

Making each of the newly created layers current, draw a circle of radius 40 on each layer to give six coloured circles in different places on the screen. Four of these circles will have continuous linetypes, the other two having centre linetype and hidden linetype, respectively.

Layer status

Layers can have six states these being

    (a) ON or OFF.
    (b) THAWED or FROZEN.
    (c) UNLOCKED or LOCKED.

The layer state is given in the layer control dialogue box and so far all layers have been ON, THAWED and UNLOCKED. We will now investigate the other layer state options using the six coloured circles so

	State
1. Make layer 0 current.	O . .
2. Activate the layer control dialogue box and	
(a) pick the CL layer line	
(b) pick the off box	. . .
(c) pick OK – no green circle.	
3. Activate the layer control dialogue box and	
(a) pick the DIMEN layer line	
(b) pick the freeze box	On F .
(c) pick OK – no blue circle.	
4. Layer control dialogue box again and	
(a) pick the HID layer line	
(b) pick the lock box.	On . L
(c) pick OK – yellow circle still on screen.	.
5. Layer control again and	
(a) pick the SECT layer line	
(b) pick freeze and lock boxes	On F L
(c) pick OK – no cyan circle.	
6. Last time for the layer control dialogue box and	
(a) pick the TEXT layer line	
(b) pick off, freeze, lock boxes	F L
(c) pick OK – no magenta circle.	

Your drawing screen should only display a red and yellow circle, i.e. only layers which are ON or LOCKED will be visible. Any layer which is OFF or FROZEN will not be visible. Now try the following:

1. ERASE the yellow circle – you cannot as it is on a locked layer.
2. Draw a line from the centre of the red circle to the centre of the yellow circle using the CENter icon. You can reference the yellow circle although it is on a locked layer.
3. Using the layer control dialogue box, pick Select All (all blue) then pick on, thaw, unlock then OK to 'restore' all circles.

The LAYER command

All work with layers has been achieved with the layer control dialogue box, but the command **LAYER** is available for keyboard entry. When entered the user is prompted with 12 options which allow layers to be made, set, thawed, etc. As these options are all available in the layer control dialogue box, the keyboard command is very rarely used, but it is useful to obtain a list of the available layers.

At the command line enter **LAYER<R>**

prompt	`/Make/....................../` `Lock/Unlock`	
enter	**?<R>**	
prompt	`Layer name(s) to list <*>`	
enter	***<R>**	

The screen will then display the layers created in a different format from the layer control dialogue box as shown in Fig. 16.6. This option is useful in that it gives the layer colour and colour number. The screen can be 'cancelled' by
(a) picking the top left 'disk box' then close
(b) holding done the ALT key and pressing the F4 key
(c) using CTRL-C.

Layer name	State	Color	Linetype
0	On	7 (white)	CONTINUOUS
CL	On	3 (green)	CENTER
DIMEN	On	5 (blue)	CONTINUOUS
HID	On	2 (yellow)	HIDDEN
OUT	On	1 (red)	CONTINUOUS
SECT	On	4 (cyan)	CONTINUOUS
TEXT	On	6 (magenta)	CONTINUOUS

Current layer: 0

?/Make/Set/New/ON/OFF/Color/Ltype/Freeze/Thaw/LOck/Unlock:

Fig. 16.6. The **? LAYER** option.

❑ *Summary*

1. Layers are probably the most important concept in AutoCAD LT.
2. Layers allow entities to be created with different linetypes and colour.
3. Layers are created using the layer control dialogue box.
4. Created layers are not usually 'erased'.
5. New layers can be added at any time.
6. The layer control dialogue box has two associated dialogue boxes
   (a) the SetLtype dialogue box
   (b) the SetColor dialogue box.
7. Linetypes must be loaded before they can be used.
8. The colour palette allows 255 colours if your system supports them.
9. By saving layers on the standard sheet, layers need only be created once.
10. The LTSCALE variable alters the 'appearance' of linetypes.
11. The current layer name and colour appears in the menu bar.
12. Layers can have the following states
    ON: all entities are displayed and can be edited.
    OFF: entities are not displayed and therefore will not be edited.
    FREEZE: similar to OFF, but allows faster regeneration.
    THAWED: undoes a frozen layer.
    LOCK: entities (a) are displayed
                    (b) CANNOT be edited
                    (c) CAN BE REFERENCED.
    UNLOCK: undoes a locked layer.
13. Care has to be taken when editing a drawing with layers which have been turned OFF – more on this later.
14. The layer states in the layer control dialogue box are
    On . .   layer is ON
    . . .   layer is OFF
    On F . layer is ON but FROZEN
    On . L layer is ON but LOCKED

Activity

There are no direct activities with layers, other than to say that all future drawings will use the standard sheet with the created layers.

Exit AutoCAD LT (but do not save the circles) and have a break. If you have worked through this chapter you have certainly earned it.

17. User exercise 2

With the last chapter on layers being rather long, we will now create a simple drawing to use with some other commands, so

1. Load AutoCAD LT if you are not in it.
2. Select the New icon and
   (a) enter **A:STDA3** as the Prototype name
   (b) enter **A:USEREX** as the new drawing name
   (c) pick OK.
3. This will load your standard sheet with the layers.
4. Check that OUT is the current layer.
5. Refer to Fig. 17.1 and
   (a) draw the original shape to the sizes given as Fig. 17.1(a). A start point is available.
   (b) Offset the three lines using the sizes given as Fig. 17.1(b).
   (c) Extend the four lines as Fig. 17.1(c).
   (d) Trim to give the final shape as Fig. 17.1(d).
6. Pick the SAVE icon to save the final shape as **A:USEREX**.

Taking stock

At this stage we have created several drawings as follows

1. Tutorials **A:TUT-1**, **A:TUT-2**, **A:TUT-3**, **A:TUT-4**, **A:TUT-5**, and **A:TUT-6**.
2. A standard sheet **A:STDA3**.
3. A working drawing **A:WORKDRG** – the shape with three circles.
4. A user exercise **A:USEREX**.

The **A:STDA3** standard sheet will be used for all tutorial work, while **A:WORKDRG** and **A:USEREX** will be used throughout the book to demonstrate AutoCAD LT commands.

Exercise

Before leaving this chapter, we will use the user exercise drawing to demonstrate an interesting effect.

1. Make CL the current layer, i.e. green, centre lines.
2. Offset any line of the red shape by 20.
3. Why is this offset line a red continuous line and not a green centre line when CL is the current layer?
4. The reason is that the line selected to be offset, was created on the OUT layer and is therefore a red continuous line. It will therefore be offset as a red continuous line irrespective of the current layer.
5. This can cause some confusion to new users, and I hope that my explanation will help to overcome this confusion.
6. Now exit AutoCAD LT *without* saving the changes.

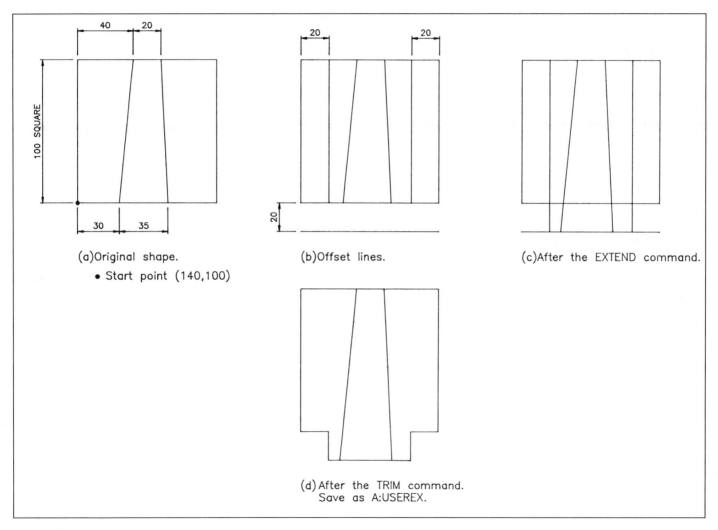

Fig. 17.1. A:USEREX construction.

18. Text

Text should be added to drawings wherever possible. This text may simply be a name and date, but could also be a parts list, a company title block, notes on costing, etc. The text command in AutoCAD LT can be activated by

(a) selecting the TEXT icon from the toolbox.
(b) selecting from the menu bar **Draw**

Text

We will demonstrate how text can be added to a drawing with the user exercise from the previous chapter, so

1. Load AutoCAD LT.
2. Open your **A:USEREX** drawing.
3. Make TEXT the current layer and refer to Fig. 18.1.
4. Select the text icon and

prompt	Justify/Style/<Start point>
enter	**30,230<R>**
prompt	Height<?>
enter	**10<R>**
prompt	Rotation angle<?>
enter	**0<R>**
prompt	Text
enter	**TXET EXRECISE<R>** (deliberately wrong spelling!!!)
prompt	Text
enter	**<RETURN>** to end text sequence.

5. Now select from the menu bar **Draw-Text** and

prompt	Justify/Style/<Start point>
enter	**200,10<R>**
prompt	Height<10>
enter	**5<R>**
prompt	Rotation angle<0>
enter	**30<R>**
prompt	Text
enter	**AutoCAD LT is a draughting package**
prompt	Text
enter	**<RETURN>**

6. Activate the text command again and pick a start point in the lower left area on the screen, and

prompt	Height and enter **8<R>**
prompt	Rotation angle and enter **0<R>**
prompt	Text and enter **YOUR NAME<R>**
prompt	Text and enter **YOUR AGE?<R>**
prompt	Text and enter **THE DATE<R>**
prompt	Text and **<RETURN>** to end sequence.

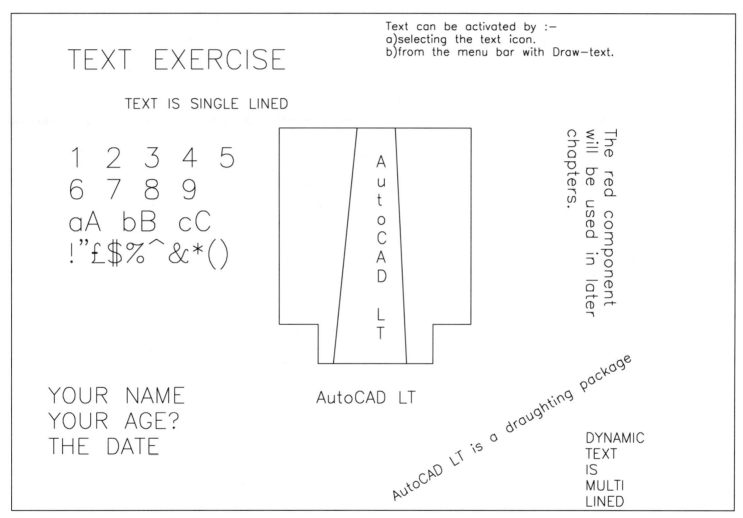

Fig. 18.1. Text exercises with **A:USEREX**.

Editing existing text

Text can be edited as it is entered from the keyboard if the user spots the mistake, but if the text is on the screen when the error is noted, then the **Edit Text** command is required. The first item of text entered (TXET EXRECISE) was deliberately misspelt to enable us to investigate how text can be edited. The command is activated from the menu bar with **Modify**
> **Edit Text**

prompt	`<Select a TEXT or ATTDEF object>?` `Undo`
respond	**pick the TXET EXRECISE item**
prompt	`Edit text dialogue box with:` TXET EXERCISE
respond	(a) move arrow to TX|ET EXERCISE and left click
	(b) backspace to give T|ET EXERCISE
	(c) move the arrow to TE|T EXERCISE and left click
	(d) enter X to give TEXT EXERCISE
	(e) move the arrow to TEXT EXR|ECISE and left click
	(f) backspace to give TEXT EX|ECISE
	(g) move the arrow to TEXT EXE|CISE and left click
	(h) enter R to give TEXT EXER|CISE
	(i) pick OK
prompt	`<Select a TEXT or ATTDEF object>/ Undo`
respond	right click to end sequence.

Your text item should be correctly spelled.

Note that this method is very useful in editing existing text items. The user could have erased to text item completely and re-entered it using the text command.

DTEXT and TEXT

AutoCAD LT allows two 'types' of text to be added to drawings:

(a) DTEXT – dynamic text which allows multiple lines of text to be added with the one text command. The user also 'sees' the text on the screen as it is entered from the keyboard.
(b) TEXT –   is a single line of text not 'seen' as it is entered.

The icon and menu bar selection methods both give DTEXT, and the TEXT command can only be activated from the keyboard (as can DTEXT).

1. At the command line enter **DTEXT<R>** then
    start point – 300,40
    height – 5
    rotation – 0
    text – DYNAMIC**<R>**
    text – TEXT**<R>**
    text – IS**<R>**
    text – MULTI**<R>**
    text – LINED**<R><R>**
2. Now enter **TEXT<R>** at the command line and
    start point – 60,210
    height – 5
    rotation – 0
    text – TEXT IS SINGLE LINED**<R>**
    This item of text will be inserted at the desired point but
    (a) you do not see the text as it is entered from the keyboard.
    (b) only one line is entered and the command is automatically exited.
3. Now add other text items as Fig. 18.1.
4. Save your drawing, then open **A:STDA3** for the text justification exercise.

Text justification

Screen text can be 'justified', i.e. positioned in different ways, AutoCAD LT allowing six justifications these being:

- left (normal) which is the default justification
- aligned
- centred
- fitted
- middle
- right.

The justification point(s) can be entered as co-ordinates or picked using the mouse.

1. Refer to Fig. 18.2, activate the **TEXT** command and

    enter **30,240<R>**   for the start point

        10<R>   for the height

        0<R>   for the rotation angle

        This is<R>

        NORMAL(LEFT)<R>

        Justified<R>

        Text<R><R>   – yes, two returns!

2. Repeat the text command and

prompt	justify/Style/<Start point>
enter	**J<R>**
prompt	Align/Fit/Center/Middle/Right
enter	**C<R>** for Center option
prompt	Center point
enter	**100,175<R>**
prompt	Height
enter	**10<R>**
prompt	Rotation angle
enter	**0<R>**
prompt	Text and enter **This is<R>**
prompt	Text and enter **CENTRE<R>**
prompt	Text and enter **Justified<R>**

    prompt   Text and enter **Text<R><R>**

3. Using text command with the **J** option and:

prompt	Align/Fit/Center/Middle/Right
enter	**R** for Right option
prompt	End point
enter	**360,190<R>**
prompt	Height and enter **10<R>**
prompt	Rotation angle and enter **0<R>**
prompt	Text and enter **This is<R>**
prompt	Text and enter **RIGHT<R>**
prompt	Text and enter **Justified<R>**
prompt	Text and enter **Text<R><R>**

4. Activate the text command and enter **J** then **F** (for Fit) and:

prompt	First text line point and enter **20,90<R>**
prompt	Second text line point and enter **150,90<R>**
prompt	Height and enter **10<R>**
prompt	Text and enter **This is FITTED text<R><R>**

5. With text again enter **J** then **M** and:

prompt	Middle point and enter **200,175<R>**
prompt	Height **10** and Rotation angle **0**
prompt	Text and enter **This is<R>**
prompt	Text and enter **MIDDLE<R>**
prompt	Text and enter **Justified<R>**
prompt	Text and enter **Text<R><R>**

6. For the last time use the text command with the **J** and **A** option and:

prompt	First text line point and enter **20,50<R>**
prompt	Second text line point and enter **150,50<R>**
prompt	Text and enter **This is ALIGNED text<R><R>**

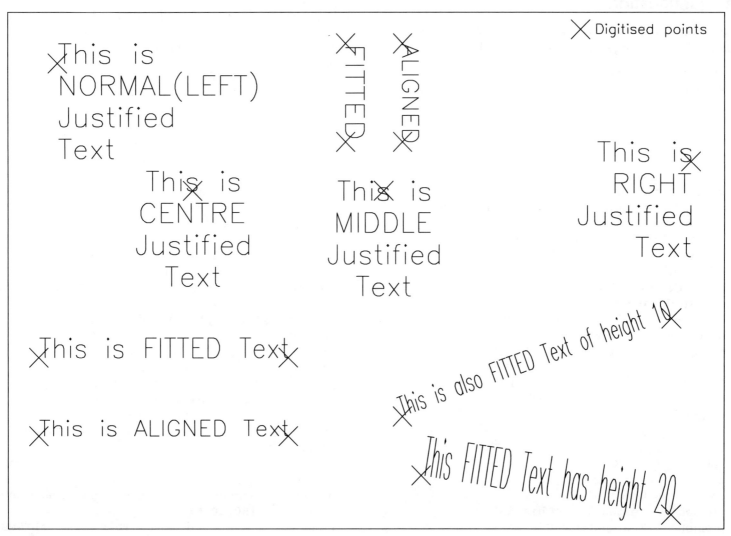

Fig. 18.2. Text justification.

Now try some text justification options of your own, then quit AutoCAD LT, saving your drawing if you want, but we will not refer to it again.

The 'pick' points with test justification are

left	the leftmost end of the text item.
centre	a baseline centre point for the text item.
middle	a text item middle point.
right	the rightmost end of the text item.
fit	two endmost points for fitting the text item.
align	two endmost points for fitting the text item.

Text style

When the text command is activated, one of the options available to the user is Style. This is an option which allows different text styles to be set, but at present we will leave this to a later chapter when we will investigate text styles and fonts.

❏ *Summary*

1. Text can be entered using DTEXT or TEXT.
2. TEXT only allows a single line entry.
3. DTEXT allows multiple text lines and the user 'sees' the text being entered on the screen.
4. DTEXT is activated from the icon or the menu bar.
5. TEXT is entered from the keyboard.
6. The text start point, centre point, fitted points etc, can be entered as co-ordinates or picked with the mouse.
7. Text can be justified six ways.
8. Screen text can be edited in dialogue box form.
9. Fitted text and Aligned text are similar
   (a) the user selects the start and end points on a 'line'
   (b) fitted text demands a height
   (c) aligned text requires no height, and the text is 'adjusted' to suit the two pick points.
10. Centre text and middle text are similar
   (a) the user selects the centre/middle point
   (b) centred text is about the text BASELINE
   (c) middle text is about the text MIDDLE.
11. Multiple text lines are justified according to the selection.

Activity

Attempt Tutorial 7 which consists of two simple components with some text items. Use your standard sheet, beginning a new drawing with a prototype name **A:STDA3** and a new drawing name of **A:TUT-7**.

Use your layers correctly, i.e. draw the outline shape on the OUT layer and add the text items on the **TEXT** layer. Do not attempt to dimension the drawing yet.

19. Dimensioning 1

AutoCAD LT has automatic dimensioning, i.e. the user simply selects the entity to be dimensioned and AutoCAD LT calculates the length, radius or angle and displays the actual dimension with arrows, extension lines, etc.

Associative dimensions

When associated dimensions are used all dimension lines, arrows, text, etc. which make up the dimension are treated as a single entity with the following features

    (a) they can be edited using AutoCAD LT commands
    (b) they change if the entity being dimensioned changes
    (c) their appearance can be altered.

The associative dimension effect is either on or off and by selecting **Settings** from the menu bar, a tick at the Associative Dimensions means that they are on. It is usual to have Associative Dimensioning on when dimensioning.
    The basic dimension types (shown in Fig. 19.1) which are available are:

1. Linear
    (a) horizontal, vertical, aligned, rotated
    (b) baseline, continue.
2. Ordinate   Automatic, X-Datum, Y-Datum.
3. Radial   Diameter, Radius.
4. Angular.
5. Leader   used to take dimensions 'outside' text.

Dimensioning A:WORKDRG

To demonstrate dimensioning open drawing **A:WORKDRG** and refer to Fig. 19.2. This drawing was created on layer 0 only and there should be no other layers? Check with the Layer Control dialogue box.
    When dimensioning it is usual to use the object snap to ensure the correct selection of the entity. I generally set a running object snap to ENDpoint, but we will use the toolbox icons for the object snap selection.

Linear dimensioning

1. From the menu bar select **Draw**
                            Linear Dimensions
                            Horizontal

prompt	First extension line origin or <RETURN> to select
respond	**ENDpoint icon and pick line d1**
and	cursor snaps to left-end of line
prompt	Second extension line origin
respond	**ENDpoint icon and pick line d2**
prompt	Dimension line location(Text/Angle)
and	drag effect is obtained
respond	**pick a point d3 below the line being dimensioned**
prompt	Dimension text<215>
respond	**<RETURN>**

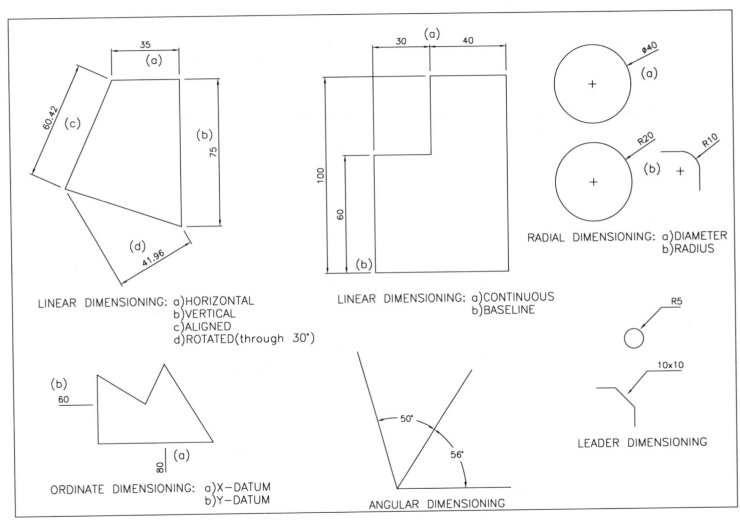

Fig. 19.1. Basic dimension types.

The dimension will be inserted at the desired point with text, arrows, etc., added. Use the erase icon and pick any point on the dimension then **<RETURN>**. The complete dimension will be erased as it is a single entity, i.e. it is an associative dimension. Now repeat the dimension selection and add the dimension again.

2. Now select **Draw-Linear Dimensions-Horizontal** and

prompt	`First extension line origin or <RETURN> to select`
respond	**ENDpoint icon and pick line d4**
prompt	`Second extension line origin`
respond	**ENDpoint icon and pick line d5**
prompt	`Dimension line location(Text/Angle)`
respond	**pick a point d6 above dimension**
prompt	`Dimension text<80>`
respond	**right click**
prompt	`Command Line`
respond	**Select Draw-Linear Dimensions-Baseline**
prompt	`Second extension line origin`
respond	**ENDpoint icon and pick line d7**
prompt	`Dimension text<150>`
respond	**right click**

3. Select from the menu bar **Draw**
> **Linear Dimensions**
> **Vertical**

prompt	`First extension line and` **ENDpoint** `line d8`
prompt	`second extension line and` **ENDpoint** `line d9`
prompt	`Dimension line location and` **pick point d10**
prompt	`Dimension text<25> and` **right click**
prompt	`Command line`

respond	**select Draw-Linear Dimensions-Continue**
prompt	`Second extension line and` **ENDpoint** `line d11`
prompt	`Dimension text<45> and` **right click**
prompt	`Command line`
respond	**select Draw-Linear Dimensions-Continue**
prompt	`Second extension line and` **ENDpoint** `line d12`
prompt	`Dimension text<80> and` **right click**

Diameter dimensioning

From the menu bar select **Draw**
> **Radial Dimensions**
> **Diameter**

prompt	`Select arc or circle`
respond	**NEArest icon and pick circle d13**
prompt	`Dimension text<30>`
respond	**right click**
prompt	`Enter leader length for text`
respond	**pick a point 'outside' circle**

Radius dimensioning

From the menu bar select **Draw**
> **Radial Dimensions**
> **Radius**

prompt	`Select arc or circle`
respond	**NEArest icon and pick circle d14**
prompt	`Dimension text<20>`
respond	**right click**
prompt	`Enter leader length for text`
respond	**pick a point 'outside' circle**

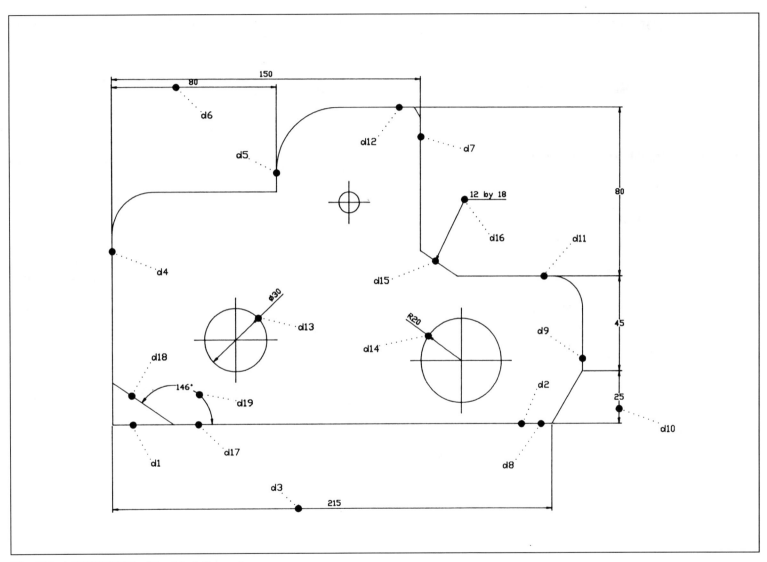

Fig. 19.2. A:WORKDRG with added dimensions.

Leader dimensioning

Select **Draw-Leader** and:

prompt	Leader start
respond	**NEArest icon and pick line d15**
prompt	To point
respond	**pick a point d16**
prompt	To point
respond	**right click or <RETURN>**
prompt	Dimension text<20?>
enter	**12 by 18<R>**

Angular dimensioning

Select **Draw-Angular Dimension**

prompt	Select arc, circle, line or RETURN
respond	**NEArest icon and pick line d17**
prompt	Second line
respond	**NEArest icon and pick line d18**
prompt	Dimension arc line location(Text/ Angle)
respond	**pick a point d19**
prompt	Dimension text<146>
respond	**right click**
prompt	Enter text location
respond	**right click**

Hopefully your **A:WORKDRG** will be dimensioned as show in in Fig. 19.2, but it may not be. Some users may have their dimension text aligned differently from mine.

The dimension 'layout' in Fig. 19.2 is not 'ideal' and there are a few points worth mentioning:

1. The Baseline dimensions are not spaced out.
2. The vertical dimension text is horizontal and not aligned with the dimension line.
3. The gap between the entity being dimensioned and the dimension extension line is not very big.
4. The diameter dimension has lines through the circle centre.

Dimension settings

Dimensions have settings which can be altered by the user, and allows the dimensions to be set to a required standard which may be British Standards, ANSI (American), DIN (German) or individual company standards. The dimensions used in Fig. 19.2 have used the AutoCAD LT default dimension settings and have not (as yet) been altered to our own personal requirements. The dimension settings can be obtained in dialogue box format by selecting from the menu bar with

> **Settings**
> **Dimension Style...**

The resulting Dimension Styles and Setting dialogue box is shown in Fig. 19.3 and has the following other dialogue box selections:

(a) Dimension Lines
(b) Extension Lines
(c) Arrows
(d) Text Location
(e) Text Format
(f) Scale and Colors

Several of these dialogue box selections will be discussed in the next chapter, so at present cancel the Dimension Style and Setting dialogue box and save your drawing as A:WORKDRGA not as **A:WORKDRG**.

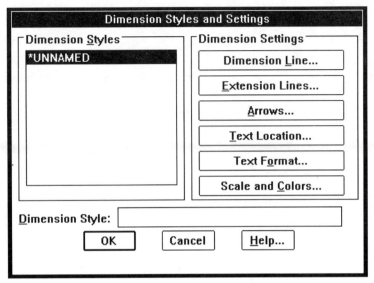

Fig. 19.3. Dimension Styles and Setting dialogue box.

Dimension terminology

Dimensions have there own terminology and Fig. 19.4 explains some of this terminology for

1. Dimension line terminology.
2. Interior/basic example.
3. Arrows, ticks and dots.
4. Dimension text Alignment.

There is other terminology used with dimensions, but Fig. 19.4 should give the user a reasonable working start.

DEFPOINTS layer

Activate the layer control command to display the Layer Control dialogue box. We have only used layer 0 with our **A:WORKDRG**, but there is a DEFPOINTS layer. This layer is automatically created every time any entity is dimensioned. It can be frozen, changed colour etc. but will not affect the dimensions on the screen as they were created on layer 0. Even when a separate layer is used for dimensioning, the DEFPOINTS layer will still be created.

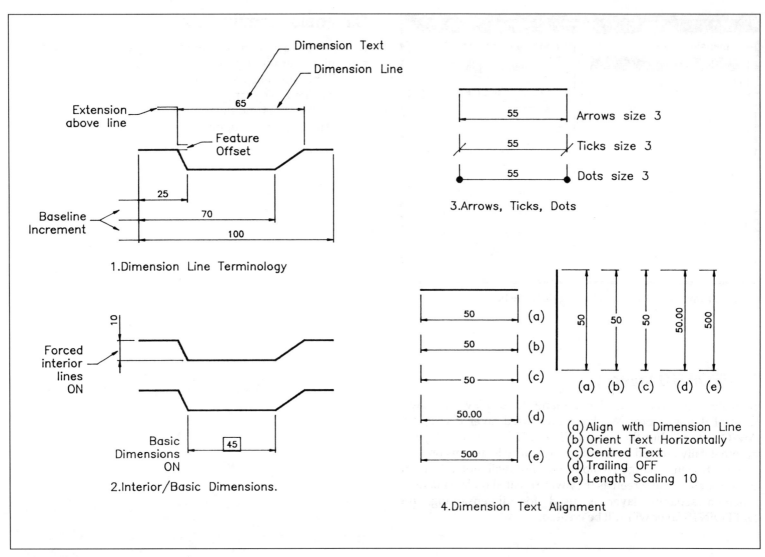

Fig. 19.4. Dimension line terminology.

The RETURN option

The first prompt when using the Linear Dimensions command was 'First extension line or RETURN to select'. This prompt allows the user to select a single entity for linear dimensioning. Activate the vertical option from the linear dimensions command and

prompt	First extension line or <RETURN> to select
respond	**<RETURN>**
prompt	Select line, arc or circle
respond	**pick the left vertical line of component**
prompt	Dimension line location
respond	**pick a point to the left**
prompt	Dimension text<40>
respond	**right click**

Select the horizontal option from the linear dimensions command and enter **<RETURN>** at the first prompt, then

(a) pick any circle
(b) pick a point below circle for dimension line location
(c) right click.

The **<RETURN>** option is generally easier to use when dimensioning as it only requires the user to select the entity to be dimensioned. I must admit to not using this option very much, preferring to select my entity to be dimensioned using the icon selection method.

Now exit AutoCAD LT, discarding changes.

❏ *Summary*

1. AutoCAD LT has automatic, associative dimensions.
2. Dimensioning can be linear, radial, angular, leader or ordinate which has not yet been covered.
3. Dimensions can be set to a required format using the Dimension Style and Settings dialogue box.
4. The diameter and degrees symbols are automatically entered when using radial and angular dimensions.
5. Object snap modes are usually used to select entities.
6. A layer DEFPOINTS is created when dimensioning.

20. Dimensioning 2 and standard sheet 3

In the last chapter we investigated how dimensions could be added to a drawing. In this chapter we will 'set' the dimensions to our own requirements (well mine) using our A:STDA3 standard sheet. This will then allow all future new drawings to have the same dimension format. We will use the Dimension Style and Settings dialogue box repeatedly in this chapter, and the changes will be given as a sequence of steps. The various individual dialogue boxes which are available will not be displayed, as the user should by now be familiar with them and know how to alter values.

1. Open your **A:STDA3** standard sheet drawing.
2. From the menu bar select **Settings-Dimension Styles...**
3. At the Dimension Style name box enter **STDA3** then **<R>** and the message New style STDA3 created from *UNNAMED appears at the bottom of the dialogue box.
4. Select Dimension Lines... and alter:
   (a) forced interior lines: off, i.e. no cross
   (b) basic dimensions: off, i.e. no cross
   (c) text gap: 2
   (d) baseline increment: 10
   (e) OK.
5. Select Extension Lines... and alter:
   (a) extension above line: 1.5
   (b) feature offset: 2.5
   (c) visibility: draw both
   (d) center mark : 2

(e) mark with center lines: off
(f) OK.
6. Select Arrows... and alter:
   (a) arrows active, i.e. black dot
   (b) arrow size: 3
   (c) OK.
7. Select Text Location... and alter:
   (a) text height: 3
   (b) tolerance height: 2
   (c) horizontal: default
   (d) vertical: above
   (e) alignment: align with dimension line
   (f) OK.
8. Select Text Format... and:
   (a) Length scaling: 1
   (b) Trailing: off, i.e. no cross
   (c) Show alternative units: off, i.e. no cross
   (d) Tolerances: off (see the separate chapter on this topic)
   (e) OK.
9. Select Scale and Color... and :
   (a) feature scaling : 1
   (b) OK
10. Pick OK from the Dimension Style and Settings dialogue box to save the dimensions which we have set as the style **STDA3**.
11. Now pick the save icon to save the STDA3 dimension style in the A:STDA3 standard sheet.

12. The **A:STDA3** standard sheet has the following personal settings
    (a) drawing aids, e.g. grid, snap, blips
    (b) a border in which all drawings are completed
    (c) various layers, e.g. OUT, CL, DIMEN, etc.
    (d) a dimension text style STDA3.

Using the STDA3 dimension text style

With OUT as the current layer use absolute co-ordinate entry with the following commands to create the shape in Fig. 20.1

LINE		CIRCLE	
From	60,90	1. CEN	80,160
To	95,90	RAD	15
To	125,120	2. CEN	115,145
To	140,80	RAD	10
To	160,200		
To	50,185		
To	close		

With DIMEN the current layer and STDA3 the dimension text style, add all the dimensions as Fig. 20.1. using the information given about baseline and continuous.

Ordinate dimensions

This type of dimension was not covered in the previous chapter, and we will investigate its use with our STDA3 dimension style. With OUT as the current layer use the LINE command with absolute co-ordinate input and the following data:

From	245,90
To	280,90
To	280,110
To	330,110
To	345,190
To	310,190
To	310,160
To	265,160
To	265,140
To	250,140
To	250,115
To	245,115
To	close

From the menu bar select **Draw**
                          Ordinate Dimensions
                          X-Datum

prompt	Select Feature
respond	**pick lower left-hand corner of drawn shape** (SNAP ON helps)
prompt	Leader endpoint (Xdatum/Ydatum)_x Leader endpoint
enter	**@0,–10<R>**
prompt	Dimension text<245.00>
respond	**right click**

Repeat the ordinate dimensions selection with Y-datum and

prompt	Select Feature
respond	**pick the same point as before**
prompt	Leader endpoint(Xdatum/Ydatum)_y Leader endpoint
enter	**@–10,0<R>**
prompt	Dimension text<90.00>
respond	**right click**

Using the above procedure add the other ordinate dimensions to the created shape. It is very easy. At the 'Select Feature' prompt, pick a point on the shape. Try to 'line up' the leader endpoints with the dimension already entered. This could be by co-ordinate entry (as our example), or by picking a point on the screen. Figure 20.1 gives the complete shape with ordinate dimensions added.

The dimension text default

When an entity is selected for dimensioning, AutoCAD LT gives the actual dimension as <???>. This is the default dimension text value. The user can:

   (a) accept this value with **<RETURN>**
   (b) enter a value from the keyboard.

While accepting the default value is satisfactory, it is sometimes beneficial to enter the actual dimension from the keyboard. I have illustrated the effect in Fig. 20.1 with three horizontal line of length 15, these being:

   (a) accepting the default 15.00
   (b) entering 15 from the keyboard
   (c) cheating by entering 99.

The benefit of entering the dimension value from the keyboard can be seen from example (b) where the dimension text is placed between the extension lines. The default example (a) put the dimension text 'outside' the extension line due to its 'size'. This is only one benefit of entering the dimension text from the keyboard. I personally use this method at all times and would recommend that the user does likewise, but it is your decision.

❏ *Summary*

1. Dimension styles can be set to user requirements.
2. STDA3 is our standard dimension style.
3. The standard sheet **A:STDA3** has the dimension style STDA3 set.
4. Ordinate dimensions offer another method of adding dimensions.
5. The dimension text value can be 'overwritten' by the user with keyboard entry.

Activity

I have included four activities for dimensioning. This may seem excessive but it will give the user practice with:

(a) drawing more components
(b) using the standard sheet with layers
(c) adding text
(d) adding dimensions.

   In each of the activities, the user should

1. Use the new drawing icon.
2. Enter the Prototype name as A:STDA3
3. Enter the new drawing name as A:TUT-??
4. Complete the drawing
5. Pick the save icon to save the drawing as A:TUT-??

   The activities are

(a) Tutorial 8 – two simple shapes to get you started.
(b) Tutorial 9 – three components with hints for construction.
(c) Tutorial 10 – two components with more thought needed.
(d) Tutorial 11 – much easier than it looks.

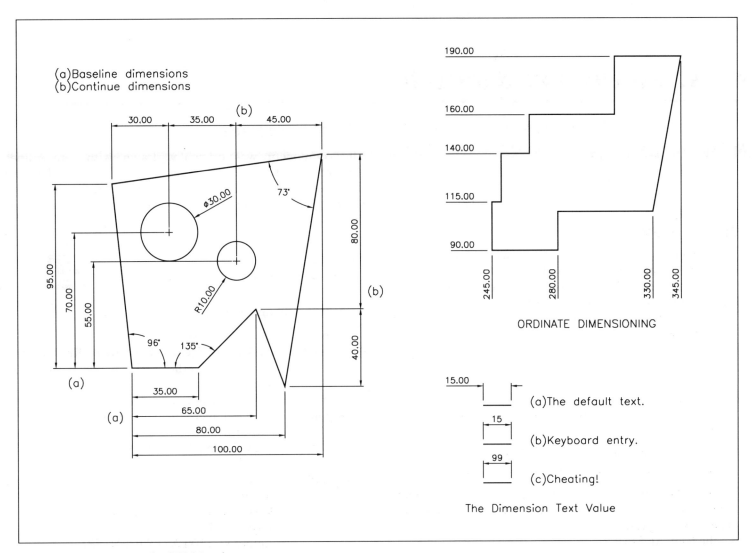

Fig. 20.1. Dimensions using the STDA3 style.

21. Construct and Modify

In this chapter we will investigate several of the **Construct** and **Modify** commands and will also use the selection set. The commands which will be discussed are

Construct   Copy, Mirror
Modify   Move, Rotate, Scale, Stretch, Change Properties.

Getting ready

1. Open your **A:WORKDRG** drawing which was created earlier. Although it was used for dimensioning it should not have been saved with the dimensions added. If it was, then erase all dimensions to leave the basic component shape.
2. Draw a border using the **LINE** command
   from 0,0
   to   380,0
   to   380,270
   to   0,270
   to   close
3. The component was drawn on layer 0. Make two new layers:

   CL   colour green with CENTER linetype
   DIMEN   colour blue with CONTINUOUS linetype.

   You may have to load the linetype file for this. If you cannot remember how this was achieved, refer to the chapter dealing with layers.
4. Set the LTSCALE to 0.5
5. Ensure layer 0 is current.

Change properties

The component was originally drawn with centre lines through the three circles, but these lines were not 'real' centre lines. We will now make these lines 'real' centre lines using the Change Properties command. The command can be activated from

Menu Bar   *Icon*
Modify
Change Properties

Activate the change properties command and

prompt	Select objects
respond	**pick the six 'centre lines' then <RETURN>**
prompt	Change Properties dialogue box as shown in Fig. 21.1
prompt	pick Layer...
respond	Select Layer dialogue box as shown in Fig. 21.2
respond	**pick CL line** (turns blue)
then	**pick OK**
prompt	Change Properties dialogue box with
	Colour...: BYLAYER (green)
	Layer...: CL
	Linetype...: BYLAYER (CENTER)
respond	**pick OK**

The six lines should now appear as green centre lines as they have been changed to the CL layer. The Change Properties command allows the following to be changed in dialogue box format for any entity:

(a) colour
(b) layer
(c) linetype.

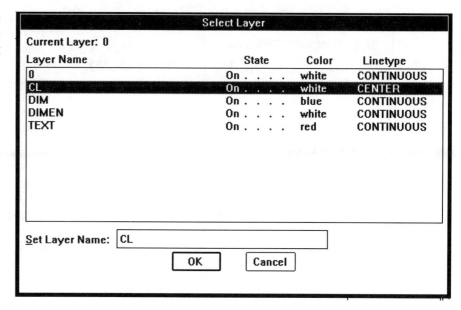

Fig. 21.2. Select Layer dialogue box.

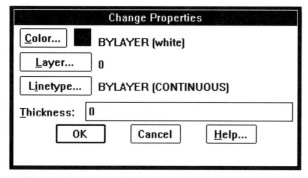

Fig. 21.1. Change Properties dialogue box.

Copy

Refer to Fig. 21.3, select the **COPY** icon and

prompt	Select objects
enter	**C<R>** for crossing
prompt	First corner
respond	**pick a point d1**
prompt	Other corner
respond	**pick a point d2**
prompt	Select objects
respond	from menu bar select **Assist**
	Select
	Add

prompt	Select objects
respond	**pick entities d3,d4,d5 then <RETURN>**
prompt	<Base line or displacement>/ Multiple
respond	**INTersection icon and pick point d6**
prompt	Second point of displacement
and	note ghost image when mouse is moved
enter	**@300,0<R>**

Your drawing should be similar to Fig. 21.4 and you may be a bit worried as part of the drawing is off the screen. This can happen with several commands, such as **COPY, MOVE, PAN** for example, but all is not lost. At the command line enter **ZOOM<R>** then **A<R>** and your drawing should appear smaller, but the copied component should be visible in total. You may want to reposition the toolbox? Figure 21.5 gives the effect after the ZOOM command.

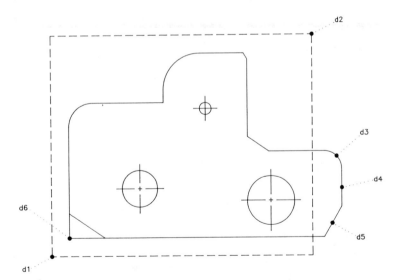

Fig. 21.3. A:WORKDRG with points for the **COPY** command.

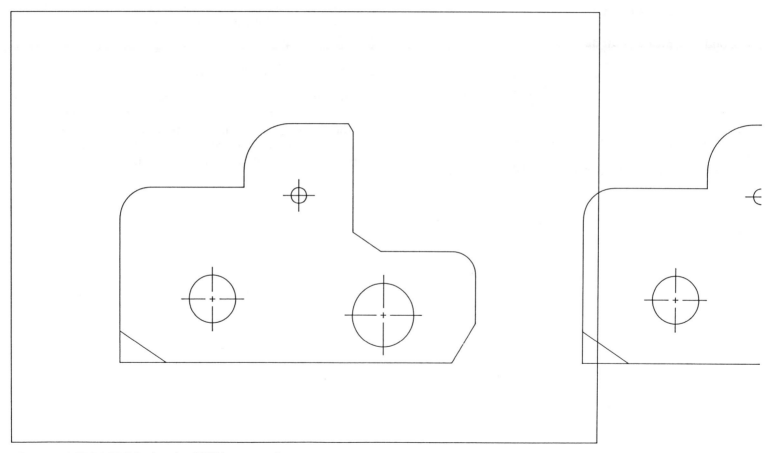

Fig. 21.4. A:WORKDRG after the COPY command.

Move

Refer to Fig. 21.5 and select the **MOVE** icon and

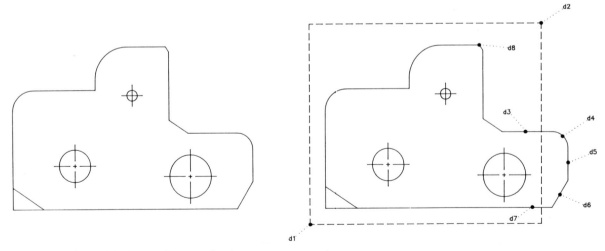

prompt	Select objects
enter	**W<R>** for window
prompt	First corner
respond	**pick a point d1**
prompt	Other corner
respond	**pick a point d2**
prompt	Select objects
respond	from menu bar select **Assist**
	Select
	Add
prompt	Select objects
respond	**pick entities d3,d4,d5,d6,d7**
prompt	Select objects
respond	from menu bar select **Assist-Select-Remove**

prompt	Remove objects
respond	**pick the three circles then <RETURN>**
prompt	Base point or displacement
respond	**INTersection icon and pick point d8**
prompt	Second point of displacement
enter	**395,295<R>**

This will give Fig. 21.6, with the copied component having been moved but the three circles have been 'left behind' as they were removed from the MOVE command.

Transparent command

In both the **COPY** and **MOVE** commands we used Assist from the menu bar to add/remove entities from the command. This type of usage where a command is activated while still using the original command is called **TRANSPARENCY**. It is very useful, but only certain commands are transparent.

Fig. 21.5. A:WORKDRG after ZOOM A, with points for the move command.

Rotate

Refer to Fig. 21.6 and select the **ROTATE** icon and

prompt	`Select objects`
respond	from menu bar select **Assist-Select-WPolygon**
prompt	`First polygon point` and pick point d1
prompt	`Undo/<Endpoint of line>` and pick point d2
prompt	`Undo/<Endpoint of line>` and pick point d3
prompt	`Undo/<Endpoint of line>` and pick point d4
prompt	`Undo/<Endpoint of line>` and pick point d5
prompt	`Undo/<Endpoint of line>` and pick point d6 then **<RETURN>**
prompt	`24 found?`
and	`Select objects`
respond	**right click**
prompt	`Base point`
respond	**CENtre icon and pick circle d7** (Note the ghost image)
prompt	`<Rotation angle>/Reference`
enter	**90<R>** to give Fig. 21.7.

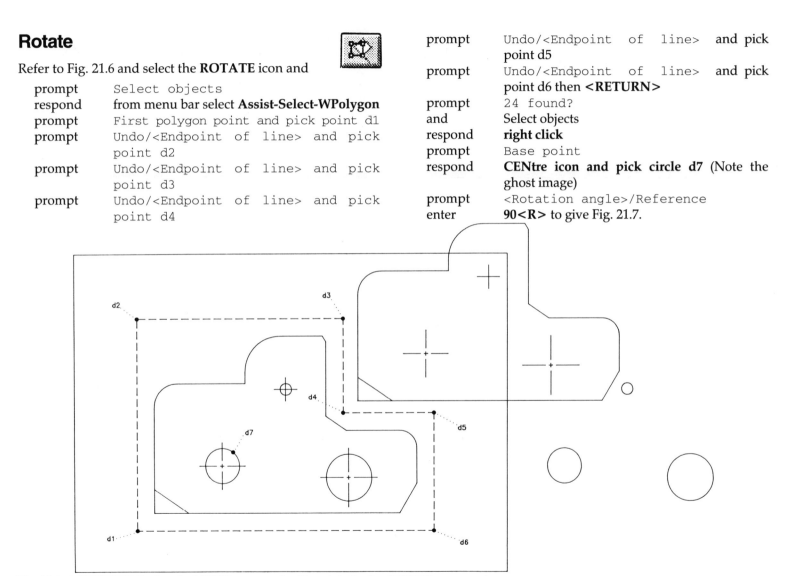

Fig. 21.6. A:WORKDRG after the MOVE command with points for the ROTATE command.

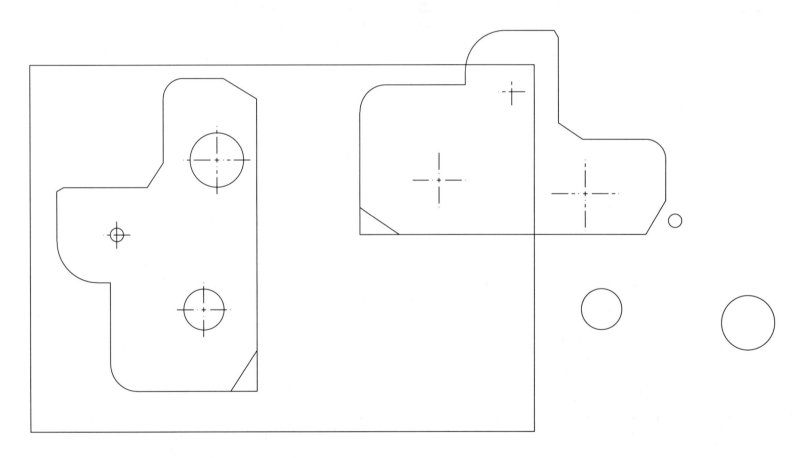

Fig. 21.7. A:WORKDRG after the ROTATE command.

Stretch

Our drawing is becoming cluttered, so erase rotated component and the three circles. This will leave the 'moved' component with centre lines.

1. Move the component from the base point 395,295 to the point 70,50 (window option).
2. Make DIMEN layer current and dimension the four lines shown in Fig. 21.8 as follows:
   (a) one horizontal and one vertical accepting the dimension text default value
   (b) one horizontal and one vertical entering the dimension from the keyboard.
3. Make layer 0 current and freeze layer CL.
4. Select the **STRETCH** icon and

    prompt   Select objects to stretch by window or polygon

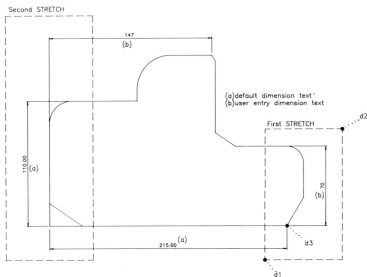

Fig. 21.8. A:WORKDRG with the STRETCH points.

Select objects	
enter	**W<R>**
prompt	First corner
respond	**pick a point d1**
prompt	Other corner
respond	**pick a point d2**
prompt	9 found?
Select objects	
respond	**right click or <RETURN>**
prompt	Base point or displacement
respond	**INTersection icon and pick point d3**
prompt	Second point of displacement
enter	**@50,0<R>**

The component will be stretched. Has the base horizontal dimension changed?

5. Repeat the STRETCH command by selecting the icon again, and select the other window as shown in Fig. 21.8. Select any suitable base point and enter a displacement of @−20,0 to give Fig. 21.9. Note that the original horizontal line has dimension 215.00; the dimension after first **STRETCH** is 265.00, i.e. +50; and the dimension after the second **STRETCH** is 285.00, i.e. +20.
6. The top horizontal dimension is still 147. This was one of the dimensions which was entered from the keyboard and has been unaffected by the **STRETCH** command, i.e.
   (a) default dimensions are stretched
   (b) keyboard entry dimensions are not stretched.

Scale

Select the **SCALE** icon and

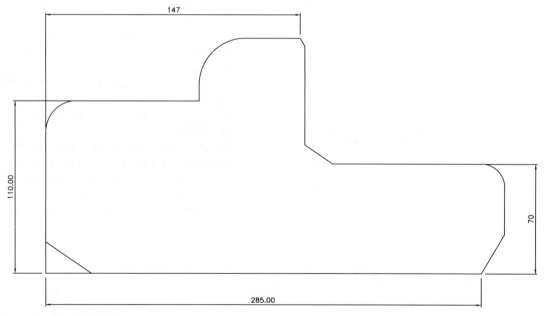

prompt	Select object
enter	**W<R>** and window complete component including dimensions
prompt	19 found?
then	Select objects
respond	**right click**
prompt	Base point
respond	**pick the lower left-hand corner of component**
prompt	<Scale factor>/Reference
enter	**0.5<R>**

The component will be redrawn at 0.5 full size as Fig. 21.10 with

(a) default dimensions have been scaled to 142.50 and 55.00
(b) keyboard entry dimensions are still 147 and 70.

Question: which dimensions are correct for the scale operation?

Fig. 21.9. A:WORKDRG after the STRETCH command.

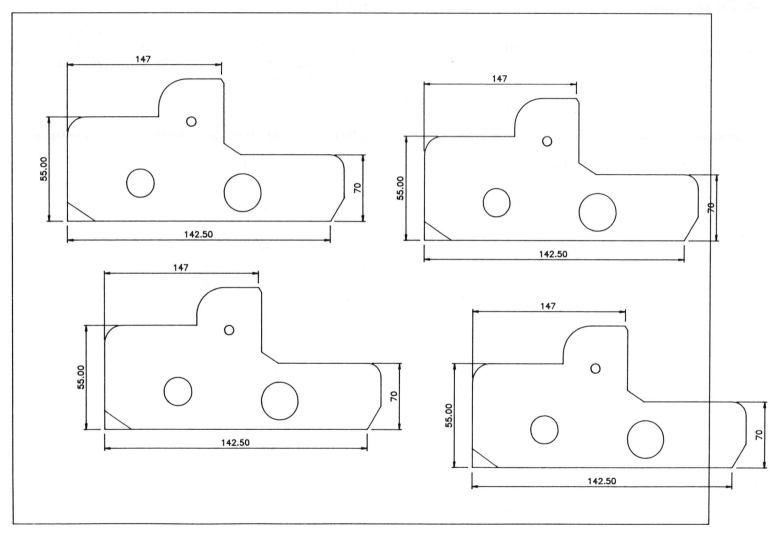

Fig. 21.10. A:WORKDRG after the **SCALE** and multiple **COPY** commands.

Multiple copy

The **COPY** command allows single or multiple coping of any selection, so from the menu bar select **Construct**

Copy

prompt	Select objects
respond	**W<R>** and window the scaled component and dimensions then **<R>**
prompt	\<Base point or displacement>/ Multiple
enter	**M<R>** for multiple option
prompt	Base point
respond	**pick lower left-hand corner of component**
prompt	Second point of displacement
enter	**30,160<R>** – absolute entry
prompt	Second point of displacement
enter	**@200,–20<R>** – relative entry (outside border?)
prompt	Second point of displacement
enter	**@200<30<R>** – polar entry
prompt	Second point of displacement
respond	**right click**

You now have three copies of the scaled component with dimensions as Fig. 21.10. Now Thaw the CL layer and note

(a) the multiple copies have no green centre lines
(b) the green centre lines are in their 'original' position.

This can happen when layers are turned off or frozen and the **MOVE**, **COPY**, etc. commands are used. Entities which are drawn on layers turned off or frozen will not be moved, copied etc., *so beware*!

Mirror

Erase the three multiple copies (with dimensions) and freeze the DIMEN and CL layers to leave the original scaled component and refer to Fig. 21.11. From the menu bar select **Construct**

Mirror

prompt	Select objects
respond	**W<R>** and window the component then **<R>**
prompt	First point of mirror line
enter	**40,140<R>**
prompt	Second point
enter	**200,140<R>**
prompt	Delete old objects<N>
respond	**right click**

Repeat the Mirror command selecting Previous, and pick the mirror lines as indicated in Fig. 21.11. In each case do not delete old objects, unless you want to try entering **Y** at the prompt. The mirror line points can be

(a) entered as co-ordinates
(b) picked on the screen
(c) referenced to existing entities.

If you thaw the DIMEN layer you will find that the dimensions have not been mirrored? Now save your drawing (if you want) giving it a different name from **A:WORKDRG**. We will probably not use the altered drawing again.

This has been quite a long exercise as the commands used a very common in draughting. Try them using some creations of your own as they are fairly easy to follow.

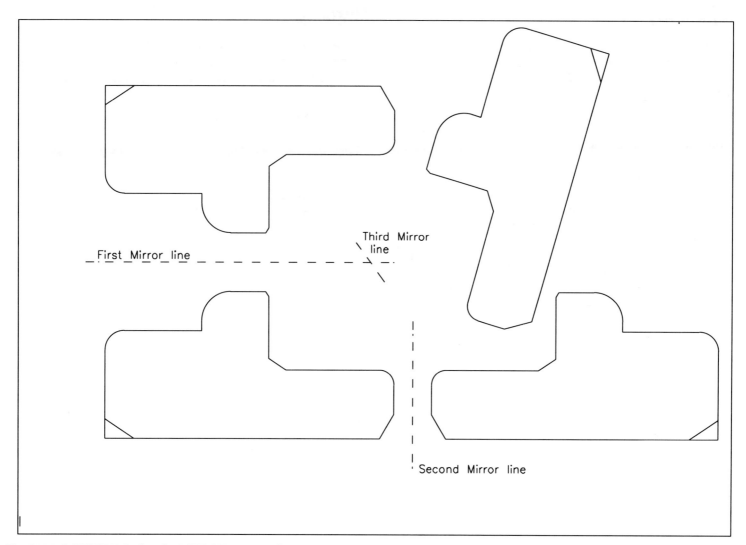

Fig. 21.11. A:WORDRG after the MIRROR command.

❏ *Summary*

1. **COPY, MOVE, SCALE, ROTATE, CHANGE PROPERTIES, STRETCH** can be activated from the menu bar or from the toolbox icons.
2. MIRROR is activated from the menu bar.
3. The selection set is useful for selecting objects.
4. The selection set allows entities to be added or removed from the selected objects.
5. The base point can be
   (a) entered as co-ordinates
   (b) picked from the screen
   (c) referenced to existing entities.
6. Entities on layers which are turned off or frozen are not copied, moved, etc.
7. Default dimensions are stretched and scaled but keyboard entry dimensions are not.
8. All the commands can be entered from the keyboard.

Activities

Three fairly simple activities have been included for this chapter. Each activity should use layers correctly and you should begin a new drawing using your standard sheet method

(a) A:STDA3 as Prototype drawing name.
(b) A:TUT-?? as New Drawing Name

The activities are

1. Tutorial 12: a decoder type circuit using multiple copies.
2. Tutorial 13: an interesting template with mirror.
3. Tutorial 14: a memory cell with mirror and copy.

22. The selection set

The selection set has been used in previous chapters. It is the name for the 'select objects' prompt options with many of the AutoCAD LT commands, e.g. ERASE, COPY, etc. The selection set option can be entered from the keyboard (e.g. W or C) or by selecting from the menu bar

Assist
Select ⟶ Last
All
Fence
WPolygon
CPolygon
Add
Remove
Previous

Using the menu bar procedure illustrates *transparency*, i.e. one 'command' being used 'inside' another one. The options available with the selection set are

Window – all entities within a user specified rectangular window
Crossing – all entities crossing/within a user-specified rectangular window
Last – selects the last entity drawn
All – all entities on the screen are selected
WPolygon – all entities within a user specified polygon window
CPolygon – all entities crossing/within a user specified polygon window

Add – add selected objects to the defined selection set
Remove – remove selected objects from the defined selection set
Previous – select the previous selection set.

The selection set usage is shown in

1. Figure 22.1 using the COPY command with
   (a) window then removing three lines
   (b) CPolygon then adding two circles
   (c) WPolygon then adding two lines.
2. Figure 22.2 with the FENCE option
   (a) using COPY
   (b) using TRIM
   (c) using EXTEND.

The selection set should be used at all times to assist the user, and as such there are no individual activities.

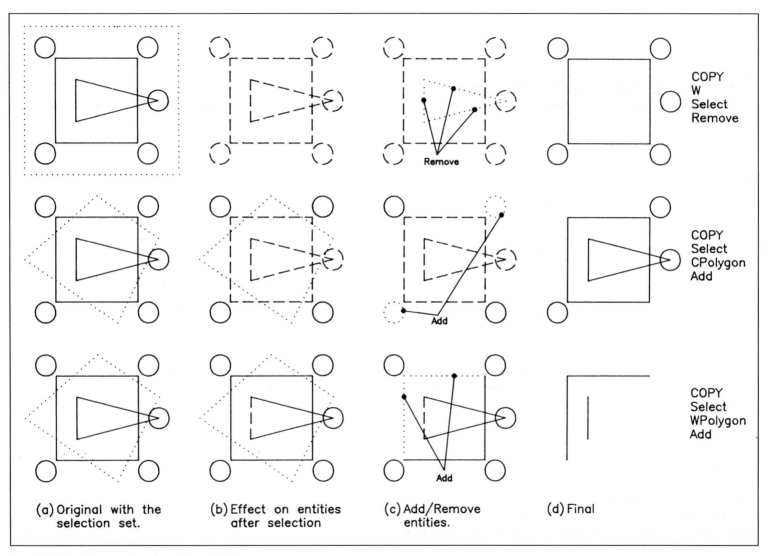

Fig. 22.1. Selection set usasge with the COPY command.

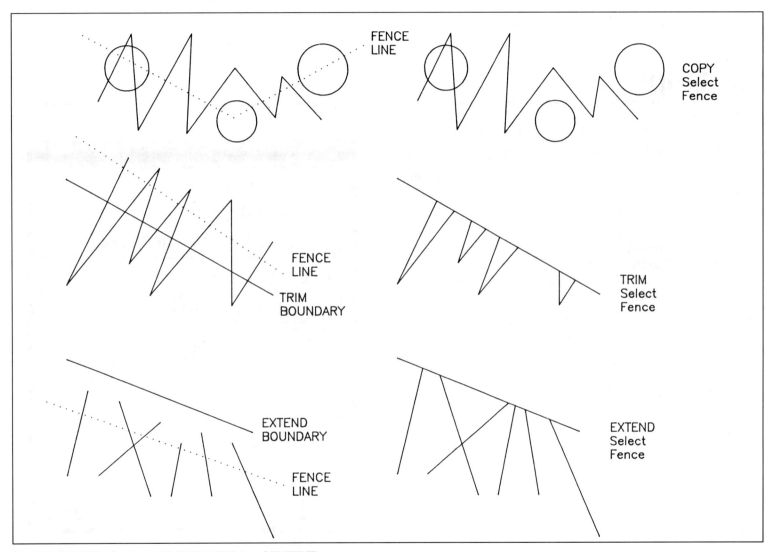

Fig. 22.2. FENCE selection with COPY, TRIM and EXTEND.

23. Grips

The small box which appeared attached to the cross-hairs of the on-screen cursor is called the grips box, and in an earlier chapter we entered some keyboard commands to 'turn the grips off'. Grips can be activated using a dialogue box, so from the menu bar select **Settings**

> **Grips Style...**

prompt   Grips dialogue box as shown in Fig. 23.1 opposite

respond   **Enable the grips with an** ×

                i.e. grips *on* – × in box, grips *off* – no × in box

then   **pick OK**

When the grips are enabled, the grip box will be attached to the cross-hairs. The grips dialogue box allows the user to:

(a) set the grip box size
(b) set the grip colours – which we will leave as blue (unselected) and red (selected).

What do grips do?

Grips provide the user with five commands which be activated without using the icon or menu bar selections. The five commands are STRETCH
> MOVE
> ROTATE
> SCALE
> MIRROR

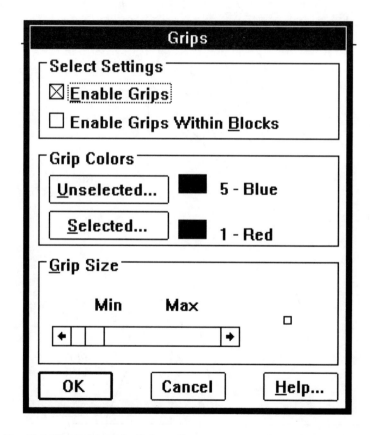

Fig. 23.1. The Grips Style dialogue box.

Notes
1. The grip box should not be confused with the object snap box used to reference entities. Although they are similar in appearance, they are entirely different concepts.
2. When a **DRAW** command is selected (e.g. **LINE**), the grips box will disappear from the cross-hairs.
3. Grips are selected using the left button on the mouse.

How grips work

With AutoCAD LT, the user first selects the command and then the entity, e.g. to copy entities the sequence is
    (a) activate the **COPY** command
    (b) select the entities to be copied.
    Grips work in the opposite 'sense' from the normal selection process, in that the user selects the entities first and then the command. With grips, it is possible to select individual entities, or entities within a window/crossing rectangle.

To demonstrate the effect refer to Fig. 23.2 and

1. Select an area on the screen which has nothing drawn.
2. Move the screen cursor to this area.
3. Pick any point on the screen with a left click.
4. Move the cursor upwards/downwards to the right of this picked point and observe that a 'solid window type box' is obtained.
5. Move the cursor upwards/downwards to the left of this picked point and observe that a 'dotted crossing type box' occurs.
6. Now right click to cancel the grip selection.

When an entity is selected with the grips box, 'blue' boxes will appear at the object snap points and the selected entity will change appearance

    line: boxes at the endpoints and the midpoint
    circle: boxes at the circle centre and the four quadrants
    arc: boxes at the arc endpoints and midpoint.

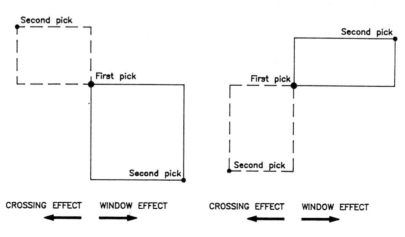

Fig. 23.2. Selections with the grip box.

There are three different types of grip as shown in Fig. 23.3, and these are
- Cold grips: appear on the selected entities in blue, but the entity is not highlighted. The grip options cannot be used with the entity.
- Warm grips: appear in blue on highlighted (dashed) entities. The grip options can be used.
- Hot grips: appear as a solid (red) box when a grip box is picked, and acts as a base for the grip options.

Grips worked example

1. Open your A:STDA3 standard sheet and refer to Fig. 23.4.
2. Draw a 50 unit square in the middle of the screen and draw a circle of radius 15 at the square 'centre' – Fig. 23.4(a).
3. Move the cross-hairs to the bottom line of the square and 'pick' it with a left click. Blue grip boxes will appear at the line end-points and at the line midpoint. The line will also change appearance (warm grip) – (b).
4. Move to the left hand box and pick it with a left click. The box will appear as a red solid (hot grip) – (c)
5. When the hot grip appears (red box) observe the prompt line

prompt	***STRETCH***
	\<Stretch to point>/Base point/Copy/Undo/ eXit
respond	right click
prompt	***MOVE***
	\<Move to point>/ . . .
enter	@–10,–20\<R>

Three things should have happened
(a) the command line is returned
(b) the bottom line of the square has been moved
(c) the grip boxes are still attached to the line (warm) – (d).

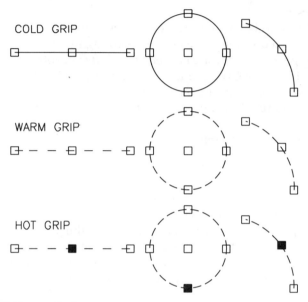

Fig. 23.3. Types of grip.

6. Move to the circle and pick it with a left click, and grip boxes will appear – (e).
7. Move to the bottom grip box of the circle and pick it to make it hot – (f) and

prompt	***STRETCH*** and right click
prompt	***MOVE*** and right click
prompt	***ROTATE***
	\<Rotational angle>/ . . .
enter	–90\<R>

The line and circle will be rotated as (g), and they are still active, i.e. warm.

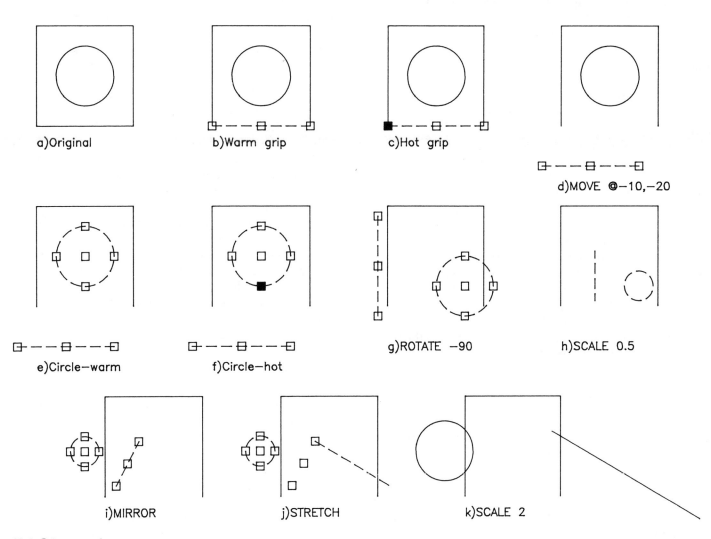

Fig. 23.4. Grip example.

8. Make the circle centre grip box hot by picking it and

prompt	***STRETCH*** and right click
prompt	***MOVE*** and right click
prompt	***ROTATE*** and right click
prompt	***SCALE***
	<Scale factor>/...
enter	**0.5<R>**

The line and circle will be scaled by a factor of 0.5 as (h) and still be warm.

9. Make the top box of the line hot (red box) and

prompt	***STRETCH*** and right click
prompt	***MOVE*** and right click
prompt	***ROTATE*** and right click
prompt	***SCALE*** and right click
prompt	***MIRROR***
	<Second point>/...
enter	**@–5,–20** <R> to give fig(i)

10. Grips still warm, so select the bottom line box and:

prompt	***STRETCH***
	<Stretch to point>/...
enter	**@50,0** <R> – (j)

11. The grips are still warm, so select the circle centre as the hot grip and SCALE it by a factor of 2.

12. The grips will still be active so
    (a) CTRL C to clear the grips from the selection set
    (b) CTRL C to remove the objects from the selection set.
13. The final drawing should resemble Fig. 23.4(k) – hopefully!

❑ *Summary*

1. Grips allow the user access to the commands **STRETCH, MOVE, ROTATE, SCALE** and **MIRROR** without selecting the icon or menu bar.
2. Grips work in the opposite 'sense' from normal AutoCAD LT commands, i.e. object first, then command.
3. Grips *do not have to be used* – they are an alternative to the normal selection process.
4. Grips are enabled/disabled using the Grip Style dialogue box
   (a) grips enabled – × in box
   (b) grips disabled – no × in box.
5. Grips can be cold, warm or hot.
6. The grip box colours are blue for cold/warm and red for hot.
7. The grip colours can be changed using the dialogue box.
8. If the user does not intend to use grips, then I recommend that they are disabled.

Activity

An activity with grips is difficult, but I have managed to think one up for you. Tutorial 15 shows different positions of a robot arm
(a) original position
(b) upper arm rotation – need to 'pick' two circles and two lines. The base point for rotation is the centre grip of larger circle
(c) lower arm rotation – add the lines and circles to the grips and pick the largest circle as the hot grip
(d) upper arm again – what to pick?
(e) both arms – two separate rotations?

This activity only uses the **ROTATE** grip option, but it is quite interesting to attempt. I have included sizes as a guide, but you should be able to create the robot arm to your own sizes if you want. The drawing itself is a reasonable exercise.

24. The BREAK command

The **BREAK** command is used to 'split' entities into a number of distinct parts – to allow hatching for instance (this will be discussed later). The command can be activated
- (a) from the toolbox icon
- (b) by entering **BREAK** at the command line
- (c) from the menu bar with **Modify**
  Break

To demonstrate the command we will use an earlier drawing so

1. Open **A:USEREX** and refer to Fig. 24.1. As this drawing was used to demonstrate text, there may text on the screen. Erase it all.
2. Before proceeding, check that the top and bottom lines of the component have been drawn as single entities. They should be, but if they are not, erase the line entities and draw in two single lines.
3. Select the **BREAK** icon and

prompt	Select objects
respond	**pick line d1** – roughly at point indicated in Fig. 24.1(b)
prompt	Enter second point (or F for first point)
respond	**pick point d2** – roughly at point indicated.

4. The top line should be erased between the two selected points as shown in Fig. 24.1(c).
5. Now enter **U<R>** to undo the **BREAK** command, and return the top line as a single entity again.
6. From the menu bar select **Modify-Break** and

prompt	Select objects
respond	**pick line d3** – Fig. 24.1(d)
prompt	Enter second point (or F for first point)
enter	**F<R>**
prompt	Enter first point
respond	**INTersection icon and pick point d4**
prompt	Enter second point
enter	**@<R>**

7. Nothing appears to have happened, but if you select **ERASE** and pick the right end of the top line then only that segment will be erased. Remember to enter **U<R>** to restore this erased segment.
8. Now repeat the break sequence, selecting line d5, enter F, and then INTersection icon and pick point d6 as (d).
9. The effect of the break can be shown in (e) with the **ERASE** command. Try this if you want, but make sure you restore the lines with **U<R>**.
10. Now save your 'broken' drawing as **A:USEREX** as it will be used to demonstrate hatching.

Note

The entry @ is very useful with **BREAK.** It assumes that the second point entry is *coincident with the first point*. The user can still select the second point with INTersection and picking the point, but using @ is easier.

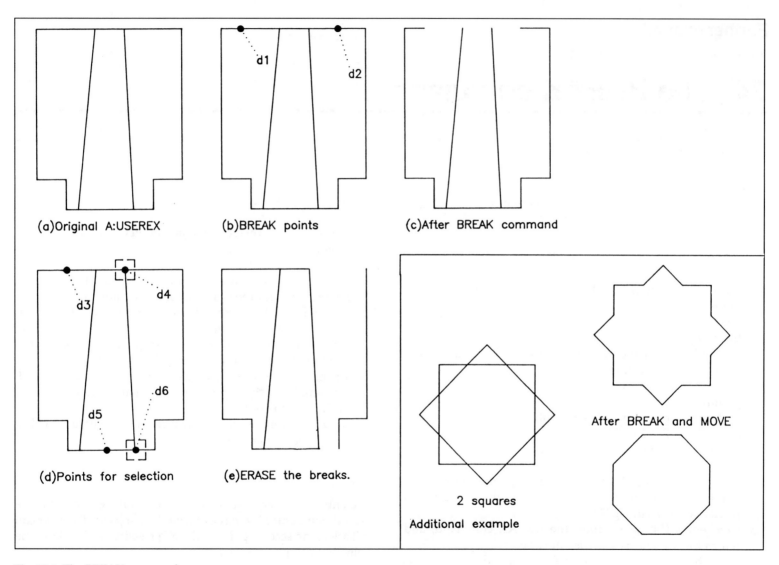

(a)Original A:USEREX

(b)BREAK points

(c)After BREAK command

(d)Points for selection

(e)ERASE the breaks.

2 squares

Additional example

After BREAK and MOVE

Fig. 24.1. The BREAK command.

Further example

It may be necessary to use the **BREAK** command twice at the same point if two lines intersect. Referring to Fig. 24.1, find a clear area on the screen and draw two squares roughly in the orientation shown. Using the **BREAK** command, break the lines at the intersection points with the sequence:

(a) **BREAK** command
(b) pick the required line
(c) enter F
(d) pick the INTersection point
(e) enter @.

This sequence must be completed 16(?) times. Now use the **MOVE** command to separate the two distinct parts of the component.

Now draw a circle with a line through it, and using the **BREAK** command select the circle as the object. Try and break the circle at one of the intersection points and you will find that it cannot be achieved. The message

```
Arc cannot be full 360 degrees
```

will appear at the prompt line.

❏ *Summary*

1. **BREAK** is a modify command and can be activated from the icon, menu bar or keyboard entry.
2. The command allows the user to select two points on an entity.
3. The @ symbol can be used for coincident first and second points.
4. Circles cannot be broken.
5. Using **TRIM** can sometimes give the same effect as **BREAK**.

25. Viewing a drawing

Up until now we have drawn entities on the screen without attempting to 'look' at them in detail. AutoCAD LT has two view commands which are **PAN** and **ZOOM**. The commands are usually activated from the **View** menu bar selection. or by entering the command at the keyboard.

Pan

1. Open your **A:WORKDRG** drawing and erase any dimensions and text. If you do not have a border, use the **LINE** command and draw from (0,0); to @380,0; to @0,270; to @-380,0; to close. This border will be used as a reference in the exercise.
2. From the menu bar select **View-Pan** and
   ```
   prompt    Displacement
   enter     0,0<R>
   prompt    Second point
   enter     10,10<R>
   ```
   The complete drawing will move nearer the centre of the screen, but the lower left-hand corner of the border will still be (0,0). Check it.
3. Enter **PAN<R>** using the keyboard then for displacement: enter **0,0<R>**; second poin enter **@500,0<R>.**
4. Nothing on the screen?

Zoom

This command allows the user to 'zoom in/out' on selected areas of a drawing. There are six options available, these being
   ALL
   CENTER
   EXTENTS
   PREVIOUS
   WINDOW
   SCALE

Each option can be activated with **View-Zoom-Option** or by keyboard entry.

Zoom all

Your screen should still be blank, so select **View-Zoom-All** and the original **A:WORKDRG** drawing will be restored.

Zoom previous

1. Now select **View-Zoom-Previous** and your screen will again be blank. We have returned to the PAN (@500,0) drawing.
2. Repeat the View-Zoom-Previous selection and you should have the first pan drawing.
3. Repeat the selection and the original drawing will be returned.

Zoom window

This is perhaps the most useful of the zoom options, as it allows the user to 'magnify' parts of a drawing.

1. Select **View-Zoom-Window** and
prompt	First corner
enter	**190,30<R>**
prompt	Other corner
enter	**390,225<R>**

   The right end of the component will be displayed at a much greater size i.e. we have 'zoomed into' an area.
2. Now View-Zoom-Window, and zoom in on the circle by placing a window around it. Hopefully your circle will 'fill the screen'.
3. Restore the original drawing with the Zoom-Previous option twice.

Zoom center

1. Select **View-Zoom-Center** and
prompt	Center point
enter	**190,130<R>**
prompt	Magnification or height<?>
enter	**100<R>**

2. Now Zoom-All to restore original drawing.
3. Repeat the Zoom-Center option and enter
Center point	**0,0<R>**
Magnification	**500<R>**

   You should have a smaller drawing at the top right of the screen, with the lower left-hand corner of the drawing still (0,0).
4. Now Zoom-Previous – original?

Zoom scale

Select **View-Zoom-Scale** and enter **0.5<R>** at the prompt. The drawing should be at the centre of the screen and be at 0.5 full size. Now restore the original drawing.

Aerial view

The aerial view command allows the user to pan and zoom a drawing interactively, i.e. as you use the command, your actual on-screen drawing will change accordingly. The command is really for very large drawings to allow the user to 'see' different areas before selecting the one required. The command is activated from the menu bar with **Settings-Aerial View** and the result is the Aerial View dialogue box as Fig. 25.1.

The aerial view dialogue box has the typical Windows control keys: the ▼ button cancels the dialogue box and the ▲ button maximises the dialogue box.

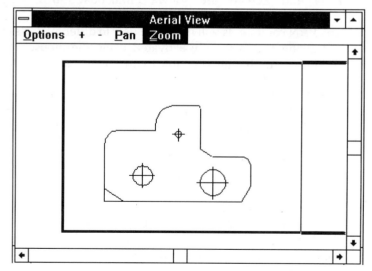

Fig. 25.1. Aerial View dialogue box.

The options available are

Zoom blue   zoom command active
Pan blue   pan command active
+   increases drawing size
–   decreases drawing size
options   global view; locate; statistics

The aerial view dialogue box has a black bordered box which allows the user to interact between the aerial view and the actual drawing. By using a left click, and repositioning the black box window, the actual aerial view will be obtained with the drawing when the dialogue box is cancelled.

Recommendation

1. The **ZOOM** command should be used constantly. As you are creating a drawing zoom in on the working area to allow ease of construction. When you have finished, zoom previous/all then zoom in on the next area. This will make life easier for you.
2. Use the **PAN** command with care, but of your drawing disappears, use the zoom all command.

❏ *Summary*

1. **PAN** and **ZOOM** are **View** commands and usually activated from the menu bar.
2. The **PAN** commands will move the user to different parts of a drawing and is usually activated using the mouse and picking points. It is also possible to use co-ordinate input for the command.
3. With **PAN**, the user's drawing can 'disappear' quite easily.
4. The **ZOOM** commands allows areas of a drawing to be looked at in greater detail. This is a 'zoom in' effect.
5. There are six options with the zoom command:
   ALL – displays the complete drawing
   CENTER zooms the drawing about a centre point supplied by the user as co-ordinate input or screen picked point. The option also requires a magnification factor
   EXTENTS zooms the actual drawing to the screen extents
   PREVIOUS returns the drawing as it was before the zoom command. This can be used repetitively, and is usually used after a **ZOOM** window

   WINDOW probably the most useful option as it allows the user to zoom in on selected areas. This may be to draw more detail or to modify detail which could not be achieved with the normal drawing. It is usually activated by the user picking a window, but co-ordinate entry is also possible.
   SCALE zooms the drawing to a scale factor entered by the user.
6. While the zoom options are usually activated with the menu bar selection of View-Zoom-Option, they can also be activated by keyboard input, e.g.:
   ZOOM<R> then **W<R>** for the window option
   ZOOM<R> then **A<R>** for the all option.
7. The aerial view commands allows the user interactive panning and/or zooming of a drawing. It is usually only used with very large drawings.

26. Hatching

Hatching (or sectioning) must be added by the user to the required area. There is only one command, and this can be activated in any of the following ways:

(a) from the toolbox icon
(b) by entering HATCH at the command line
(c) from the menu bar with **Draw-Hatch...**

The icon/keyboard entry methods are usually used for user-defined hatch patterns, while the menu bar selection is used to access the stored hatch patterns via a dialogue box.

User-defined hatch patterns

User-defined hatch patterns are line hatch patterns where the user defines the angle of the hatch pattern and the spacing between the lines. We will demonstrate its use with a worked example so

1. Open your ASTDA3 standard sheet and refer to Fig. 26.1.
2. With OUT the current layer, draw a 50 unit square and multiple copy it to nine different areas on the screen. Add any other lines as shown in Fig. 26.1 (having snap on will help).
3. Make SECT (cyan) the current layer.
4. Select the HATCH icon and

prompt	`Pattern(? or name/U, style)`
enter	**U<R>** – for user
prompt	`Angle for crosshatch lines`
enter	**45<R>**

prompt	`Spacing between lines`
enter	**3<R>**
prompt	`Double hatch area <N>`
enter	**<RETURN>**, i.e. accept the <N> default
prompt	`Select objects`
respond	**pick the four lines of one square then <R>**

The square will be hatched as shown in Fig. 26.1(a).

5. Repeat the HATCH icon selection accepting the defaults (which will be our entries from step 4) and pick the lines as indicated in (b) and (c).
6. Enter HATCH at the command line and

prompt	`Pattern` and enter **U<R>**
prompt	`Angle` and enter **45<R>**
prompt	`Spacing` and enter **3<R>**
prompt	`Select objects`
enter	**W<R>** and window a square
prompt	`4 found`
enter	**<RETURN>**

The windowed square will be hatched as Fig. 26.1(d).

7. Now repeat the **HATCH** command using the window option and select the square at (e).
8. Figure 26.1 shows other hatch results with part (f) showing window selection with entries of U,45,3,Y for double hatching; (g) window selection with U,–45,5,N; (h) picking lines indicated with U,45,3,N and result not as expected; (i) using the BREAK command (4 times?) then picking four lines. The entry is U,45,3,N; (j) circles can also be hatched.

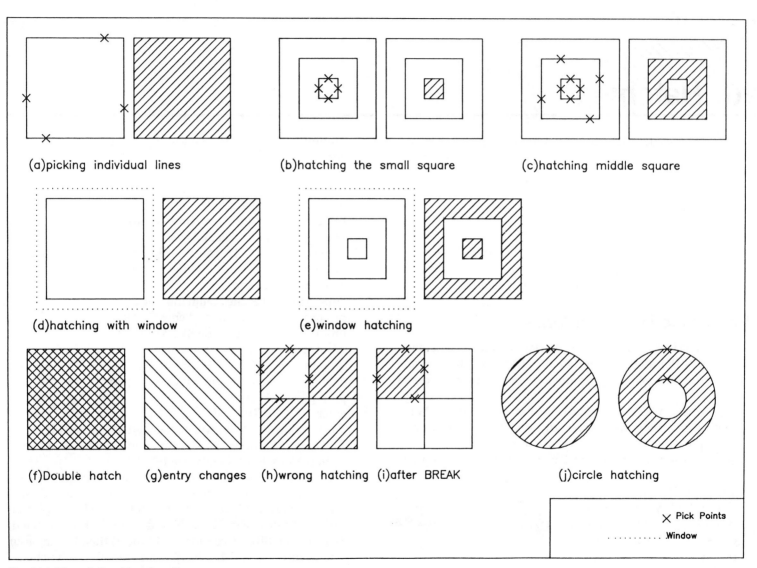

Fig. 26.1. User-defined hatch patterns.

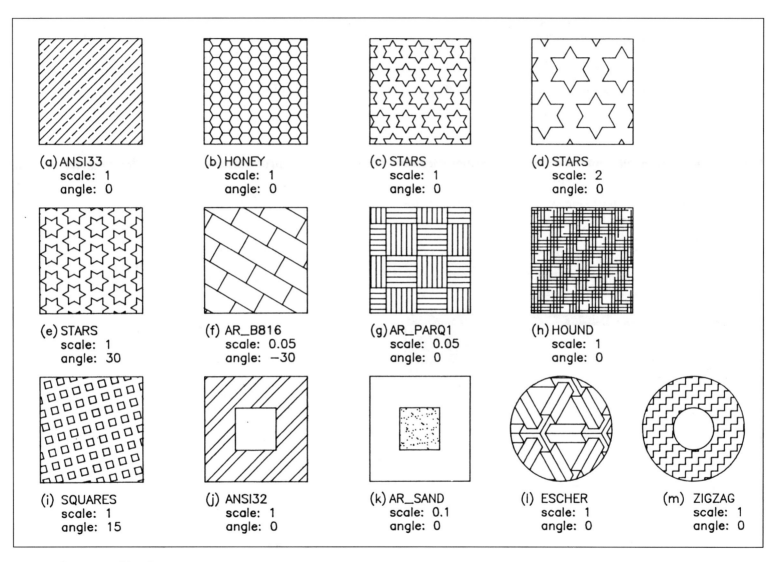

(a) ANSI33
    scale: 1
    angle: 0

(b) HONEY
    scale: 1
    angle: 0

(c) STARS
    scale: 1
    angle: 0

(d) STARS
    scale: 2
    angle: 0

(e) STARS
    scale: 1
    angle: 30

(f) AR_B816
    scale: 0.05
    angle: −30

(g) AR_PARQ1
    scale: 0.05
    angle: 0

(h) HOUND
    scale: 1
    angle: 0

(i) SQUARES
    scale: 1
    angle: 15

(j) ANSI32
    scale: 1
    angle: 0

(k) AR_SAND
    scale: 0.1
    angle: 0

(l) ESCHER
    scale: 1
    angle: 0

(m) ZIGZAG
    scale: 1
    angle: 0

Fig. 26.2. Some stored hatch patterns.

9. Draw some other shapes and try the HATCH command on them. Enter different angles and line spacings until you become familiar with their effect on the hatch result.
10. Erase a hatch pattern – all of it is erased.
11. Save the drawing if you want, but we will not use it again.

AutoCAD LT's stored hatch patterns

AutoCAD LT has several hatch patterns which can be accessed by the user using a dialogue box and hatch pattern icons. Again, let us demonstrate them with a worked example, so

1. Open A:STDA3 and refer to Fig. 26.2. Draw a 50 unit square on OUT layer and multiple copy it several times. Make SECT layer current.
2. From the menu bar select **Draw-Hatch...**

prompt	Select Hatch Pattern dialogue box (as Fig. 26.3)

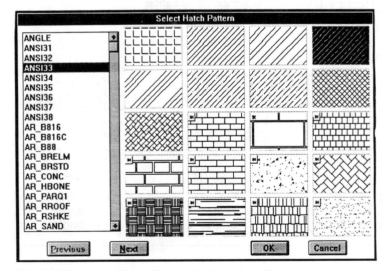

Fig. 26.3 The Select Hatch Pattern dialogue box (first screen).

respond	**pick ANSI33** from list – turns blue
and	one hatch icon is highlighted in black
then	**pick OK** to return to drawing screen
prompt	Scale pattern<1.0000>
enter	**1<R>**
prompt	Angle for pattern<0>
enter	**0<R>**
prompt	Select objects
enter	**W<R>** and window a square then **<R>**

The square will be hatched with the ANSI33 hatch pattern as shown in Fig. 26.2(a).

3. Repeat the Draw-Hatch... selection and

prompt	first hatch icon screen
respond	**pick Next** – second hatch icon screen
respond	pick the bottom left icon – turns black
and	HONEY name highlighted in blue in list
then	**pick OK** – drawing screen
prompt	Scale for pattern <1.000> and right click
prompt	Angle for pattern <0> and right click
prompt	Select objects and window a square then right click

The resultant hatching is shown in Fig. 26.2(b).

4. Draw-Hatch... again and

prompt	first hatch icon screen
respond	left click on scroll bar area of list until the hatch word 'STARS' appears
then	**pick STARS** – turns blue
and	icon in black
then	**pick OK**
prompt	Scale for pattern<1.0000> and right click
prompt	Angle for pattern<0> and right click
prompt	Select objects and window a square then right click.

The square will be hatched as Fig. 26.2(c).

5. Figure 26.2 gives other hatching from the stored patterns
   (d) STARS : scale 2, angle 0.
   (e) STARS : scale 1, angle 30
   (f) AR_B816 : scale 0.05, angle –30
   (g) AR_PARQ1 : scale 0.05, angle 0
   (h) HOUND : scale 1, angle 0
   (i) SQUARES : scale 1, angle 15
   (j) ANSI32 : scale 1, angle 0
   (k) AR_SAND : scale 0.1, angle 0
   (l) ESCHER : scale 1, angle 0
   (m) ZIGZAG : scale 1, angle 0.

Hatch pattern options

Selection of the HATCH icon gives the following options at the command line

(a) **Pattern name**: the user can enter the hatch pattern name (e.g. STARS) and the prompts are Scale factor, Angle. It iseasier to use the dialogue box, as you then see all the hatch names.

(b) ?: entering **?<R>** at the prompt gives

prompt `Pattern(s) to list<*>`
enter **<RETURN>**
prompt the AutoCAD LT text screen with a list of the hatch pattern names and a description of each as shown in Fig. 26.4.

(c) **U**: user-defined patterns which have been discussed.

(d) **Style**: allows the user to select two variants of the user-defined command. By entering (a) u; (b) u, o; (c) u,i at the prompt, different hatch result are obtained. Refer to Fig. 26.5 which shows:
   (a) the normal **U** entry window hatching
   (b) the **u,o** entry – o meaning outer.
   (c) the **u,i** entry – i for ignore.

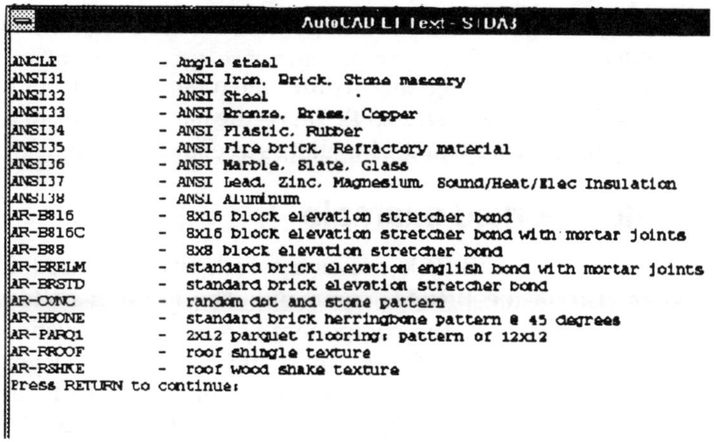

```
ANGLE      - Angle steel
ANSI31     - ANSI Iron, Brick, Stone masonry
ANSI32     - ANSI Steel
ANSI33     - ANSI Bronze, Brass, Copper
ANSI34     - ANSI Plastic, Rubber
ANSI35     - ANSI Fire brick, Refractory material
ANSI36     - ANSI Marble, Slate, Glass
ANSI37     - ANSI Lead, Zinc, Magnesium, Sound/Heat/Elec Insulation
ANSI38     - ANSI Aluminum
AR-B816    -  8x16 block elevation stretcher bond
AR-B816C   -  8x16 block elevation stretcher bond with mortar joints
AR-B88     -  8x8 block elevation stretcher bond
AR-BRELM   -  standard brick elevation english bond with mortar joints
AR-BRSTD   -  standard brick elevation stretcher bond
AR-CONC    -  random dot and stone pattern
AR-HBONE   -  standard brick herringbone pattern @ 45 degrees
AR-PARQ1   -  2x12 parquet flooring: pattern of 12x12
AR-RROOF   -  roof shingle texture
AR-RSHKE   -  roof wood shake texture
Press RETURN to continue:
```

Fig. 26.4. AutoCAD LT hatch pattern text screen.

Problems with hatching

Using the hatch command is not all plain sailing as there are several pitfalls which the user may come across. The most common are shown in Fig. 26.5 and are:

1. No hatch pattern being shown – Fig. 26.5(d). This is due to the hatch pattern scale factor being too large and the message `Hatching did not intersect the figure` will be displayed at the prompt line. Repeat the command entering a smaller scale factor.
2. Hatching takes ages to appear. This is due to the hatch pattern scale factor being too small. *This is serious!* If it happens terminate the hatch operation immediately with CTRL C. If the hatch operation is allowed to continue, there is a chance that the disk will become full (especially if a floppy is used).

Always start a new hatch pattern with a large scale factor (5/10) and work downwards until you get the pattern you want.

3. Incomplete hatching due to gaps – Fig. 26.5(e). Redraw the shape.
4. Unexpected hatching due to the hatch 'shape' not being properly defined – Fig. 26.5(f). This is the hardest problem to overcome and we will deal with it as a separate section.

A hatch worked example

1. Open your **A:USEREX** drawing which was last used to demonstrate the **BREAK** command. The top and bottom horizontal lines of the component should be two distinct entities. Refer to Fig. 26.6 and make **SECT** the current layer.
2. Select the **HATCH** icon and use entries of U, 45, 3 and N in response to the prompts then pick lines d1–d6 as Fig. 26.6(a).
3. The hatching should be as Fig. 26.6(b).
4. Repeat the hatch command with the same entries and pick lines d7–d12 as Fig. 26.6(c) and note the 'appearance' of lines d7 and d9 when selected.
5. The resultant hatching is not correct – Fig. 26.6(d). This is due to the lines d7 and d9 extending beyond the 'hatch area'.
6. Erase the wrong hatching.
7. Break lines d7 and d9 at the appropriate point – easy?
8. Repeat the hatch command to give the correct hatching – (e).
9. Save if you want, but we will not use this drawing again.

How can the user ensure hatching will always be correct?

Wrong hatching is a nuisance and can cause frustration to the user. There are several methods which can be used to ensure that the hatching will always be correct and these are
1. Make sure the shape to be hatched has been drawn as a series of connected lines, arcs, etc. This is not always possible, and it is really impracticable and bad draughting.
2. Break all entities at the appropriate points to leave the shape to be hatched. Again this is also impracticable, especially with complex shapes.

3. Draw around the required shape using a construction line, then adding the hatching to this created shape. The use of layers makes this option fairly easy. I call this option the **TRACE** layer method.
4. Draw round the required shape with a polyline, then add the hatch pattern to this polyline. Very similar to option 3. We will discuss polylines in the next chapter.

Note for AutoCAD R12 users
AutoCAD LT does not have the **BHATCH** command which allows the user to select points within a shape for hatching. As all R12 users will know this command overcame all the hassle with polylines, layers, etc. It is a mystery to me why AutoDESK did not include BHATCH in the AutoCAD LT package. Perhaps AutoCAD LT is thought of as a 'taster' prior to purchasing 'big brother' R12 or even R13?

Using a TRACE layer for hatching

A worked example will be used to demonstrate how an 'awkward' shape can be hatched.
1. Open your **A:STDA3** standard sheet. Use the layer control dialogue box to add a new layer **TRACE**, colour yellow with continuous linetype. Pick the **SAVE** icon to update your standard sheet.
2. Refer to Fig. 26.7 and with OUT the current layer draw two 50 unit squares in the orientation shown in (a). Snap on will help.
3. We want to produce the hatching as Fig. 26.7(b).
4. With **SECT** layer current, use the **HATCH** icon with entries of U,45,3,N to the prompts, then window the complete shape. The resulting hatching is nice, but not as expected – (c). Now **ERASE** the hatching by picking one point on it then <R>.
5. We could hatch the component using the **BREAK** command (16 times?) at the line intersections, but we will use the trace layer method.
6. Set a running object snap to INTersection.

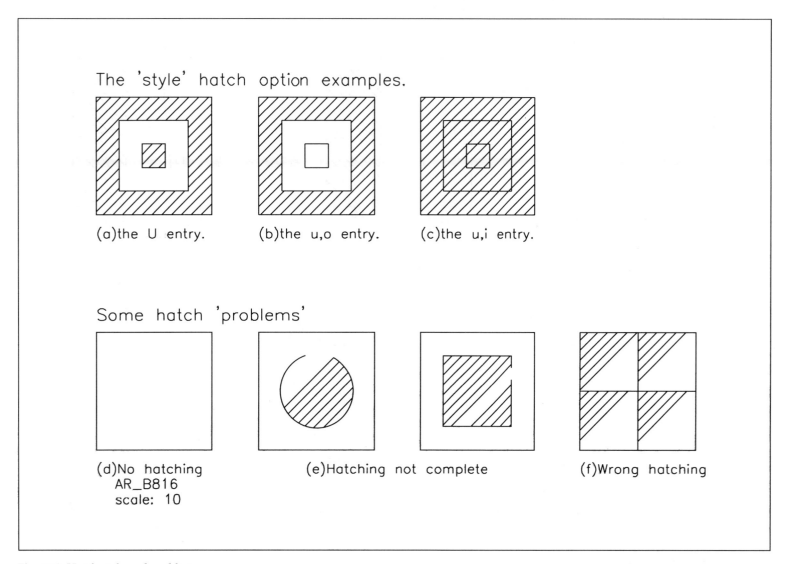

The 'style' hatch option examples.

(a)the U entry.   (b)the u,o entry.   (c)the u,i entry.

Some hatch 'problems'

(d)No hatching   (e)Hatching not complete   (f)Wrong hatching
   AR_B816
   scale: 10

Fig. 26.5. Hatch style and problems.

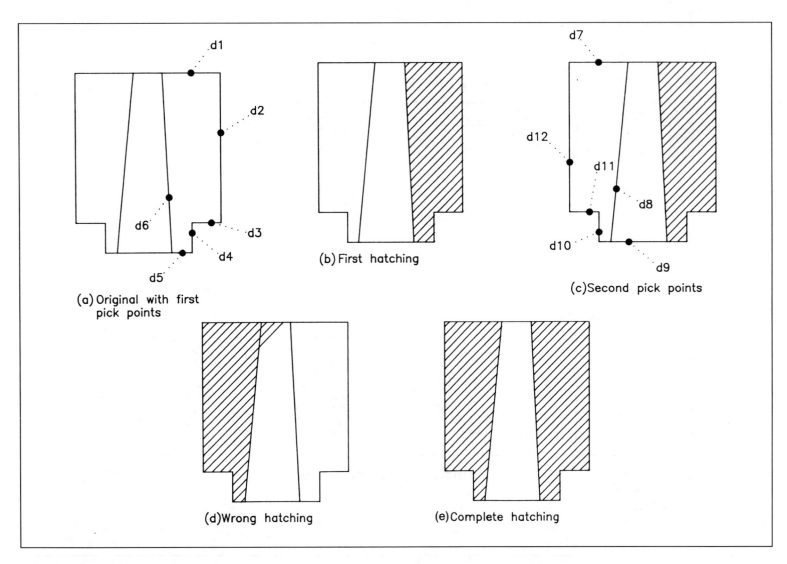

Fig. 26.6. A:USEREX as hatch example.

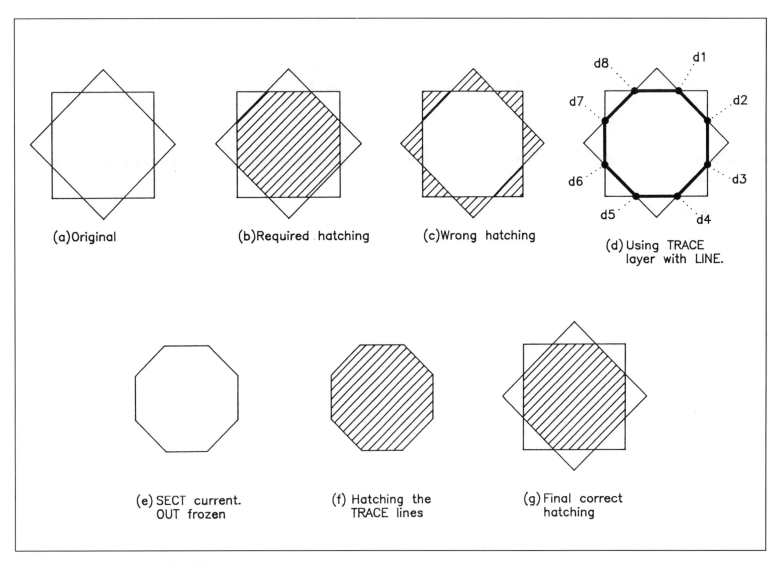

Fig. 26.7. Hatching using the TRACE layer.

7. Make **TRACE** layer current.
8. Use the **LINE** command to draw around the shape to be hatched, picking the points d1–d8 as Fig. 26.7(d).
9. Cancel the running object snap.
10. Make **SECT** layer current and freeze layer **OUT** to leave the yellow trace outline as Fig. 26.7(e).
11. Use the hatch command with U,45,3,N and window the yellow shape. Cyan hatching is added as Fig. 26.7(f).
12. Now thaw layer OUT, make it current and freeze the TRACE layer.
13. The hatching will now be perfect – Fig. 26.7(g).

❏ *Summary*

1. Hatching is a draw command activated from the icon or menu bar.
2. The icon selection method is for user-defined hatch patterns.
3. With user-defined patterns, the user has control over the hatch pattern angle, the spacing between lines and double hatching.
4. The menu bar selection allows access to the stored hatch patterns.
5. Stored hatch patterns are in icon form in a dialogue box.
6. With stored patterns, the user controls the scale factor and the angle.
7. When using stored hatch patterns *always use a large scale factor* to start with. Work downwards until the hatching is correct.
8. Hatching may not be as expected.
9. The user can select individual entities or a window.
10. Hatching is a single entity and all hatching is erased with a single pick.
11. All hatching should be created on the SECT layer.
12. LTSCALE does not affect hatch patterns.

While the method seems very cumbersome it always works and gives the correct hatching. I would recommend that all hatching be completed using this method, the steps being:
1. Draw the component as normal.
2. With **TRACE** layer current, draw around the shapes to be hatched using a running object snap (INT,END)
3. Make **SECT** layer current and freeze OUT, CL, HID, DIMEN, etc but not **TRACE**.
4. Hatch the yellow shapes.
5. Thaw frozen layers and freeze **TRACE** layer.

Activities

Many users may not use hatching in their draughting work, but they should still be familiar with the process. I have included four interesting drawings for you to attempt, and they will test your CAD draughting skills.
1. Tutorial 16: A simple cover plate drawing. Use the **MIRROR** command will make the drawing easy for you. The hatching is fairly easy but the trace method should still be used.
2. Tutorial 17: a bearing block. The drawing requires some thought to complete, and **MIRROR** will help again. For the hatching, the trace method requires a circle/arc to be added. Hatch with ANSI35.
3. Tutorial 18: this will really test you. The steam expansion box drawing is much easier than you would think, but it takes some thought. Getting started is the main problem. The hatching is simple?
4. Tutorial 19: The gasket cover is a traditional type of engineering drawing and is quite a challenge. I used offset and trim a lot. The difficulty with the trace layer is when the fillet radii need to be included. This is a typical draughtspersons type of drawing.

27. Polylines

A polyline is an entity which can consist of line and arc segments and can also be drawn with varying width. It has its own editing facilities and is activated by an icon or from the menu bar. As usual we will use examples to demonstrate it.

1. Open your **A:STDA3** standard sheet and refer to Fig. 27.1
2. Select the **POLYLINE** icon and

prompt	`From point`
enter	**15,185<R>**
prompt	`Arc/Close/Halfwidth/`
	`Length/Undo/Width/<Endpoint of line>`
enter	**@50,0<R>**
prompt	`Arc/Close........` and enter **@0,50<R>**
prompt	`Arc/Close........` and enter **@–50,0<R>**
prompt	`Arc/Close........` and enter **@0,–50<R>**
prompt	`Arc/Close........` and enter **<RETURN>**
	to end sequence

3. **From the menu bar select** Draw-Polyline and enter
   From point **80,185<R>**
   Endpoint **@50,0<R>**
   Endpoint **@0,50<R>**
   Endpoint **@–50,0<R>**
   Endpoint **C <R>** to close the square.
4. Now select the COPY icon and pick any single point on the **second** square then **<R>**. Multiple copy from the base point of (80,185) to the points (145,185); (225,185); (305,185); (15,80); (80,80) and (145,80).

Note that when the polyline was picked, all four lines where highlighted, i.e. it is a single entity.

5. Set a fillet radius of 5 and chamfer distances of 10.
6. Select from the menu bar **Construct-Fillet** and

prompt	`Fillet Polyline/Radius.....`
enter	**P<R>**
prompt	`Select 2D polyline`
respond	**pick the first square drawn**
prompt	`3 lines were filleted – fig(a).`

7. Repeat the fillet polyline selection and pick the second square drawn, and the last prompt will be: `4 lines were filleted` – Fig. 27.1(b).
8. Figures 27.1(a) and (b) show the difference between a closed polyshape and a **<RETURN>** closed polyshape.
9. Select from the menu bar **Construct-Chamfer** and

prompt	`Chamfer Polyline/ Distance ....`
enter	**P<R>**
prompt	`Select 2D polyline`
respond	**pick the third square drawn**
prompt	`4 lines were chamfered` (see Fig. 27.1(c)).

10. Now select **Construct-Offset** and:

prompt	`Offset distance or through`
enter	**10<R>**
prompt	`Select object to offset`
respond	**pick the fourth square drawn**
prompt	`Side to offset?`
respond	**pick a point outside polyline** then right click

The complete square is offset by 10 – Fig. 27.1(d).

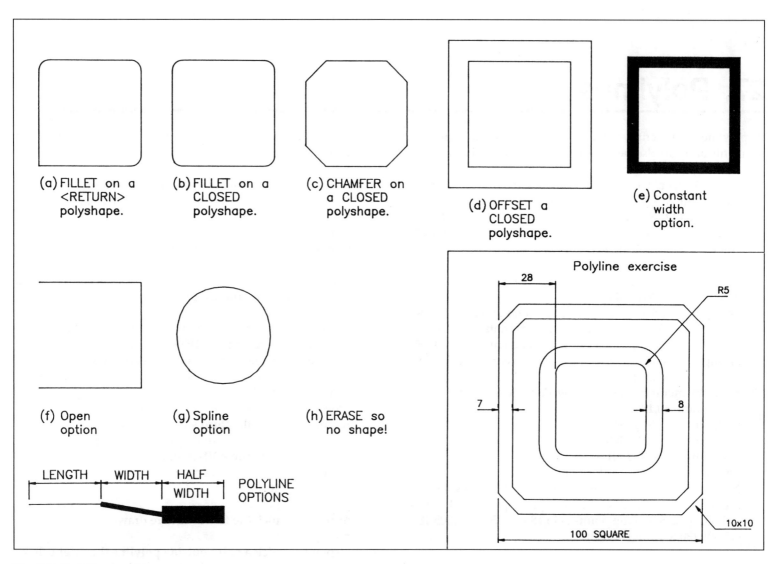

Fig. 27.1. Polyline examples.

11. From the menu bar select **Modify-Edit Polyline** and

    prompt   `Select polyline`

    respond   **pick the fifth square drawn**

    prompt   `Open/Join/Width..........`

    enter   **W<R>** – for width

    prompt   `Enter new width for all segments`

    enter   **5<R>**

    prompt   `Open/Join...............`

    respond   right click to end sequence.

    The complete square is drawn with the line width 5 as Fig. 27.1(e).

12. Repeat the Edit Polyline command and pick the sixth square drawn. At the prompt enter **O<R>** and the last segment drawn will be removed, i.e. the polyline has been opened – Fig. 27.1(f).

13. Edit Polyline again picking the seventh square drawn. At the prompt line enter **S<R>** (for spline) and a circle will result as Fig. 27.1(g).

14. Now erase the eighth square with a single pick – Fig. 27.1(h). There is obviously nothing there as it has been erased!

We will investigate the Edit Polyline options in greater detail in the next chapter.

Polyline exercise

Select a suitable area on the screen and draw a 100 unit square as a closed polyshape. With the sizes given in Fig. 27.1, use **OFFSET**, **FILLET** and **CHAMFER** to complete the component. It is much easier than you think.

Polyline options

The polyline command has several options available to the user, and these are displayed at the prompt line when the start point has been selected. These options can be activated by entering the CAPITAL letter displayed with the options. The available options are:

Arc	draws an arc segment
Close	closes a polyline shape, i.e. to start point
Halfwidth	start and end polyline halfwidth entered
Length	length of line segment entered
Undo	undoes the segment drawn
Width	start and end width entered
Endpoint	point picked or co-ordinates entered.

These options are very easy to use. Select the POLYLINE icon and then

enter	10,25 as the start point
enter	**L** then 35 as the length of the line segment
enter	**W** then 2 as start width, 2 as end width and @30,–5 as end point
enter	**H** then 4 as start and end halfwidths and @30,5 as end point
enter	**U** to undo halfwidth option
enter	**H** then 4 as start and end halfwidths and @30,0 as end point
enter	**<RETURN>** to end sequence.

Your complete drawing should be as Fig. 27.1. Save it if you want, but it is not needed for future work.

Line and arc segments

A continuous polyline entity can be created from a series of line and arc segments of varying width, and we will demonstrate how to construct one with a new example. This will entail several of the options available to the user. The component will also be used to investigate the polyline editing facilities. The exercise is given as a LONG series of stepped sequences, so open your A:STDA3 standard sheet with OUT as the current layer. Refer to Fig. 27.2.

Select the POLYLINE icon and

Prompt	*Enter*	
1. From point	**40,40<R>**	(pt 1)
2. Arc/Close/Halfwidth......	**L<R>**	
3. Length of line	**45<R>**	(pt 2)
4. Arc/Close/Halfwidth......	**W<R>**	
5. Starting width<0>	**0<R>**	
6. Ending width<0>	**10<R>**	
7. Arc/Close/Halfwidth......	**@150,0<R**	(pt 3)
8. Arc/Close/Halfwidth......	**A<R>**	
9. Angle/CEnter/CLose.......	**@50,50<R>**	(pt 4)
10. Angle/CEnter/CLose.......	**L<R>**	
11. Arc/Close/Halfwidth......	**W<R>**	
12. Starting width<10>	**10<R>**	
13. Ending width<10>	**0<R>**	
14. Arc/Close/Halfwidth......	**@0,120<R>**	(pt 5)
15. Arc/Close/Halfwidth......	**210,250<R>**	(pt 6)
16. Arc/Close/Halfwidth......	**W<R>**	
17. Starting width<0>	**0<R>**	
18. Ending width<0>	**5<R>**	
19. Arc/Close/Halfwidth......	**@50<–90<R>**	(pt 7)
20. Arc/Close/Halfwidth......	**A<R>**	
21. Angle/CEnter/CLose.......	**@–60,0<R>**	(pt 8)
22. Angle/CEnter/CLose.......	**CE<R>**	
23. Center point	**110,210<R>**	(pt 9)
24. Angle/Length/<End point>	**A<R>**	
25. Included angle	**120<R>**	(pt 10)
26. Angle/CEnter/CLose.......	**L<R>**	
27. Arc/Close/Halfwidth......	**W<R>**	
28. Starting width<5>	**5<R>**	
29. Ending width<5>	**0<R>**	
30. Arc/Close/Halfwidth......	**40,225<R>**	(pt 11)
31. Arc/Close/Halfwidth......	**C<R>**	
32. A closed polyshape.		

That's all there is to it! With a bit of luck your polyshape will be the same as Fig. 27.2. There is a lot of steps in this, but this is normal when constructing a polyshape with line and arc segments. The line segments have their own options, as do the arc segments. The problem with 'complicated' polyshapes is that it is not easy to correct individual parts which are wrong, and it is usual to erase the shape and start again.

The entries will have introduced the user to the polyarc options which allow the user to specify angles, centres, radii, widths, etc.

To demonstrate an arc polyshape construction, select the icon and:

Prompt	*Enter*
1. From point	**90,120<R>**
2. Arc/Close/Halfwidth......	**A<R>**
3. Angle/CEnter/CLose.......	**W<R>**
4. Staring width<0>	**0<R>**
5. Ending width<0>	**5<R>**
6. Angle/CEnter/CLose.......	**D<R>**
7. Direction from start point	**@0,–10<R>**
8. End point	**140,70<R>**
9. Angle/CEnter/CLose.......	**CE<R>**
10. Center point	**140,100<R>**

11.	Angle/CEnter/CLose.......	**A<R>**
12.	Included angle	**150<R>**
13.	Angle/CEnter/CLose.......	**W<R>**
14.	Starting width<5>	**5<R>**
15.	Ending width<5>	**15<R>**
16.	Angle/CEnter/CLose.......	**155,100<R>**

17. Angle/CEnter/CLose.......   **<RETURN>**
18. A nice curly shape?

At this stage save your drawing as **A:?????** as it will be used in the next chapter to demonstrate the editing of polylines.

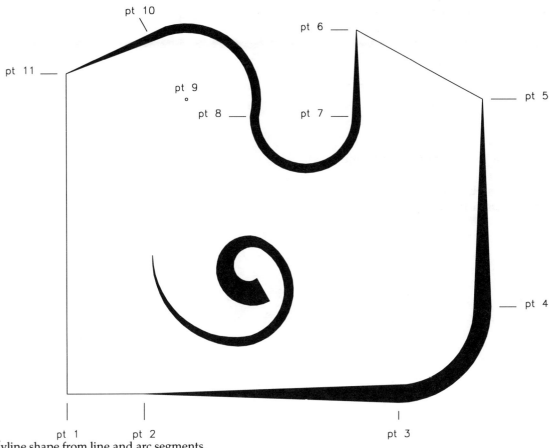

Fig. 27.2. Polyline shape from line and arc segments.

❏ *Summary*

1. A polyline is a single entity which can be made from several line and arc segments.
2. Polylines can have varying start and end widths.
3. A polyshape which is to be 'closed' should be completed with the Close option and not with **<RETURN>**.
4. Polylines allow easy filleting, chamfering, offsetting and erasing.
5. Polylines have their own editing commands.

Activity

One activity is included for you to attempt using polylines. This is:

Tutorial 20: some simple shapes obtained using the width option of the command. Some also include polyarcs.

28. Modifying polylines and arcs

Polylines have their own editing command which is activated from the menu bar with **Modify-Edit** polyline. The command has several options and is best demonstrated by example, so open the·polyline/polyarc drawing created in the last chapter and refer to Fig. 28.1.

From the menu bar select **Modify**
                    Edit Polyline

prompt	Select polyline
respond	**pick any point on the large polyshape**
prompt	Open/Join/Width/Edit vertex/Fit/Spline/Decurve/Ltype gen/Undo/eXit<X>
enter	**W<R>** – the width option
prompt	Enter new width for all segments
enter	**3<R>** – Fig. 28.1(b)
prompt	Open/Join................
enter	**D<R>** – the decurve option (Fig. 28.1(c))
prompt	Open/Join................
enter	**F<R>** – the fit option (Fig. 28.1(d))
prompt	Open/Join................
enter	**S<R>** – the spline option (Fig. 28.1(e))
prompt	Open/Join................
enter	**O<R>** – the open option (Fig. 28.1(f))
prompt	Open/Join................
enter	**D<R>** – Fig. 28.1(g)
prompt	Open/Join................
enter	**W<R>**
prompt	Enter new width for all segments
enter	**0<R>** – Fig. 28.1(h)
prompt	Open/Join................
enter	**X<R>** – to end the Edit Polyline command.

The command is very interactive, and if the result is not as expected the Undo option is very helpful. At this stage, I would imagine that the **Edit Polyline** command will not be used too often with new AutoCAD LT users.

Activate the **Edit Polyline** command again and select any point on the polyarc, and at the prompts enter

1. **C<R>** for close – Fig. 28.1(b)
2. **U<R>** to undo close – Fig. 28.1(c)
3. **W<R>** then **2<R>** for constant width – Fig. 28.1(d)
4. **D<R>** to decurve – Fig. 28.1(e)
5. **S<R>** for spline – Fig. 28.1(f)
6. **F<R>** to fit – Fig. 28.1(g)
7. **C<R>** to close –Fig. 28.1(h)
8. **X<R>** to exit command.

Your drawing should now resemble Fig. 28.1(h) and should now be saved for reference if you want. We will probably not refer to this drawing again.

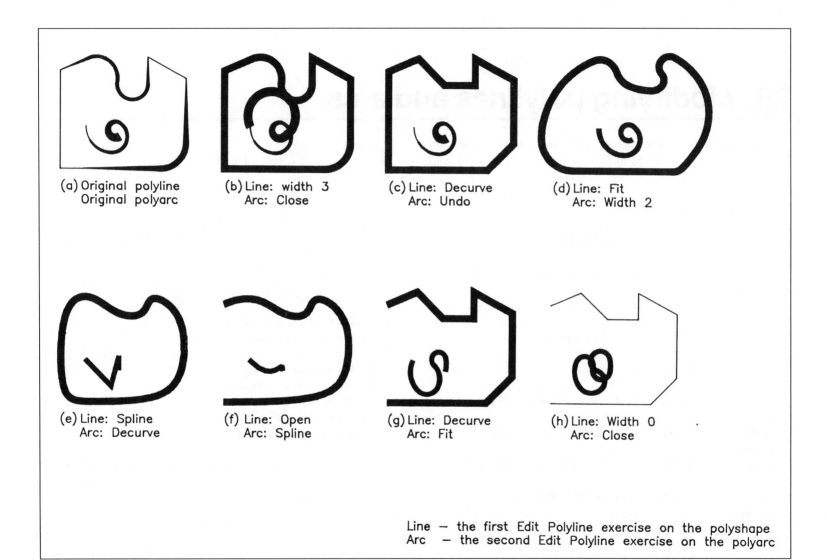

(a) Original polyline
Original polyarc

(b) Line: width 3
Arc: Close

(c) Line: Decurve
Arc: Undo

(d) Line: Fit
Arc: Width 2

(e) Line: Spline
Arc: Decurve

(f) Line: Open
Arc: Spline

(g) Line: Decurve
Arc: Fit

(h) Line: Width 0
Arc: Close

Line — the first Edit Polyline exercise on the polyshape
Arc — the second Edit Polyline exercise on the polyarc

Fig. 28.1. Edit polyline example.

Edit vertex option

The **Edit Polyline** command has ten options available for selection. Most of them 'redraw' the polyshape after a single keyboard entry, e.g. (F)it, (S)pline, etc., but the (E)dit vertex option is slightly different, in that the user is faced with another set of options. We will demonstrate this option with a new example, so open your A:STDA3 standard sheet and refer to Fig. 28.2.

1. Draw an 80 unit *closed* square polyshape, and multiple copy it to two other places on the screen.
2. Activate the **Edit Polyline** command and:

prompt	`Select polyline`
respond	**pick the first square**
prompt	`Open/Join................`
enter	**W<R>** and **8<R>** for new width
prompt	`Open/Join................`
enter	**E<R>** – the edit vertex option
prompt	`Next/Previous/Break/` `Insert/Move/Regen/` `Straighten/Tangent/Width/ eXit`
and	an × at the first vertex of the square (lower left-hand corner?)
enter	**W<R>** – the width option
prompt	`Enter start width <8.00>` and enter **8** `<R>`
prompt	`Enter ending width <8.00>` and enter **0** `<R>`
prompt	`Next/Previous.............`
enter	**N<R>** – the next option
and	× moves to the next vertex (lower right-hand corner?)
prompt	`Next/Previous.............`
enter	**W<R>**
prompt	`Enter start width<8.00>` and enter **0<R>**
prompt	`Enter ending width<0.00>` and enter **4<R>**
prompt	`Next/Previous.............`

enter	**N<R>**
and	× moves to next vertex (top right hand?)
prompt	`Next/Previous.............`
enter	**X<R>** to exit the edit vertex option
prompt	`Open/Join................`
enter	**X<R>** to exit the edit polyline command.

The result is Fig. 28.2(a), i.e. two of the line segments have had their widths individually altered between selected vertices.

3. Repeat the **Edit Polyline** command and pick the second square

prompt	`Open/Join................`
enter	**E<R>**
prompt	`Next/Previous.............`
and	× at first vertex (lower left hand?)
enter	**M<R>** – the move option
prompt	`Enter new location`
enter	**@20,20<R>**
prompt	`Next/Previous.............`
enter	**N<R>** – X at next vertex
prompt	`Next/Previous.............`
enter	**N<R>** – X at next vertex (top right hand?)
prompt	`Next/Previous.............`
enter	**M<R>**
prompt	`Enter new location`
enter	**@–20,–20<R>**
prompt	`Next/Previous.............`
enter	**X<R>** to exit edit vertex option
prompt	`Open/Join................`
enter	**X<R>** to exit edit polyline command.

The result should be Fig.28.2(b), i.e. we have moved two of the vertices to give a 'rhombus' shape.

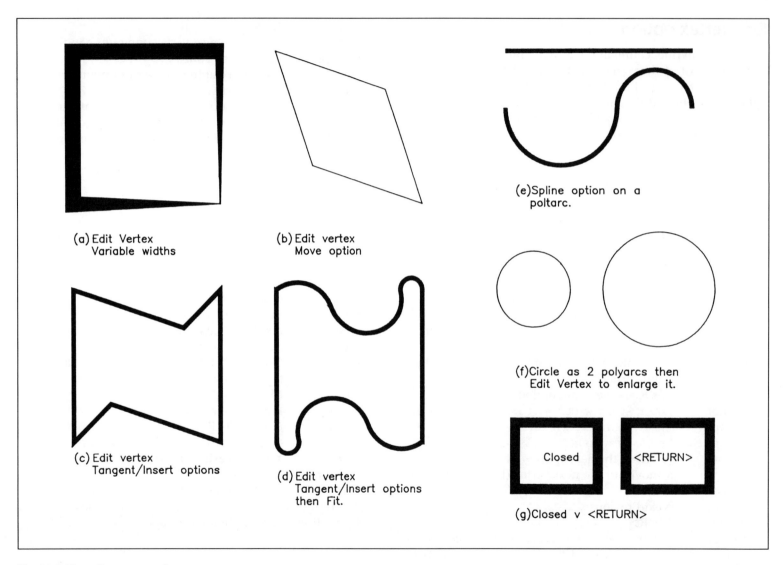

(a) Edit Vertex
Variable widths

(b) Edit vertex
Move option

(e) Spline option on a
poltarc.

(c) Edit vertex
Tangent/Insert options

(d) Edit vertex
Tangent/Insert options
then Fit.

(f) Circle as 2 polyarcs then
Edit Vertex to enlarge it.

Closed   <RETURN>

(g) Closed v <RETURN>

Fig. 28.2. The edit vertex option.

4. Activate the **Edit Polyline** command again and pick the third of the polyline squares, and use the width option to set a constant width of 2 for all segments. Select **E** for edit vertex and:

prompt	Next/Previous...........
enter	**N<R>** until × is at lower left-hand corner
prompt	Next/Previous...........
enter	**T<R>** – the tangent option
prompt	Direction of tangent
respond	**pick a point vertically below the** ×
and	arrowed line results?
prompt	Next/Previous...........
enter	**I<R>** – the insert option
prompt	Enter location of new vertex
enter	**@20,20<R>**
prompt	Next/Previous.... and enter **N<R>**
prompt	Next/Previous.... and enter **N<R>**
	(× at top right hand?)
prompt	Next/Previous....
enter	**T<R>**
prompt	Direction of tangent
respond	**pick a point vertically above the** ×
and	arrowed line?
prompt	Next/Previous....
enter	**I<R>**
prompt	Enter location of new vertex
enter	**@–20,–20<R>** – Fig. 28.2(c)
prompt	Next/Previous....
enter	**X<R>** to end edit vertex option
prompt	Open/Join........
enter	**F<R>** – Fig. 28.2(d)
prompt	Open/Join........
enter	**X<R>** to end the edit polyline command.

The sequence completed used the same co-ordinate input as the previous sequence (i.e. @20,20 and @–20,–20) but the result was entirely different. In the previous sequence a rhombus shape resulted from the entry, but in the last sequence the two vertices did not move. This was a result of the (T)angent option, which fixed the actual vertices.

Figure 28.2 also illustrates some other interesting uses of the **Edit Polyline** command: part (e) shows the effect of the spline option on a continuous polyarc, (f) shows a circle drawn as two polyarcs, then the edit vertex option used to move the vertices – scale effect and (g) shows why a polyline should be closed with the close option and not with **<RETURN>** – bottom left-hand corner.

Activity

While there is no set activity for the **Edit Polyline** command, it is recommended that the user investigates the options available with a simple polyshape of their own creation.

❏ *Summary*

1. Polyshapes can be copied, scaled, moved, etc.
2. Polyshapes have their own edit command – **Edit Polyline**.
3. The options available allow the user several useful options

Open	opens a closed polyshape – the last segment is removed
Width	allows a constant width for all segments to be entered.
Decurve	removes all curves and returns polylines.
Fit/Spline	advanced options.
Undo	undoes the last option entered.

4. The edit vertex option of the **Edit Polyline** command has several options

Next/Previous	moves an × to the next/previous vertex
Move	moves the current vertex by co-ordinate input or screen selection.
Width	allows variable widths to be entered.

5. AutoCAD R12 users can use **PEDIT** at the command line.

29. Point, polygon and solid

These are three drawing commands which are interesting and allow some scope to the user. They will be demonstrated by a worked example, so open your A:STDA3 standard sheet.

Point

A point is an entity. The appearance of the point on the screen can be altered by the user, so from the menu bar select

> **Settings**
> **Point Style...**

prompt   Point Style dialogue box as shown in Fig. 29.1
respond   **pick the style indicated then OK**
prompt   Point
enter   **50,50<R>** – refer to Fig. 29.2.
prompt   Point
enter   **350,240<R>**
prompt   Point and CTRL C to end the command.

Repeat the **Settings-Point Style...** selection and

(a) pick another point style
(b) change the point size to 10
(c) pick OK

prompt   Point and enter 20,230<R>
prompt   Point and enter 330,40<R>
prompt   Point and CTRL C

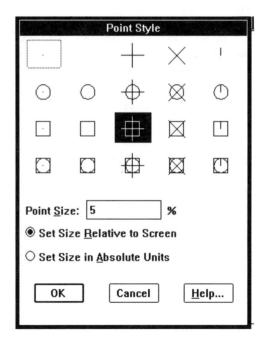

Fig. 29.1. Point Style dialogue box.

Now refer to Fig. 29.2, activate the LINE icon and:

prompt	From point
respond	**NODE icon and pick lower left point**
prompt	To point
respond	**NODE icon and pick upper right point**
prompt	To point
respond	**right click**

A line will be drawn between the selected points. The NODE selection is used with point entities.

Polygon

AutoCAD LT allows polygons to be drawn by specifying
- (a) a centre point and radius
- (b) two endpoints on an edge.

1. Select the **POLYGON** icon and

prompt	Number of sides<4?>
enter	**6<R>**
prompt	Edge/<Center of polygon>
respond	**MIDpoint icon and pick the line**
prompt	Radius of circle (and note drag effect)
enter	**40<R>**

2. Repeat the polygon icon selection and

prompt	Number of sides<6>
enter	**6<R>**
prompt	Edge/<Center of polygon>
enter	**200,145<R>**
prompt	Radius of polygon
enter	**@60,0<R>**

The two polygons which have been drawn have different 'orientations' due to the radius input. The radius can be
- (a) entered as a numeric value from the keyboard
- (b) picked as a point on the screen
- (c) referenced to existing entities, e.g. ENDpoint of a line, etc.

3. At the command line enter **POLYGON<R>** and

prompt	Number of sides<6>
enter	**5<R>**
prompt	Edge/<Center of polygon>
enter	**E<R>** – for edge option
prompt	First endpoint of edge
enter	**30,90<R>**
prompt	Second endpoint of edge
enter	**70,90<R>**

4. Repeat the polygon icon selection and enter:

sides	**7<R>**
option	**E<R>**
First endpoint	**300,70<R>**
Second endpoint	**@70<15<R>**

5. Now select **Construct-Offset** and enter an offset distance of 10

prompt	Select object to offset
respond	**pick the 5 sided polygon**
prompt	Side to offset
respond	**pick outwards**
prompt	Select object to offset
respond	**pick the 7 sided polygon**
prompt	Side to offset
respond	**pick inwards**
prompt	Select object to offset
respond	**right click** to end command.

The complete polygons are offset outward/inward by 10, i.e. a polygon is a polyline.

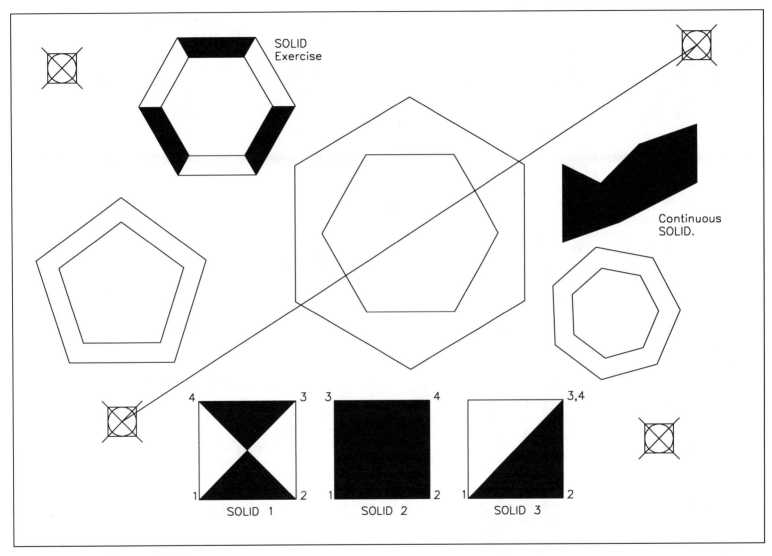

Fig. 29.2. Point, polygon and solid.

Solid

This command 'fills in' shapes according to a 'pick' order entered by the user.

1. Use the LINE icon to draw three 50 unit squares from the points (90,10); (160,10); (230,10).
2. From the menu bar select **Draw**

    Solid

prompt	First point
respond	pick point 1 of SOLID 1 (SNAP ON will help)
prompt	Second point and pick point 2
prompt	Third point and pick point 3
prompt	Fourth point and pick point 4
prompt	Third point and right click to end command.

3. Repeat the SOLID command and pick points 1–4 in the order given in SOLID 2 of Fig. 29.2.
4. Use the SOLID command again and referring to SOLID 3

prompt	First point and pick point 1
prompt	Second point and pick point 2
prompt	Third point and pick point 3
prompt	Fourth point and pick point 4
prompt	Third point and right click.

These three examples demonstrate how three- and four-sided shapes are 'filled; with the **SOLID** command. The prompts fourth point/third point are to allow continuous solid creation. Activate the solid command and

prompt	First point and enter 280,180
prompt	Second point and enter 280,140
prompt	Third point and enter 300,170
prompt	Fourth point and enter 310,159
prompt	Third point and enter 320,190
prompt	Fourth point and enter 350,170
prompt	Third point and enter 350,200

prompt	Fourth point and enter 350,200
prompt	Third point and right click.

Exercises

1. Draw a six-sided polygon, centre at 100,210 and radius 25.
2. Offset this polygon outwards by 10.
3. Use **SOLID** to produce the effect in Fig. 29.2 (ENDpoint icon helps)
4. Find the maximum number of sides allowed with the polygon command?

❏ *Summary*

1. A point is an entity, the appearance being determined by the user from the Point Style dialogue box.
2. The node icon is used to reference points.
3. When a drawing is plotted/saved with points, the points assume the appearance of the last style entered – hence in Fig. 29.2 all points have the same appearance, when the user would have been expecting two different styles of point.
4. A polygon is a multi-sided figure (more than sides) which can be drawn:
    (a) with a centre point and radius
    (b) with two endpoints on an edge.
5. A polygon is a polyline.
6. The SOLID command 'fills-in' shapes.
7. The order of selection with the solid command is important.
8. Only four-sided and three-sided figures can be solid-filled.

30. Text and dimension control codes

AutoCAD LT has certain codes which can be used with text and dimensions to underline/overscore text as well as add other symbols. The codes which are available are

%%O   toggles the *overscore* on/off
%%U   toggles the *underscore* on/off
%%D   draws the *degrees* symbol (°) (angle or temperature)
%%C   draws the *diameter* symbol (Ø)
%%P   draws the *plus or minus* (±) symbol
%%%   draws the *percent* (%) symbol

Open your A:STDA3 standard sheet and refer to Fig. 30.1
1. Select the **TEXT** icon and

prompt	justify/Style/<Start point>
enter	**30,220<R>**
prompt	Height
enter	**10<R>**
prompt	Rotation angle
enter	**0<R>**
prompt	Text
enter	**%%UAutoCAD LT%%U<R>**
prompt	Text and **<RETURN>**

The text will be inserted with an underline.
2. Repeat the **TEXT** command and

enter	45,185**<R>** as the start point
enter	15**<R>** as the height
enter	0**<R>** as the rotation angle

enter   123.45%%DF**<R>** as the text
enter   **<R>** to end sequence.

3. With the TEXT command again, enter:
   150,240**<R>** as the start point
   10**<R>** as the height
   0**<R>** as the angle
   0%%DC is %%UFREEZING%%U**<R>**<R> as the text.
4. Now add the other text in Fig. 30.1 selecting your own start point and entering your own text height.
5. Draw two horizontal lines of 100 units.
6. Use the horizontal Linear Dimension command as normal picking the endpoints of each line and at the dimension text prompt enter
   (a) for line 1 *not* %%C50
   (b) for line 2 *not even* %%O50%%DF%%O.

❏ *Summary*

Control codes are very useful additions when text is being added to a drawing. The underline (%%U) code is probably the most useful, but the degrees (%%D) and diameter (%%C) codes are used extensively. Using control codes when dimensioning, allows user text to be entered in place of the default dimension text value.

Text dimension and control codes   **143**

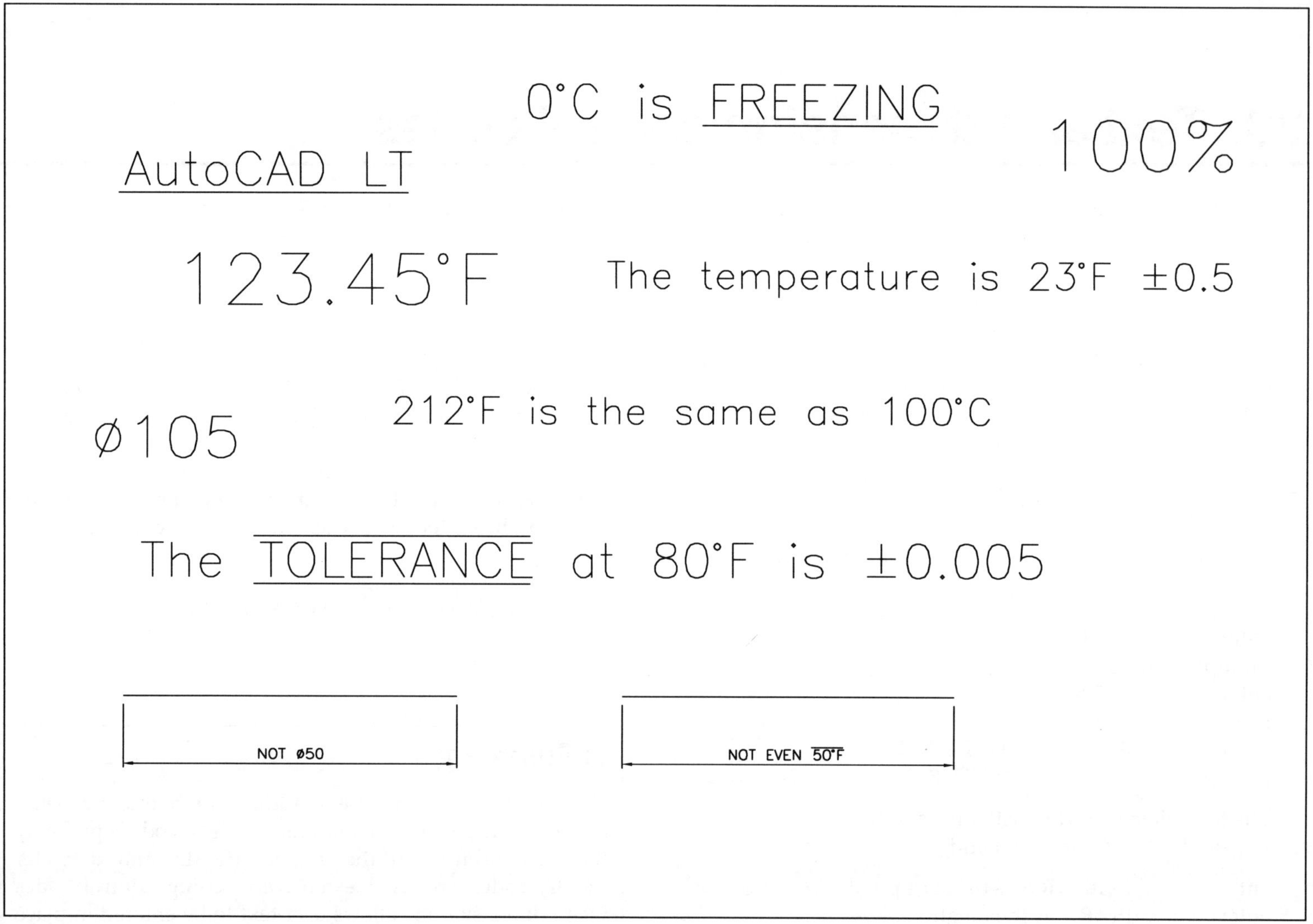

Fig. 30.1. Control codes with text and dimensions

31. Dimension styles

When we were considering how to dimension a component, it was stated that dimensions could be 'set' to specific values, e.g. dimension text height, dimension text position, arrow size, etc. This would allow dimensions to be 'customised' to a specific standard and/or to a customer's requirement. One of AutoCAD LT's advantages is that these different dimension styles can be saved for future recall. This means that the user can have several dimension styles with a variety of different values and use a specific style for a particular application.

To achieve these dimension styles, use is made of the Dimension Style and Settings dialogue box, and we have used this dialogue box to set a dimension style called STDA3. In this chapter we will create four new dimension styles and use each one to dimension different linear, circular and angular entities.

Making the new dimension styles

1. Open your A:STDA3 standard sheet.
2. From the menu bar select **Settings**
   Dimension Style...
3. The dimension style dialogue box will appear with
   (a) STDA3 as a named dimension style in blue
   (b) STDA3 at the Dimension Style name box (also in blue) indicating that it is the current dimension style. A flashing | will also be displayed after the 3.

4. Use the mouse to position the arrow to the right of the 3, then:
   (a) right click
   (b) delete STDA3 with five backspaces.
5. Enter **BOBST1<R>** at the Dimension Style name box and:
   (a) prompt New style BOBST1 created from STDA3 appears at the bottom of the dialogue box.
   (b) BOBST1 is added (in blue) to the Dimension Styles list.
6. Pick (left click) STDA3 from the Dimension Styles list and:
   (a) it turns blue
   (b) STDA3 will appear in the Dimension Style name box.
7. Position the arrow to the right of the 3 and delete STDA3 as before.
8. Enter **BOBST2<R>** at the Dimension Style name box and:
   (a) prompt New style BOBST2 created from STDA3 appears as before
   (b) BOBST2 is added to the Dimension Styles list.
9. Repeat steps 6, 7 and 8 entering BOBST3 and then BOBST4 as the dimension names, both being created from STDA3.
10. Pick STDA3 from the Dimension Styles list and then pick OK.
11. You will be returned to the drawing screen.
12. Select **Settings-Dimension Styles...** again and your dialogue box will appear as Fig. 31.1, i.e. four new dimension styles have been made.
13. Cancel the dialogue box.

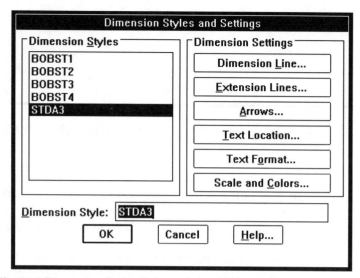

Fig. 31.1. Dimension Styles dialogue box with four styles set up.

Customising the new dimension styles

The procedure which follows may seem rather involved and tedious, but it is essential if the new dimension styles have to be customised correctly. Once the user becomes accustomed to the method described it will become simple – I hope.

1. Once again select **Settings-Dimension Styles...**
2. Pick **BOBST1** from the Dimension Styles list (turns blue) and the name **BOBST1** will appear in the Dimension name box.
3. From the dialogue box, select the following dialogue box names, and alter the variable stated to the value given, picking OK when all the values have been set

    (a) Dimension Lines   Basic Dimension: ON, i.e. × in box.
    (b) Extension Lines   Center Mark Size: 0
    (c) Arrows   Size: 5
    (d) Text Location   Vertical: Centred.

4. Pick OK from the Dimension Style and Settings dialogue box to set the dimension style **BOBST1** to the altered values.
5. Now repeat steps 1–4 for the other three new dimension styles, using the appropriate dialogue box to set the following values

Dimension style BOBST2

    (a) Extension lines   Center Mark Size: 3.
                                  Center Lines ON, i.e. × in box
    (b) Text location   Horizontal: Force Text Inside
                                  Alignment: Orient Text
                                              Horizontally
    (c) Text format   Trailing: OFF, i.e. no × in box.

Dimension style BOBST3

    (a) Arrows   Ticks: ON, i.e. black dot in box
                                  Tick size: 3
    (b) Text location   Text Height: 4
    (c) Text format   Show Alternate Units: ON, i.e. ×
                                              in box
                                  DP: 2

Dimension style BOBST4

    (a) Arrows   Dots: ON, i.e. black dot in box
                                  Dot size: 3
    (b) Text location   Vertical: Centred
                                    Alignment: Orient Text
                                              Horizontally
    (c) Text format   Length Scaling: 100.

Using the customised dimension styles

Refer to Fig. 31.2 and create five of each of the following entities

- (a) horizontal lines of length 70
- (b) horizontal lines of length 10
- (c) vertical lines of length 70
- (d) vertical lines of length 10
- (e) circles of radii 20
- (f) angled lines of a reasonable length.

1. Activate the Dimension Style dialogue box.
2. Make STDA3 the current dimension style by
   - (a) picking STDA3 from the dimension styles list (turns blue)
   - (b) check the name STDA3 appears in the dimension name box
   - (c) pick OK.
3. Now dimension one of each of the drawn entities using
   - (a) linear dimensions – horizontal and vertical
   - (b) radial dimensions – diameter
   - (c) angular dimensions.
4. Make BOBST1 the current dimension style, and dimension another set of entities.
5. Repeat the entity dimensioning making each dimension style current.

Your final result should be similar to Fig. 31.2. Save at this stage.

Problems with dimension styles

Dimension styles allow the user a great deal of scope for customising dimensions to individual requirements. They, however, have one disadvantage which can be a bit of a nuisance. If a saved dimension style has a variable altered, then all dimensions which used that saved style will also be altered.

We will demonstrate this with the following example:
1. Make BOBST1 the current dimension style.
2. Using the Dimension Styles dialogue box, alter the following:
   - (a) Extension Lines: Visibility: Suppress both.
   - (b) Arrows: Arrow Size: 5
   - (c) Text Location   Vertical: Relative
                            Relative Position: –5
3. Pick OK from the Dimension Styles and Settings dialogue box.
4. Five entities on the screen should have their dimension styles redrawn with
   - (a) rather large arrows.
   - (b) the dimension text below the dimension line
   - (c) no dimension extension lines.
5. Now set BOBST1 back to the original values (if you can?)
6. Exit without saving.

❏ *Summary*

1. Dimension Styles can be set by the user.
2. Dimension Styles can be saved.
3. There is no limit to the number of dimension styles which can be saved.
4. Saved Dimension Styles allow customisation of dimensions to different standards and/or customer requirements.

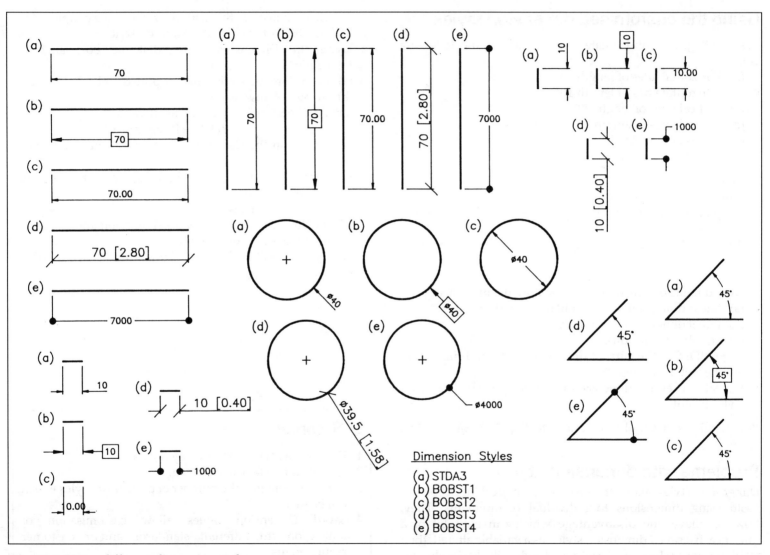

Dimension Styles

(a) STDA3
(b) BOBST1
(c) BOBST2
(d) BOBST3
(e) BOBST4

Fig. 31.2. Using different dimension styles.

32. Tolerances and limits

Many engineering drawings require dimensions to be added which display tolerances or limits, and AutoCAD LT allows this facility using the Text Format selection from the Dimension Styles and Settings dialogue box. There are three options available:

(a) none, i.e. 'normal' dimensions
(b) variance on – this is AutoCAD LT's tolerance
(c) limits on.

The three effects are shown in Fig. 32.1, which has been displayed with the units set to a precision of four decimal places.

Notes

1. Only one option can be on at the one time, i.e. it is not possible to display dimensions with both tolerances and limits.
2. To obtain variance or limit dimensions the user *must accept* the default dimension text value, i.e. you will not get variance/limit dimensions if you enter a dimension text value from the keyboard.
3. When the Variance/Limits option is selected from the dialogue box, the user enters:

    (a) the upper value, e.g. 0.05
    (b) the lower value, e.g. 0.02.

    These are equivalent to a +ve (upper) or −ve (lower) variance/limit.

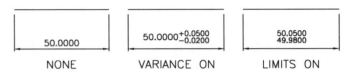

Fig. 32.1. Effect on dimensions of varaince and limits.

4. The units must be set to the required precision (i.e. decimal places) to obtain the correct dimension display. This is obtained from the Units Style... dialogue box, under Settings.
5. Because variance and limits cannot both be on at the same time, it is necessary to make different dimension styles for the two options.
6. If two different variance/limit values are required in a drawing, a different dimension style must be made for each value.

Worked example

1. Open your A:STDA3 standard sheet and refer to Fig. 32.2.
2. With OUT the current layer, draw a horizontal line of 80 units, and multiple copy it to nine other places on the screen.
3. Using the Dimension Styles and Settings dialogue box, make ten new dimension styles from the original STDA3 style. Mine were called: DIMVAR1, DIMVAR2, DIMVAR3, DIMVAR4, DIMVAR5, DIMLIM1, DIMLIM2, DIMLIM3, DIMLIM4 and DIMLIM5.

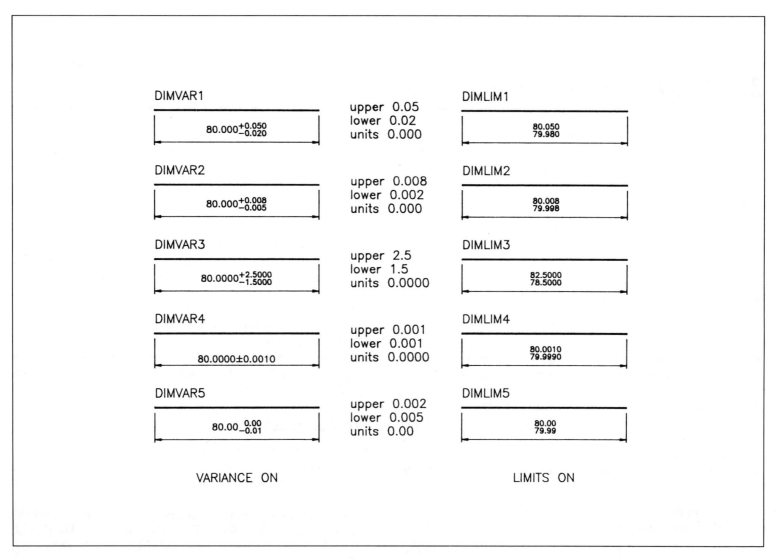

Fig. 32.2. Variance and limit values on dimensions.

5. Using the Text Format dialogue box, set the following for each new dimension style:

All VARIANCE ON

DIMVAR1
Upper limit	0.05
Lower limit	0.02
Unit precision	0.000

DIMVAR2
Upper value	0.008
Lower value	0.002
Unit precision	0.000

DIMVAR3
Upper value	2.5
Lower value	1.5
Unit precision	0.0000

DIMVAR4
Upper value	0.001
Lower value	0.001
Unit precision	0.0000

DIMVAR5
Upper value	0.002
Lower value	0.005
Unit precision	0.00

All LIMITS ON

DIMLIM1
Upper value	0.05
Lower value	0.02
Unit precision	0.000

DIMLIM2
Upper value	0.008
Lower value	0.002
Unit precision	0.000

DIMLIM3
Upper value	2.5
Lower value	1.5
Unit precision	0.0000

DIMLIM4
Upper value	0.001
Lower value	0.001
Unit precision	0.000

DIMLIM5
Upper value	0.002
Lower value	0.005
Unit precision	0.00

6. Now set DIMVAR1 as the current dimension style and dimension the first horizontal line.
7. Set DIMLIM1 as the current dimension and dimension the next line.
8. Repeat the dimensioning of each line, making each dimension style current in turn.
9. Draw some other entities, e.g. vertical lines, circles, etc and add dimensions to each. You may want to alter some of the other variables, but this is your choice.

❏ **Summary**

1. Tolerances (variance) and limits can be added to dimensions.
2. A dimension style must be made for each variance/limit required.
3. The unit precision affects the variance/limits dimension.
4. If a variance/limit value is altered, all existing dimensions which have used that style will be 'updated'.
5. Only default dimension text values will display variance/limits dimensions.

Activity

It is now some time since we have attempted any activities, and I have included two for you to try:
1. Tutorial 21 – a simply component to draw with several tolerance and limit dimensions added. I used offset and trim quite a bit to draw the component. You will need to make several dimension styles to obtain the actual dimensions shown.
2. Tutorial 22 – an engineering type component. This drawing does not have any tolerance/limit dimensions but it requires you to use the text control codes as well as dimension styles – I used two.

33. The ARRAY command

ARRAY is a command which allows the multiple copying of objects into a rectangular or polar (circular) pattern. The command will be demonstrated by a worked example so:
1. Open your A:STDA3 standard sheet and refer to Fig.33.1.
2. With OUT the current layer make the basic shape to the sizes given then multiple copy it to the points indicated at A, B, C and D using the donut marker as the base point.
3. Erase the original shape when you have completed the copy command.

Rectangular array

From the menu bar select **Construct**

                   Array

prompt	Select objects
respond	**window the shape at A then \<R\>**
prompt	Rectangular or Polar array(R/P)\<?\>
enter	**R\<R\>**
prompt	Number of rows(—)\<1\>
enter	**3\<R\>**
prompt	Number of columns(|||)\<1\>
enter	**5\<R\>**
prompt	Unit cell or distance between rows(—)
enter	**30\<R\>**
prompt	Distance between columns (|||)
enter	**25\<R\>**

The shape at A will be copied 14 times into a three row and five column pattern. This is the basis of all rectangular arrays.

Polar array with rotation

Repeat the **Construct-Array** selection and

prompt	Select objects
respond	**window the shape at B then \<R\>**
prompt	Rectangular or Polar(R/P)\<R\>
enter	**P\<R\>**
prompt	Center point of array
enter	**300,195\<R\>**
prompt	Number of items
enter	**10\<R\>**
prompt	Angle to fill (+=ccw,-=cw)\<360\>
enter	**360\<R\>** – for full circle
prompt	Rotate objects as they are copied\<Y\>
enter	**\<RETURN\>** i.e. accept the Y default

The shape at B is copied into a circular pattern about the selected centre point, and the shape is also rotated (i.e. aligned) about the centre point.

Polar array without rotation

Repeat the array command and window the shape at C. Enter **P** for polar, **(215,75)** as the centre point, **10** as the number of items, **360** as the angle to fill and enter **N** to the rotate prompt. The resultant pattern is not as 'neat' as the array with rotation.

Partial polar array

The two previous polar arrays had an angle to fill of 360 degrees, i.e. the array was a full circular fill. The user can specify the angle which the array is to 'fill' about the centre point. Repeat the array command and window the shape at D then

prompt	`Center point of array`
enter	**60,70<R>**
prompt	`Number of items`
enter	**7<R>**
prompt	`Angle to fill.........`
enter	**−130<R>**
prompt	`Rotate...............`
enter	**Y<R>**

Your final arrays should now be similar to Fig. 33.1. Save if you wish to.

The array command is very useful especially with engineering type drawings where (for example) a number of holes are required on a PCD.

Refer to Fig. 33.2 and:
1. Open A:STDA3
2. Draw three circles:
   (a) radius 20 on layer OUT
   (b) radius 50 on layer OUT
   (c) radius 35 on layer CL.
3. Multiple copy the three circles to three other parts of the screen.

4. Draw the centre line and circle using the reference sizes given, and multiple copy them to the four sets of circles using the END and CENTRE icon selections.
5. Complete Fig. 33.2. Use the **ARRAY** command, selecting the copied line and circle. Polar array with the following information:
   (a) 4 items, angle 360
   (b) 6 items, angle 360
   (c) 8 items, angle 240
   (d) 10 items, angle −200.

❏ *Summary*

1. **ARRAY** is a **Construct** command.
2. Arrays allow multiple copying in rectangular or polar patterns.
3. Rectangular arrays must have at least 1 row and 1 column.
4. Polar arrays require a centre point for rotation, and this can be:
   (a) entered as co-ordinates from the keyboard
   (b) referenced to an existing entity, e.g. circle centre.
5. Polar arrays allow the object to be rotated about the centre point.

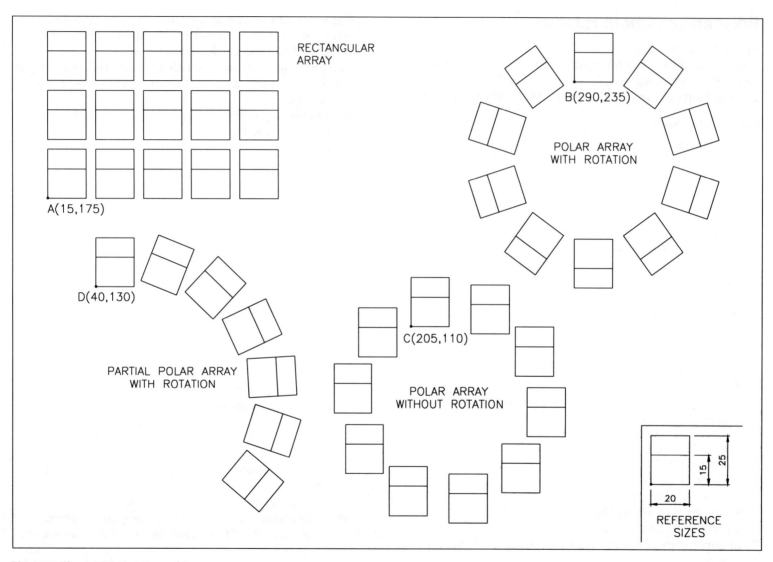

RECTANGULAR ARRAY

A(15,175)

B(290,235)

POLAR ARRAY WITH ROTATION

D(40,130)

PARTIAL POLAR ARRAY WITH ROTATION

C(205,110)

POLAR ARRAY WITHOUT ROTATION

25
15
20

REFERENCE SIZES

Fig. 33.1. The **ARRAY** command 1.

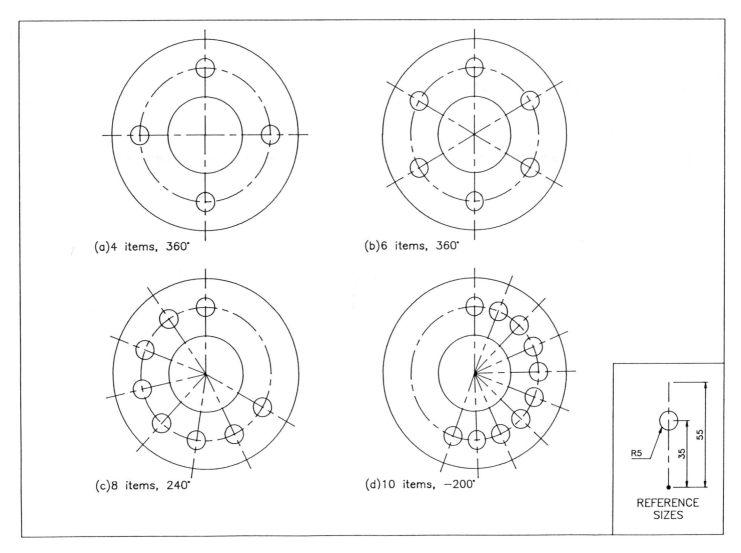

Fig. 33.2. The **ARRAY** command 2.

34. User exercise 3

This is a simple exercise using the array command, but the drawing will be saved for the later chapter dealing with text styles and fonts, so refer to Fig. 34.1 and

1. Open your A:STDA3 standard sheet with OUT layer current.
2. Draw a 35 unit square, the lower left corner being at (20,70).
3. Select Construct-Array and window the square then enter:

   R   – for rectangular
   4   – for the rows
   2   – for the columns
   40 – as the row distance
   40 – as the column distance.

4. Save the resultant arrayed drawing as **A:USEREX3**.

(20,70)

Fig. 34.1. User exercise 3.

Activities

As stated earlier, **ARRAY** is of the most useful commands available in AutoCAD LT. Four activities are included for you to attempt, and have tried to vary the exercises to give added problems. For these activities, remember to use your standard sheet, beginning a new drawing with:

(a) Prototype name – A:STDA3
(b) New drawing name – A:TUT23, etc .

The drawing should be dimensioned, which will also test your skills.

1. Tutorial 23: a simple drawing but the construction of the actual tooth requires a bit of thought. Position the two centre lines then the three circles. Draw the L-shapes tooth and then move it to its start position. The **ARRAY** command does the rest.
2. Tutorial 24: an engineering type drawing using the **ARRAY** command for the counterbored circles and the slots. This drawing is harder than it looks, especially as it involves hatching and dimensioning.
3. Tutorial 25: the light bulb problem, which I consider to be one of the hardest drawings in the book. It is fairly straightforward until you attempt the R10 radius arc.
4. Tutorial 26: a bit of light relief. The ARRAY command is very good for producing designs, the result only being limited by the users imagination. The two designs in this exercise involve using both rectangular and polar arrays, and are

Design A

The basic shape is from lines drawn about a 30 unit square. I used a snap and grid of 5 and then drew a few lines. The basic 'square' was rotated twice and the rectangular array had two rows and two columns. The polar array had the basic square copied then rotated 45 degrees before the command was activated.

Design B

A set of five lines polar arrayed about the circle centre. The actual polar array of the basic shape was through a fill angle of 180 degrees.

35. Getting some assistance

AutoCAD LT allows the user to 'interrogate' entities to obtain information about co-ordinates, distances and areas. The commands are all activated from the menu bar with **Assist** and are

ID Point
Distance
Area
List
Time

Refer to Fig. 35.1 and:

1. Open your A:STDA3 standard sheet.
2. With the LINE command, draw a rectangle from the point (30,170) the sides being 95 and 65 long. Draw in a diagonal – Fig. 35.1(a).
3. Draw a circle, centre (230,210) with radius 45 – Fig. 35.1(b).
4. Draw a triangular polyshape of width 0 from the point (45,45) the horizontal side being 60 long and the vertical side 90. Close the triangle – Fig. 35.1(c).
4. Draw an 80 unit square from the point 155,35 and add a 20 unit square and a 10 radius circle anywhere within this square – Fig. 35.1(d).
5. Draw a polyshape as Fig. 35.1(e), the straight side being 70 long and the arc radius 40. Offset the shape 20 'inwards'.

Note that the letters in Fig.35.1 are for reference only.

Point identification

1. From the menu bar select **Assist**
                              ID Point

prompt	IDPoint
respond	**INTersection icon and pick point A**
Display	X=30.00 Y=170.00 Z=0.00

These are the co-ordinates of point A, the Z being 0 as our drawing is a flat 2D drawing.
2. Repeat the Assist-ID Point selection and

prompt	ID Point
respond	**MIDpoint and pick the diagonal line AC**
Display	X=77.50 Y=202.50 Z=0.00

3. Select ID Point again and at the prompt:

respond	**CENter icon and pick the circle**
Display	X=230.00 Y=210.00 Z=0.00

These are the co-ordinates of the circle centre.

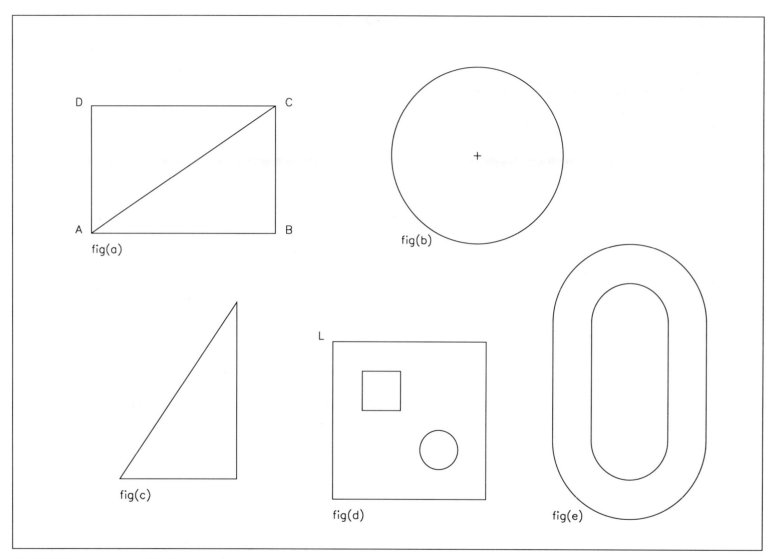

Fig. 35.1. Figures for use with distance, area, etc.

Distance

This is a command which will return the distance and angle for any two selected points.

1. Select **Assist-Distance** and

prompt	First point
respond	**INTersection icon and pick point A**
prompt	Second point
respond	**INTersection icon and pick point C**
Display	Distance=115.11,Angle in X–Y Plane= 34, Angle from X–Y Plane=0Delta X=95.00,Delta Y=65.00, Delta Z=0.00

i.e. the distance from A to C is 115.11 units and point C lies at an angle of 34 degrees from a horizontal line through point A. The horizontal distance from A to C is 95, and the vertical distance from A to C is 65.

2. Repeat the Distance command and:

prompt	First point
respond	**CENter icon and pick the circle**
prompt	Second point
respond	**INTersection icon and pick point L**
Display	Distance=121.04,Angle in X–Y Plane= 232,Angle from X–Y Plane=0, Delta X=-75.00,Delta Y=-95.00,Delta Z=0.00

Area

The area command will return the area and perimeter of a selected shape or polyshape. It also allows the user to add and subtract other shapes to the original.

1. Select **Assist-Area** and:

prompt	<First point>/Entity/Add/ Subtract
respond	**INTersection icon and pick point A –** Fig. 35.1(a)
prompt	Next point
respond	INTersection icon and pick point B
prompt	Next point and pick point C
prompt	Next point and pick point D
prompt	Next point
respond	**right click** to end the command.
Display	Area = 6175.00, Perimeter = 320.00

Are these correct for the rectangle?

2. Select **Assist-Area** again and:

prompt	<First point>/Entity/Add/ Subtract
enter	**E<R>** for entity selection
prompt	Select circle or polyline
respond	pick any point on the circle
Display	Area = 6361.73, Perimeter = 282.74

Are these correct for a circle of radius 45?

3. Repeat the area command and select any point on the triangular polyshape and:

Display	Area = 2700.00, Perimeter = 258.17

4. Select the area command again and:

prompt	`<First point>/Entity/Add/Subtract`
enter	**A\<R>** the add option
prompt	`<First point>/Entity/Subtract`
respond	pick first corner of square in fig(d)
prompt	`(Add mode)Next point and pick the next corner of square`
prompt	`(Add mode)Next point and pick the third corner`
prompt	`(Add mode)Next point and pick the fourth corner`
prompt	`(Add mode)Next point`
respond	**right click** to end point selection
display	Area = 6400.00, Perimeter = 320.00 (1)
	Total Area = 6400.00
prompt	`<First point>/Entity/Subtract`
enter	**S\<R>** the subtract option
prompt	`<First point>/Entity/Add`
respond	pick first corner of **small** square
prompt	`(SUBTRACT mode)Next point and pick second corner`
prompt	`(SUBTRACT mode)Next point and pick third corner`
prompt	`(SUBTRACT mode)Next point and pick fourth corner`
prompt	`(SUBTRACT mode)Next point`
respond	**right click** to end point selection
display	Area = 400.00, Perimeter = 80.00 (2)
	Total Area = 6000.00
prompt	`<First point>/Entity/Add`
enter	**E\<R>** for entity selection
prompt	`(SUBTRACT mode)Select circle or polyline`
respond	pick a point on small circle

Display	Area = 314.16, Perimeter = 62.83 (3)
	Total Area = 5685.84
prompt	`(SUBTRACT mode)Select circle or polyline`
respond	**right click** – to end selection
prompt	`<First point>/Entity/Add`
respond	**right click** – to end command

This is a long sequence and involves the user in several keyboard entries to select entities and/or add/subtract other shapes. The sequence gives the area and perimeter of each shape identified as well as a 'running area total'

(1) large square area 6400, perimeter 320
Total area = 6400.00
(2) small square area 400, perimeter 80
Total area = 6000.00 (large-small)
(3) small circle area 314.16, perimeter 62.83
Total area = 5685.84 (large square – (small + circle))

5. Finally repeat the area command and:

prompt	`<First point>/Entity/Add/Subtract`
enter	**A\<R>**
prompt	`<First point>/Entity/Subtract`
enter	**E\<R>**
prompt	`(ADD mode)Select circle or polyline`
respond	pick the outer polyshape in fig(e)
Display	Area = 9826.55, Perimeter = 371.33
	Total area = 9826.55
prompt	`(ADD mode)Select circle or polyline`
respond	**right click**
prompt	`<First point>/Entity/Subtract`
enter	**S\<R>**
prompt	`<First point>/Entity/Add`
enter	**E\<R>**

prompt	(SUBTRACT mode) Select circle or polyline
respond	pick the inner polyshape
Display	Area = 3656.64, Perimeter = 245.16
	Total area = 6169.91
prompt	(SUBTRACT mode) Select circle or polyline
respond	**right click** and **right click**.

List

This command returns information about a selected entity, the information being displayed in text screen format. Select **Assist-List** and

prompt	Select objects
respond	**pick any point on large circle**
prompt	text screen as Fig. 35.2
respond	study the display
then	**press key F2 to 'FLIP' back to drawing screen**

The information which is given in the text screen includes:

(a) the type of entity – CIRCLE
(b) the layer on which it is drawn – OUT
(c) whether it is in MODEL or PAPER space
(d) co-ordinate details.

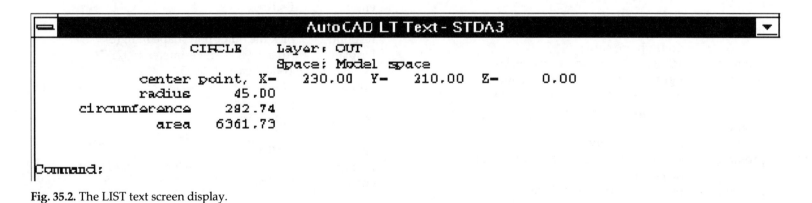

```
                    CIRCLE      Layer: OUT
                                Space: Model space
            center point, X=     230.00  Y=     210.00  Z=      0.00
                   radius     45.00
        circumference    292.74
                  area   6361.73
```

Command:

Fig. 35.2. The LIST text screen display.

Time

This can be a useful command as it gives information about the current drawing

- (a) when it was originally created
- (b) when it was last updated
- (c) the time worked on it, etc .

Select **Assist-Time** and the Time Text screen will be displayed similar to Fig. 35.3.

The user has four options

Display	displays the time screen
ON	turns the timer on.
OFF	urns the timer off
Reset	resets the timer.

To exit the Time text screen:

1. right click to exit command line
2. F2 to flip to drawing screen.

```
Command: '_time
Current time:            05 Jun 1994 at 13:34:15.010
Times for this drawing:
  Created:               08 May 1994 at 10:21:07.330
  Last updated:          22 May 1994 at 11:24:55.250
  Total editing time:    0 days 00:02:50.450
  Elapsed timer (on):    0 days 00:02:50.450
  Next automatic save in: <disabled>

Display/ON/OFF/Reset: d
```

Fig. 35.3. The LIST text screen display.

❏ *Summary*

1. Drawings can be 'interrogated' to obtain information about:

   - (a) co-ordinate details
   - (b) distances
   - (c) areas
   - (d) entity types, layers and spatial orientation
   - (e) times.

2. Distance is returned between any two selected points and gives

   - (a) the actual distance between the points
   - (b) the angle to the 'horizontal'
   - (c) the X and Y distances between the selected points.

3. Areas and perimeters are returned for selected shapes and/or polyshapes. Areas can be added or subtracted form the original shape.

36. Text fonts and styles

Text has been added to drawings without any consideration being given to the text appearance. When dealing with text, there are two concepts with which the user should be familiar, these being **fonts** and **styles**.

Font

A text font defines the pattern which is used to_draw text characters and AutoCAD LT has several text fonts available for selection in icon form, these being contained in a dialogue box. From the menu bar, select **Settings-Text Style...**

prompt	Select Text Font dialogue box (first screen) as Fig. 36.1.
respond	**pick Next**
prompt	Text Font dialogue box (second screen)
respond	**pick Cancel**

Figure 36.2 gives the appearance of several of these text fonts, as they appear on the screen using the text phrase AutoCAD LT.

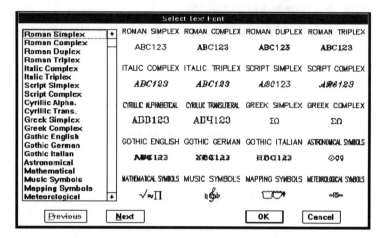

Fig. 36.1. The select text font dialogue box (first screen).

Style

A text style defines the parameters used to draw actual text, and include the text height, obliquing angle, backwards text, etc. To 'see' what style is available at present, activate the TEXT icon and:

prompt	Justify/Style/<Start point>
enter	**S<R>** – for Style
prompt	Style name (or ?)<STANDARD>
enter	**?<R>**
prompt	Text style(s) to list<*>
enter	***<R>** – for all text styles

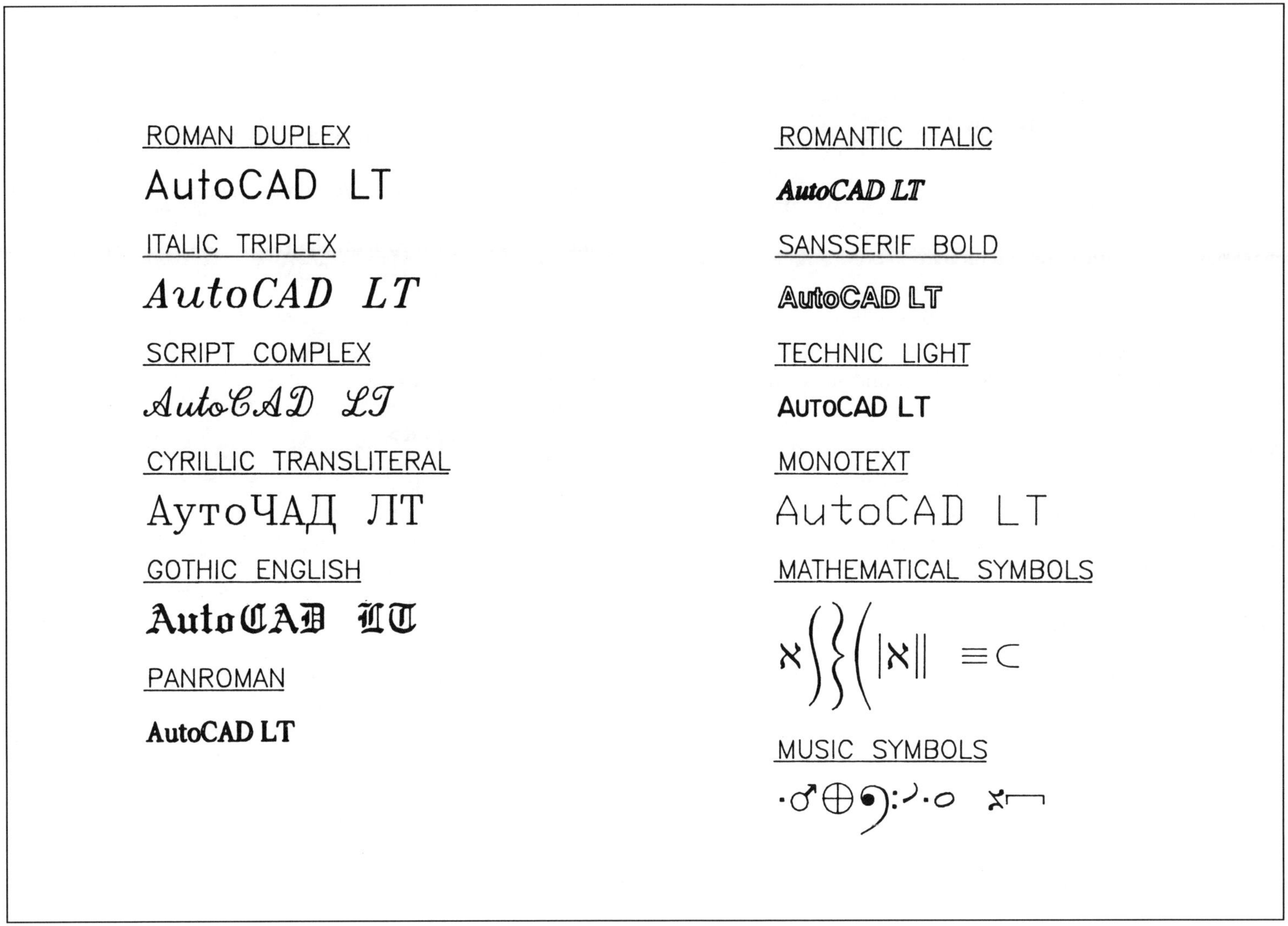

ROMAN DUPLEX

AutoCAD LT

ITALIC TRIPLEX

AutoCAD LT

SCRIPT COMPLEX

AutoCAD LT

CYRILLIC TRANSLITERAL

АутоЧАД ЛТ

GOTHIC ENGLISH

AutoCAD LT

PANROMAN

AutoCAD LT

ROMANTIC ITALIC

AutoCAD LT

SANSSERIF BOLD

AutoCAD LT

TECHNIC LIGHT

AutoCAD LT

MONOTEXT

AutoCAD LT

MATHEMATICAL SYMBOLS

$$\chi \int \left\{ \left(\| \chi \| \right. \right. \equiv \subset$$

MUSIC SYMBOLS

Fig. 36.2. Some text fonts – all AutoCAD LT (height 8).

prompt	Text screen with –
	Text styles:
	Style name: STANDARD Font files: txt
	Height: 0.0000 Width factor: 1.0000
	Obliquing angle 0
	Generation Normal
	Current text style S T A N D A R D
	Justify/Style/<Start
	point>
respond	study the screen
then	**CTRL C** to exit command
and	**F2** to flip to drawing screen.

The text style described above is AutoCAD LT's default style. It has been given the name STANDARD and uses the text font file called TXT.

Notes

1. Text fonts are 'inherent' in AutoCAD LT.
2. Text styles are defined by the user.
3. Text fonts can be used for many text styles.
4. An individual text style uses a text font.

Making text styles

To make a text style it is necessary to
  (a)   select the required text font.
  (b)   define the parameters for the actual text.
The command to make a text style is **STYLE**, but this command is not available in icon form or from the menu bar, and must therefore be entered from the keyboard. We will make six different text styles using three text fonts, the procedure being identical in each case. Open your **A:STDA3** standard sheet and refer to Fig. 36.3. These are the text styles which we will make.

At the command line enter **STYLE<R>**

prompt	Text style name(or ?)
enter	**ST1<R>**
prompt	New style
and	Select Font Style dialogue box as shown in Fig. 36.4.
respond	click on up/down arrow until romant.shx is in view
then	**pick romant.shx** (turns blue)
and	**pick OK**, i.e. ROMAN TRIPLEX selected
prompt	Height<0.0>
enter	**10<R>**
prompt	Width factor<1.0>
enter	**2<R>**
prompt	Obliquing angle<0>
enter	**10<R>**
prompt	Backwards<N>
enter	**N<R>**
prompt	Upside-down<N>
enter	**N<R>**
prompt	Vertical<N>
enter	**N<R>**
prompt	ST1 is now the current text style.

At present we will not use this text style, but will repeat the above procedure using the STYLE command to create the other five text styles. Table 36.1 gives the data for these text styles, so enter STYLE at the command line, then enter the appropriate value as the prompts appear

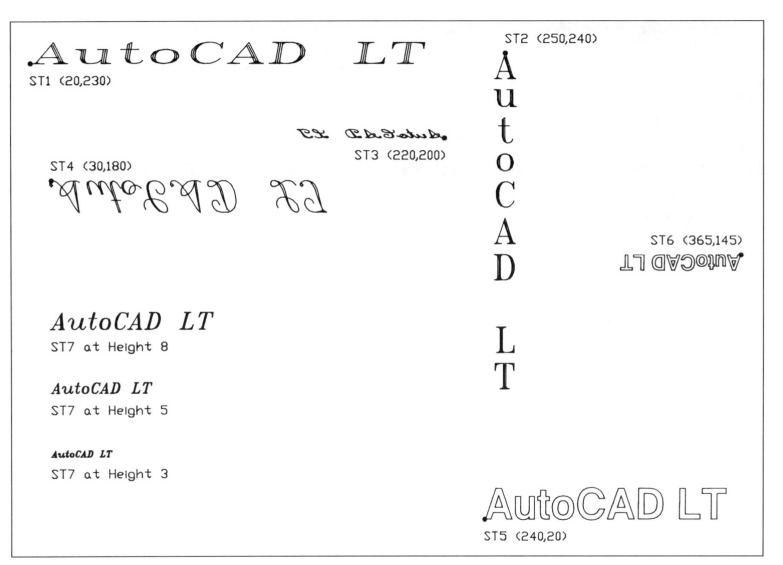

Fig. 36.3. Using created text styles.

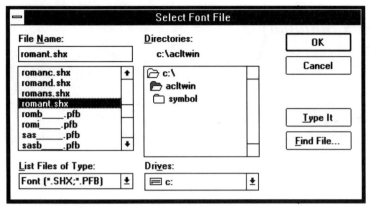

Fig. 36.4. The Select Text Font dialogue box.

Table 36.1

Style name	ST2	ST3	ST4	ST5	ST6
Font name	romant	scriptc	scriptc	sasb	sasb
Extension	shx	shx	shx	.pfb	pfb
Height	12	4	15	20	10
Width factor	1	2	1	1	1
Obliquing angle	0	10	0	0	0
Backwards	N	Y	N	N	Y
Upside-down	N	N	Y	N	Y
Vertical	Y	N	N	—	—

When all six text styles have been made, enter **STYLE**

prompt	`Text style name (or ?)<ST6>`
enter	**?<R>**
prompt	`Text style(s) to list<*>`
enter	***<R>**
prompt	Text screen with the various styles created. You may have to **<RETURN>** to 'see' them all.
then	Current text style: ST6
respond	Cancel the command and F2 to flip to drawing screen.

Using created text styles

A text style is used with the TEXT command, and only one style can be used at a time. Select the TEXT icon and

prompt	`Justify/Style/<Start point>`
enter	**S<R>** – for style
prompt	`Style name(or ?)<ST6>`
enter	**ST1<R>**
prompt	`justify/Style/<Start point>`
enter	**20,230<R>**
prompt	`Rotation angle<0>`
enter	**0<R>**
prompt	`Text`
enter	**AutoCAD LT<R><R>** – why two returns?

The phrase AutoCAD LT will be displayed at the point (20,230) and will have the ROMAN TRIPLEX text font. The actual style of the text will be as created, i.e. a height of 10, a width factor of 2, etc.

Repeat the TEXT command for the other five styles we have created, entering the style name and the start point using the information given in Fig. 36.3, e.g. ST2 at (250,240), etc.

A point of interest

When the **TEXT** command was used with the created text styles, there was no height prompt. The reason for this was that each text style had a height entered when it was being created. Thus when ST1 is used, the text height will *always* be 10, ST5 will always have a text height of 20, etc. It is recommended that when a text style is being created the height be entered as 0. This will allow the user to enter a varying height when the **TEXT** command is used. If this seems confusing make a new text style called **ST7** with

> font – italict.shx
> height – 0
> width factor – 0
> obliquing angle – 0
> backwards, upside-down, vertical – all N

Now use the **TEXT** command, entering the style as ST7. You will now have a height prompt, and you can insert the text at the required height as shown in Fig. 36.3.

Text fonts

The text icons from the Text Style... dialogue box can also be used to create a text style, the procedure being similar to that described. I would *not recommend* this method for creating text styles as the text style 'name' cannot be entered by the user, and the actual icon font name is used as the style name. This may cause confusion. Text style should be made with the **STYLE** command.

❑ *Summary*

1. **FONTS** define the pattern of text characters.
2. **STYLES** define the parameters to draw the text.
3. Text styles are created by the user with the **STYLE** command.
4. The AutoCAD LT default text style is **STANDARD**.
5. Text styles allow the user to add 'fancy text' to a drawing.

Activity

I have not included any activities with text styles, but the next chapter is an exercise which requires the user to create some styles of their own.

37. User exercise 4

Open the **A:USEREX3** drawing of the eight squares created with the ARRAY command. These should be displayed with the lower left corner at the point (20,70). (If you did not save this drawing, refer back to chapter 34 and create the squares).

1. Multiple copy the squares from the point (20,70) to the points (110,70); (200,70) and (290,70) to give four sets of eight squares and refer to Fig. 37.1.
2. Draw two horizontal lines above each set of eight squares.
3. Create two new text styles

   (a) T1 using ROMANC at a height of 12
   (b) T2 using MONOTXT at a height of 5

   In both cases accept the other defaults.
4. Select the TEXT icon and set T1 as the current text style. Add the text (F1–F9) using the centre/fit option as required. Also add the text 'ESC' and 'RETURN' to bottom the squares.
5. Dimension one of the horizontal lines and note the appearance of the dimension text.
6. Repeat steps 4 and 5 setting T2 as the current text style, adding the text HELP, FLIP.... to the squares.
7. Create the other six text styles stated in Fig. 37.1 and add repeat the text and dimensioning sequences setting each style current in turn.
8. Save this drawing as A:????? for the next chapter.

Note

When a created text style is current and a dimension is added to a drawing, the dimension text is displayed as the text style which is current.

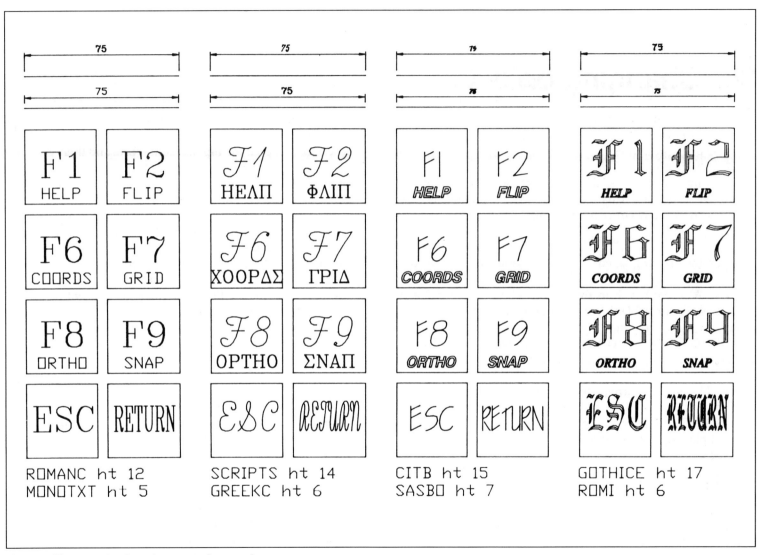

Fig. 37.1. User exercise 4 – using created text styles.

38. Changing objects

AutoCAD LT has two commands which allow certain properties of entities to be changed, the commands being
- (a) change properties
- (b) change point.

Both commands are available by selecting Modify from the menu bar, and the **Change Properties** command is also available in icon form from the toolbox.

To demonstrate the commands

1. Open the drawing saved from the previous chapter, i.e. four sets of eight squares with different text styles.
2. Erase **ALL** entities from the screen. The reason for this is that we want a blank screen, but require the text styles created in the drawing.
3. Make OUT the current layer and draw three horizontal lines. These should be red, continuous? Refer to Fig. 38.1 for the layout.
4. Set T1 as the current text style and with the **TEXT** command, enter the phrase **AutoCAD LT** at a height of **5** with the **TEXT** layer current.
5. Multiple copy this phrase to six other places on the screen.

Change properties

This command allows the user to select entities and change their
- (a) colour
- (b) linetype
- (c) layer

1. Activate the **Change Properties** icon and

prompt	Select objects
respond	**pick the top horizontal line and then right click**
prompt	Change Properties dialogue box with Color: BYLAYER(red) Layer: OUT Linetype: BYLAYER(CONTINUOUS)
respond	**pick Color...**
prompt	Select Color dialogue box
respond	**pick green from Standard Colours then OK**
prompt	Change Properties dialogue box with Color: 3green Layer: OUT Linetype: BYLAYER(CONTINUOUS)
respond	**pick OK**

The selected line will be displayed as a green continuous line.

2. Repeat the **Change Properties** icon selection and pick the middle horizontal line then right click

prompt	Change Properties dialogue box with Color: BYLAYER(red) Layer:OUT Linetype: BYLAYER(CONTINUOUS)
respond	**pick Linetype...**
prompt	Select Linetype dialogue box
respond	**pick CENTRE then OK**

prompt	Change Properties dialogue box with
	Color: BYLAYER(red)
	Layer: OUT
	Linetype: CENTRE
respond	**pick OK**

The selected line will be displayed as a red centre line.

3. Now select from the menu bar **Modify-Change Properties** and pick the third line drawn then OK. From the Change Properties dialogue box, pick **Layer...** and

prompt	Select Layer dialogue box with OUT in blue, i.e. it is current
respond	**pick CL (turns blue) then OK**
prompt	Change Properties dialogue box with
	Color:BYLAYER(green)
	Layer:CL
	Linetype: BYLAYER(CENTER)
respond	**pick OK**

The line selected will be displayed as a green centre line.

4. Repeat the Change Properties command and pick the first text item inserted, then change it's layer to 0, to give black text.

What has been achieved?

The change properties command with the lines has
1. Changed the colour to green on layer OUT.
2. Changed the linetype to CENTRE on layer OUT.
3. Changed the layer to CL.

Options 1 and 2 mean that the layer OUT (which has colour RED and linetype CONTINUOUS) has one line coloured green and another line with a CENTRE linetype. This is bad practice as all entities on the one layer should have the same colour and linetype. Option 3 is how the **Change Properties** command should be used correctly.

Note that although I have stated that it is bad practice to have different colours and linetypes on the one layer, it does not mean that it should not be done. There may be occasions when your drawing requires different colours and linetypes on the same layer.

Change point

This command is really used for text and allows the user to alter
(a) the text insertion point
(b) the text style (which must have been created)
(c) the text height
(d) the text rotation angle
(e) the actual text phrase.

The command also allows colour, linetype and layers to be changed.

1. From the menu bar select **Modify-Change Point** and

prompt	Select objects
respond	**pick a text item then right click**
prompt	Properties/<Change point>
respond	**<RETURN>**
prompt	Enter text insertion point
enter	**@50,0<R>**
prompt	Text style T1
and	New style or RETURN for no change and enter**<R>**
prompt	New height <5.00> and enter**<R>**
prompt	New rotation angle <0> and enter**<R>**
prompt	New text <AutoCAD LT> and enter**<R>**

The selected text item will be move 50 units to right.

2. Enter **CHANGE\<R\>** at the command line and

prompt	`Select objects`
respond	**pick another text item and right click**
prompt	`Properties/<Change point>`
respond	**\<RETURN\>**
prompt	Enter text insertion point and enter**\<R\>**
prompt	`Text style T1`
and	New style or RETURN for no change
enter	**T7\<R\>**
prompt	New height \<5.00\> and enter**\<R\>**
prompt	New rotation angle \<0\> and enter**\<R\>**
prompt	New text \<AutoCAD LT\> and enter**\<R\>**

The selected text item will be displayed with the T7 text style which is the Gothic English font.

3. Repeat the change command, select another text item and change its height to 15, accepting the other defaults.
4. Pick another text item and enter a rotation of −15 degrees, leaving all other prompts with their default settings.
5. Again select a text item and make the New text **TL DACotuA**.
6. Finally select your last item of text and change all the options using the following information
   (a) text insertion point: @20,0
   (b) new style: T6
   (c) new height: 8
   (d) new rotation angle: −5
   (e) new text: DRAUGHTING.
7. As stated earlier, the **Change Points** command also offers the user the same options as the Change Properties command, but does not use dialogue boxes. Activate the Change Points command and select any text item and

prompt	`Properties/<Change point>`
enter	**P\<R\>**
prompt	`Change    what    property    (Color` `/Elev/LAyer/LType/Thickness)`

enter	**LA\<R\>** – for layer
prompt	`New layer<TEXT>`
enter	**OUT\<R\>**
prompt	`Change what property.`
enter	**right click**, i.e. no more to properties to change.

The selected text item will be displayed in red as it has been changed to the OUT layer.

Your final drawing should now be similar to Fig. 38.1. Save it if you want, but we will not refer to it again.

Worked example

The **Change Points** command can be used to give some very interesting results, especially when used with the **ARRAY** command. The following example is a typical application.

1. Open A:STDA3 standard sheet and refer to Fig. 38.2.
2. Draw the arc segments as Fig. 38.2(a).
3. Add the polyline and the 0 text item using the information given.
4. Use the ARRAY command and Polar array the polyline and the 0 text:
   (a) for 4 items, the angle to fill being 30 degrees.
   (b) for 7 items, the fill angle being −60 degrees.
   In each case, the polar centre point can be obtained with the CENtre icon and selecting any arc, and the items have bo rotated as they are copied.
5. The result of the arrays should be Fig. 38.2(b).
6. Using the Change Points command, alter the actual text item to that shown in Fig. 38.2(c), the text heights being
   text item: 0–50, height 8
   text item: 60–100, height 5.

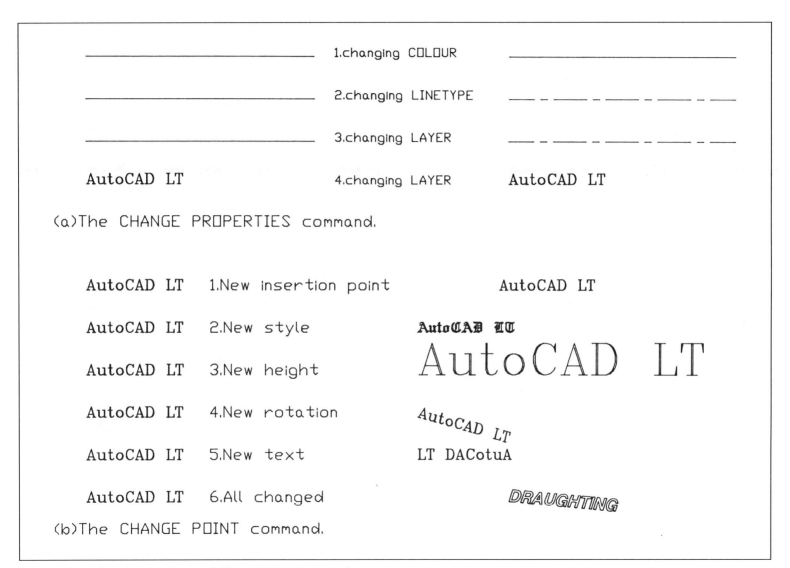

——————————————————————————— 1.changing COLOUR ———————————————————————————

——————————————————————————— 2.changing LINETYPE —— — —— — —— — — —— — — ——

——————————————————————————— 3.changing LAYER —— — —— — —— — — —— — — ——

AutoCAD LT   4.changing LAYER   AutoCAD LT

(a)The CHANGE PROPERTIES command.

AutoCAD LT   1.New insertion point   AutoCAD LT

AutoCAD LT   2.New style   **AutoCAD LT**

AutoCAD LT   3.New height   AutoCAD LT

AutoCAD LT   4.New rotation   AutoCAD LT

AutoCAD LT   5.New text   LT DACotuA

AutoCAD LT   6.All changed   DRAUGHTING

(b)The CHANGE POINT command.

Fig. 38.1. The **Change Properties** and **Change Points** commands.

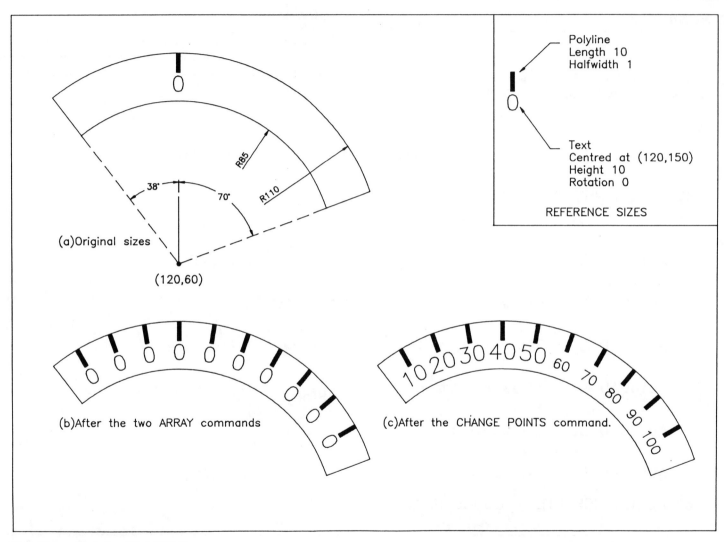

(a)Original sizes

(120,60)

R85

R110

38°

70°

Polyline
Length 10
Halfwidth 1

Text
Centred at (120,150)
Height 10
Rotation 0

REFERENCE SIZES

(b)After the two ARRAY commands

(c)After the CHANGE POINTS command.

Fig. 38.2. Change Points with **ARRAY**.

❏ *Summary*

1. The **Change Properties** command is used to change the colour, layer and linetype of any entity.
2. The **Change Points** command is used to change the insertion point, style, height and rotation angle of text entities.
3. The **Change Points** command can also be used to change actual text items, although the **Edit Text** command is more suited for this.
4. The **Change Points** command also allows colour, layer and linetype changes, but the **Change Properties** command is quicker and easier.

Activity

I have included two activities in Tutorial 27 which are based on the **ARRAY/CHANGE** worked example. They can both be drawn on the one sheet and are interesting to complete.

(a) The clock: can be drawn any size. I created a text style with the SASBO text font at a height of 15. The clock face was hatched using dots with a scale factor of 1. Note the interesting effect of the hatching around the text items. This is obtained by selecting the actual text items as objects in response to the prompt. The hands can be drawn to your own design, and the 'rim' is a donut.

(b) The speedometer: the basic sizes are given. Text style is your own.

The number of items for the array and the 'angle to fill' will need some thought and may take several attempts to get it right. The name at the bottom of the speedo was inserted by the **ARRAY/CHANGE** method, and is interesting to attempt.

39. Blocks

A block is a drawing, or part of a drawing, which can be 'stored away' for future recall *within the drawing in which it was created*. The block may be a nut, diode, tree or a complete drawing. Blocks are used when repetitive copying of entities is required, but they have another very important use in that text can be attached to them. This will be discussed in a later chapter.

To demonstrate blocks, we will create a new drawing so

1. Open your A:STDA3 standard sheet.
2. Refer to Fig. 39.1 and draw a shape similar to that shown. The actual shape sizes are unimportant but
   (a) the lower left-hand point should be at the point (80,80)
   (b) the outline should be on the OUT layer
   (c) add two or three dimensions on the DIMEN layer
   (d) add a text item on the TEXT layer.
3. At the command line enter **BLOCK<R>** and

prompt	Block name(or ?)
enter	**?<R>**
prompt	Block(s) to list<*>
enter	***<R>** – for all blocks
prompt	Text screen with

Defined blocks

User Blocks	External References	Dependent Blocks	Unnamed Blocks
0	0	0	?

i.e. there are no user blocks as we have not yet created any.

Now F2 to flip back to the drawing screen.

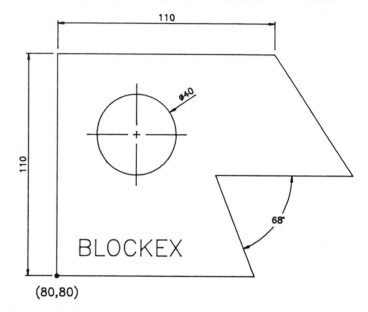

Fig. 39.1. Block model.

Creating a block

From the menu bar select **Construct**
                    Make Block...

prompt	`Block Definition dialogue box`
with	flashing cursor at the Block name box.
respond	**enter BL1 at the block name box**
then	**pick Select Point < box**
prompt	`Insertion base point`
respond	**INTersection icon and pick lower left-hand corner of shape**
prompt	Block Definition dialogue box with Base Point X: 80
	Y: 80
	Z: 0
respond	**pick Select Objects < box**
prompt	`Select objects`
respond	**enter W<R> and window the complete shape including dimensions**
prompt	`14 found (for my drawing)`
respond	**right click**
prompt	Block definition dialogue box as shown in Fig. 39.2
respond	**pick OK**

Nothing appears to have happened, but if you enter **BLOCK** at the command line, then enter **?** and ***** as before the text screen will display

                    Defined blocks
                    BL1
                    User
                    Blocks
                    1

i.e. we have created a user block called BL1.

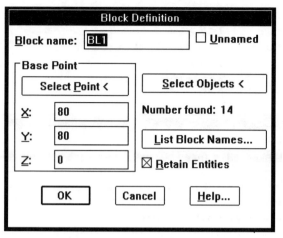

Fig. 39.2. Block Definition dialogue box.

Inserting a created block

Erase all entities from the screen (other than the border) and select from the menu bar **Draw**
                    Insert Block...

prompt	`Insert dialogue box`
respond	**pick Block... box**
prompt	`Blocks Defined in this Drawing dialogue box`
with	BL1 (I hope!)
respond	**pick BL1 and**
	(a) it turns blue
	(b) BL1 name added to selection box
	(c) pick OK
prompt	Insert dialogue box with BL1 in Block name box (Fig. 39.3)
respond	**pick OK**
prompt	Insertion point – and note block drag effect
enter	**45,120<R>**

prompt	X scale<1>/Corner/XYZ
enter	**1<R>**
prompt	Y scale factor(default=X)
enter	**1<R>**
prompt	Rotation angle<0>
enter	**0<R>**

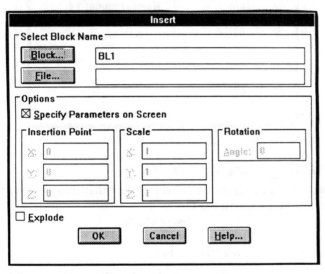

Fig. 39.3. Insert dialogue box.

Block BL1 will be inserted full size at the point (45,120). Now repeat the Insert block command using BL1 as the block name with the following insertion points, X and Y scales and rotation angles

(a) (45,120) X=1, Y=1, Rot=0 (already entered)
(b) (280,200) X=0.5, Y=0.5, Rot=0
(c) (35,25) X=1.5, Y=0.5, Rot=0
(d) (235,95) X=0.3, Y=0.3, Rot=-15
(e) (315,25) X=0.4, Y=1.2, Rot=5

The final result should be Fig. 39.4.

Notes

1. When a block has been inserted it is a **SINGLE ENTITY**. Select the ERASE icon and pick any point on the smallest block inserted (d) then right click. The complete block is erased with a single pick.
2. Blocks which have been made on several layers are inserted with the layers 'as used'. Select the Layer Control dialogue box and Freeze layer DIMEN then pick OK. There will be no blue dimensions on any of the blocks. Now Thaw layer DIMEN.
3. Blocks can be inserted at different X and Y scale factors. The default scale factors are X=Y=1 and the block is inserted full size. If the X scale factor is 2, then all x dimensions will be increased by a factor of 2.
4. When a block is scaled, any original dimensions remain unaltered, no matter if they are entered from the keyboard or accepted as default.
5. Inserted blocks can be **EXPLODED** which converts the block into its individual entities.

Select the **EXPLODE** icon and

prompt	Select objects
respond	**pick any point on block (a) then right click**

Nothing appears to have happened, but now select ERASE and pick the circle. Only the circle entity will be erased.

6. A named block can be redefined, i.e. it is possible to re-use the same block name for a new block. I would not recommend this until the user becomes proficient with blocks, as it is possible to 'loose' created blocks. If a block name is entered which already exists, the warning dialogue box is displayed as shown in Fig. 39.5.

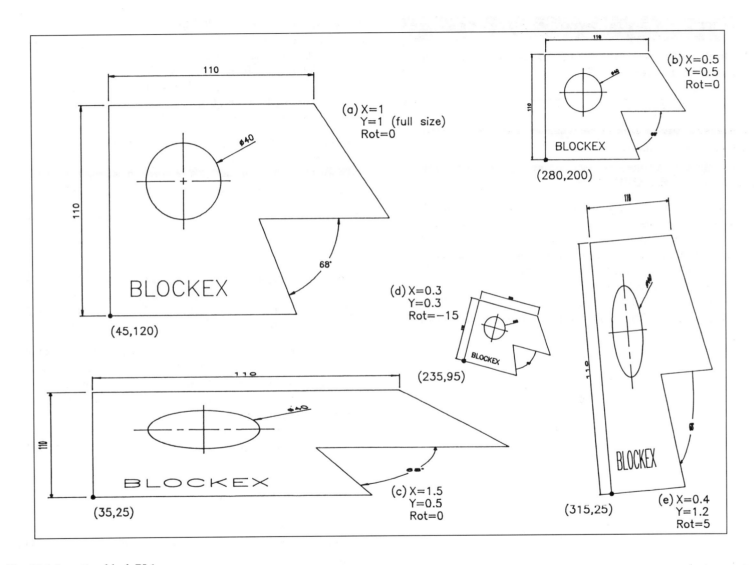

Fig. 39.4. Inserting block BL1.

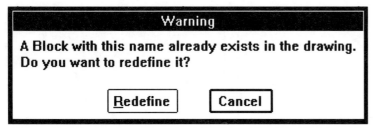

Warning

A Block with this name already exists in the drawing. Do you want to redefine it?

[Redefine] [Cancel]

Fig. 39.5. Block Warning dialogue box.

Block worked example

1. Open your A:STDA3 standard sheet and refer to Fig.39.6.
2. Make the shapes to the sizes given using the OUT and CL layers. *Do not add dimensions*. Use grid and snap to assist.
3. From the menu bar select **Construct-Make Block** and using the Block Definition dialogue box.
   (a) enter CAM as the block name.
   (b) pick Select Point and pick the given Insertion Point
   (c) pick Select Objects and window the complete CAM
   (d) pick OK.

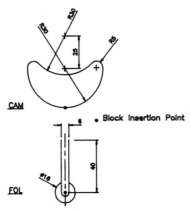

Fig. 39.6. Block sizes.

4. Repeat step 3 for the FOL block.
5. Erase all entities form the screen.
6. Select **Draw-Insert Block...** and
   (a) pick Block... from the Insert dialogue box
   (b) pick CAM from the Blocks Defined in this Drawing dialogue box then OK
   (c) pick OK from the Insert dialogue box

prompt	Insertion point and enter **80,80<R>**
prompt	X scale and enter **0.5<R>**
prompt	Y scale and enter **0.5<R>**
prompt	Rotation angle and enter **0<R>**

The cam will be inserted at half-full size at the selected point.

7. Now insert the CAM using the following information and refer to Fig.39.7

Insertion pt:	80,80	120,80	160,80	200,80	240,80	280,80	320,80
X scale	0.5	0.5	0.5	0.5	0.5	0.5	0.5
Y scale	0.5	0.5	0.5	0.5	0.5	0.5	0.5
Rotation	0	20	40	60	80	100	120

8. Repeat the Insert command entering FOL as the block name and insert it at the point (80,135) at $X=Y=1$, i.e. full size.
9. Using the ARRAY command, rectangular array the follower for 1 row and 7 columns, the column distance being 40 – why 40?
10. The followers now have to be moved vertically downwards to just touch the cams. This sounds easier than it is, but I will leave this for you to attempt.
11. Before leaving the exercise, draw a 1 wide polyline through the centres of each follower then edit this polyline to be a spline curve. This curve is the locus of the follower centres.
12. Finally linear dimension the vertical distance between the centres of the leftmost of rightmost follower circles. What was your dimension value? I got 8.88.

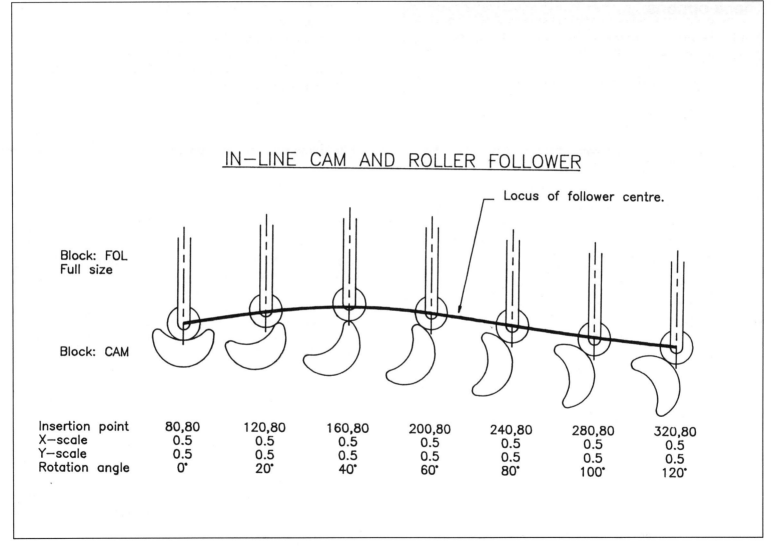

Fig. 39.7. Block exercise.

Block options

When a block is being inserted, the Insert dialogue box has two options available to the user, these being

1. Specify insertion parameters on the screen, i.e. enter the insertion point as keyboard co-ordinates.
2. Automatically explode the block as it is inserted.

The two options are activated with an × in the appropriate box, remembering that

(a) × present – option is active.
(b) no × present – option is not active.

The defaults are:

1. specify parameters on the screen active (i.e. × present)
2. explode not active (i.e. no ×).

We will investigate these options with our CAM/FOL blocks, so erase all entities from the screen then

1. Select **Draw-Insert...** from the menu bar
2. Select **Block...**
    FOL
    OK
3. De-activate the Specify Parameters on the screen box, i.e. pick the box to remove the ×. The insertion point, scales and rotation areas will now appear black, i.e. they are active.
4. Using the mouse/arrow with a left click, change the following

Insertion point	Scale	Rotation
X: 50	X: 1	Angle: 0
Y: 150	Y: 1	
	Z: 1	

5. Pick OK
6. The FOL block will be inserted full size at the point (50,150).
7. Repeat the insert command and select Block...–CAM-OK.
8. Activate the EXPLODE option (i.e. × in box) and note that only the **X: 1** scale factor is active (*Y* and *Z* being grey).

9. Insert the CAM at the point *X*: 50, *Y*: 100 with an *X* scale of 1 and an angle of 0.
10. Now using the ERASE icon
    (a) pick the FOL block – completely disappears
    (b) pick the CAM block – only entity selected is erased, as it is an exploded block.

Notes

1. It is a personal preference as to whether the insertion point is from the keyboard or dialogue box.
2. It is normal to explode blocks as they are inserted, but this does not allow X and Y scale factors.

Exploded blocks and dimensions

As stated, the explode option returns a block to its basic entities, and this can have an effect on dimensions. Erase all entities from the screen and

1. Draw a 50 unit square and dimension
    (a) a horizontal side, entering 50 from the keyboard.
    (b) a vertical side, accepting the 50 default dimension.
2. Make a block called TEST of the square and the dimensions.
3. Insert the block TEST at the point (20,20) with the explode option deactivated. The scale factor is to be X=Y=0.5 and zero rotation.
4. Insert the block (with explode activated) at the point (70,20), the scale factor being 0.5
5. Zoom in on the inserted blocks and note
    (a) the unexploded block has dimensions 50 and 50.
    (b) the exploded block has
        (i) the horizontal dimension 25 (keyboard entry)
        (ii) the vertical dimension 50 (default)
6. Exploded block dimensions are altered if they have been entered from the keyboard.

Layer 0 and blocks

So far all blocks have been created with the entities on their correct layers. Layer 0 is the AutoCAD LT 'free' layer and it can be used for block creation, but the results are not as expected.

1. Clear the screen and draw
   (a) a 50 unit square on layer 0 (black)
   (b) a 20 radius circle inside the square on layer OUT (red)
   (c) two centre lines through the circle on layer CL (green)
2. Make a block of all 7(?) entities with the name TRY. Select the lower left corner of the square as the insertion point.
3. Erase all the entities from the screen.
4. Make layer OUT current and insert the block TRY full size at the point (50,180). The square (drawn on the black layer 0) should be inserted in red, i.e. it is on layer OUT. The circle and centre lines should be as created.
5. Make layer CL current and insert block TRY full size at the point (130,180). The square should be green centre lines, i.e. it is on the layer CL.

6. Repeat the insertion of block TRY with layer HID current. The point of insertion is (210,180). The square should now be yellow with hidden linetype, i.e. it is on layer HID.
7. Make layer 0 current and insert the block at (50,70) – black square.
8. Make layer OUT current again and insert block try at the point (130,170) but this time activate the explode option in the insert dialogue box. The square should be black, i.e. it is on layer 0.
9. Explode the first three blocks inserted and the square should be black in each case, i.e. it has been 'transferred' back to layer 0.
10. Finally use the Layer Control dialogue box to freeze layer 0 and there should be no black squares.

❏ Summary

1. Blocks are entities created and used in the current drawing.
2. Blocks are used for repetitive copying of frequently used 'shapes'
3. An inserted block as a single entity.
4. Blocks can be inserted at different X and Y scale factors. This allows blocks to be scaled.
5. The explode command will return a block to its individual entities
6. An exploded block can only be inserted at the same X and Y scale factor.
7. The insertion point for a block can be entered as keyboard input or by dialogue box entry.
8. Blocks allow text to be added in the form of Attributes (later).
9. Blocks are inserted with the layers used 'intact'
10. Entities created on layer 0 are inserted on the current layer, unless the block is exploded.
11. Complete drawings can be inserted as blocks, using the File...option from the Insert dialogue box.

Activity

There are two activities for you to attempt using blocks. They are not in any order of difficulty.

1. Tutorial 28: This activity is in two parts. Tutorial 28(a) requires you to begin a new drawing and make the blocks using the sizes and names given. Proceed to Tutorial 28(b) and use these created blocks to complete the electronic circuit shown. I inserted all the blocks full size, but the rotation angle needs to be thought out. Add all the text.

2. Tutorial 29: This is also in two parts. Part (a) gives some ideas of equipment found in a child's playground. Make these as blocks using your imagination for sizes not given. The blocks have then to be used to complete the playground in part (b). I used a polyline shape for the playground boundary.

40. WBLOCKS

Blocks are useful when frequently used shapes are required in a drawing, but they are **drawing specific**, i.e. they can only be used in the drawing in which they were created. Blocks can however be made and accessed by all CAD users, i.e. they are **global** and are called WBLOCKS – for world blocks. **WBLOCKS** are used in the same way that blocks were used, with the exception that they are usually saved to a named directory. We will use our floppy disk as the named directory in our worked example.

Creating WBLOCKS

1. Open your A:STDA3 standard sheet.
2. Use the PLINE icon and draw a polyline which is 5 wide from (10,10) to (370,10); to (370,260); to (10,260); to Close.
3. Select from the menu bar **File**

	Import/Export
	Block out...
prompt	Create Drawing File dialogue box
respond	**pick Type it**
prompt	wblock File name
enter	**A:BORDER<R>**
prompt	Block name
enter	**<RETURN>**
prompt	Insertion base point
enter	**0,0<R>**
prompt	Select objects
respond	**pick any point on the polyline then<R>**

The polyline will disappear as it has been made into a WBLOCK, which a drawing in its own right.

4. Refer to Fig. 40.1 and construct a title box of your own design, using the sizes and layout given as reference.
5. Select from the menu bar **File-Import/Export-Block out...** and
   (a) pick Type it
   (b) enter the wblock file name as **A:TITLE<R>**
   (c) enter **<RETURN>** to the block name prompt
   (d) pick the lower right hand corner as the insertion point
   (e) window the complete box.
6. Now select **File-Open-No** and the Open Drawing dialogue box should display a list of drawings on your disk. The two WBLOCKS, i.e. A:TITLE and A:BORDER should be listed. Cancel the command.
7. Now quit AutoCAD LT without saving!

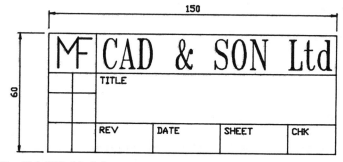

Fig. 40.1. Title block layout.

Inserting WBLOCKS

1. Start AutoCAD LT and open your A:STDA3 standard sheet.
2. Refer to Fig. 40.2 and create a factory layout of your own in the centre of the screen. Try not to have too much in the lower right corner, as the title block will be positioned there.
3. When your layout is complete select **Draw-Insert Block** from the menu bar and

prompt	Insert dialogue box
respond	**pick Block...**
prompt	empty Blocks definition box (I hope) as we have not created any blocks in this drawing
respond	**pick Cancel**
prompt	Insert dialogue box
respond	**pick File...**
prompt	Select Drawing File dialogue box
respond	**pick Drive box then a:**
prompt	list of drawing files on the A: floppy
respond	**pick border.dwg** (turns blue)
then	**pick OK**
prompt	Insert dialogue box (name as expected?)
respond	**pick OK** - if name is as required
prompt	Insertion point
enter	**0,0<R>**
prompt	X scale........
enter	**1<R>**
prompt	Y scale........
enter	**1<R>**
prompt	Rotation angle
enter	**0<R>**

The polyline border should be inserted into the drawing.

4. Repeat the step 3 insert command, selecting **title.dwg** as the file name. Insert it full size (X=Y=1) at a suitable point in the lower right corner of the drawing.
5. Complete your drawing as required.
6. Save it, but not as A:STDA3.

Notes

1. What we have achieved is to insert two drawings (A:BORDER and A:TITLE) into another drawing A:STDA3. We used our floppy disk in this example, but if the floppy had been a named directory, then anyone could have accessed the two drawings at any time. This is the benefit of creating WBLOCKS.
2. Every drawing can be considered as a WBLOCK and inserted into any other drawing. Figure 40.3 illustrates this and I have inserted Tutorials 1–4 into my A:STDA3 standard sheet at a scale factor of 0.4. The drawing may be difficult to read, but it illustrates the use of WBLOCKS.
3. Perhaps you want to add your border and title blocks to your existing A:STDA3 standard sheet and save this 'new' drawing as A:STDA3 again. This would then mean that your standard sheet has the border and title box available at all times. I'll leave this for you to decide.
4. Now is a good time to customise your standard sheet (A:STDA3) to your personal requirements.

❏ *Summary*

1. WBLOCKS are global and can be accessed by all users.
2. WBLOCKS are usually saved to a named directory.
3. WBLOCKS are created using the Blocks out command.
4. WBLOCKS are inserted in a similar manner to blocks i.e. they can be inserted from the keyboard or from the dialogue box.
5. WBLOCKS can be exploded when inserted.

Activity

I have only added one activity for WBLOCKS. Tutorial 30 is an interesting drawing to complete as it uses many of the drawing commands previously encountered. It also involves hatching, which I am sure you can manage quite easily! You can draw the component first and then insert the border and title blocks, or vice-versa. It may be better to insert first and then complete the drawing, but the choice is yours.

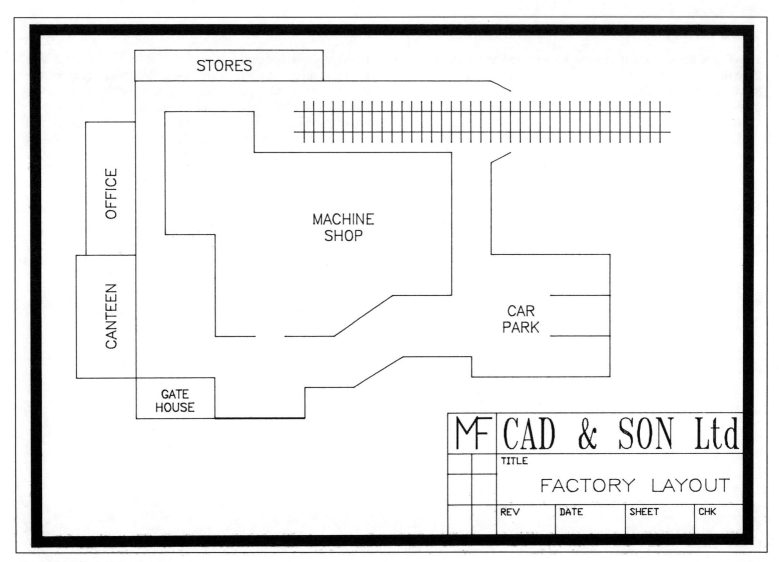

STORES

OFFICE

CANTEEN

MACHINE
SHOP

CAR
PARK

GATE
HOUSE

MF CAD & SON Ltd

TITLE

FACTORY LAYOUT

| REV | DATE | SHEET | CHK |

Fig. 40.2. WBLOCK insertion.

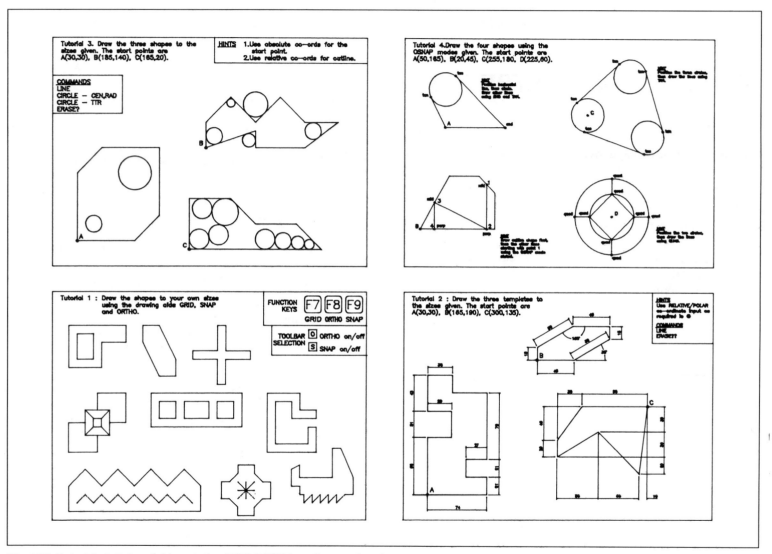

Fig. 40.3. Tutorials 1, 2, 3 and 4 inserted as WBLOCKS into the one drawing.

41. External references

External references (or XREFs) are similar to blocks and are created and inserted into drawings as if they were blocks. They have one big advantage over blocks. If an XREF block is altered, all drawings which contain the XREF are automatically altered. We will demonstrate the use of XREFs with an example.

1. Open your A:STDA3 standard sheet.
2. Refer to Fig. 41.1 and on layer OUT (red) draw the component to the sizes given, the large circle centre being at the point (100,100).
3. From the menu bar select **File**
   Import/Export
   Block out...

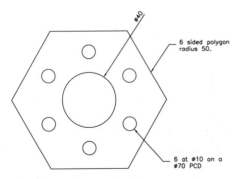

Fig. 41.1. XREF reference drawing.

6 sided polygon radius 50.

6 at ⌀10 on a ⌀70 PCD

prompt	Create Drawing File dialogue box
respond	**pick Type It**
prompt	File name
enter	**A:XREF1 <R>**
prompt	Block name and enter <RETURN>
prompt	Insertion point
enter	**100,100 <R>** – circle centre point
prompt	Select objects
enter	**W <R>** and window the complete component
prompt	8 found and component disappears.

We have made a WBLOCK of the component.

4. Open A:STDA3 again, picking 'no' to the prompt box.
5. From the menu bar select **Draw**
   External References
   Attach...

prompt	Select File to Attach dialogue box
respond	**pick Type It**
prompt	Select file to Attach
enter	**A:XREF1 <R>**
prompt	Insertion point (and drag effect)
enter	**100,180 <R>**
prompt	as blocks and accept all defaults.

This appears to be identical to inserting a block, but what has been inserted is an external reference. This XREF:

(a) can be erased
(b) cannot be exploded – try it
(c) can be updated.

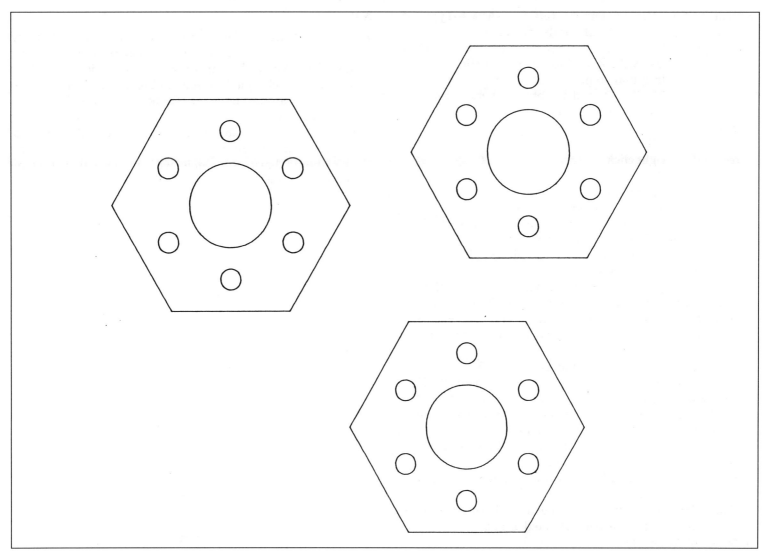

Fig. 41.2. Three inserted external references (A:XREF1)

6. Repeat the **Draw-External Reference-Attach-Type It** sequence and enter A:XREF1 as the file name.

    prompt   `Xref XREF1 has already been loaded`
                      Use XREF Reload to update its definition
                      Insertion point
    enter   **215,75** <R> and accept the other defaults.

7. Now **right click** on the mouse and

    prompt   `XREF`
                      `?/Bind/Detach..............`
    respond   **right click**
    prompt   `Xref to Attach<XREF1>`
    respond   **right click**
    prompt   `Insertion point`
    enter   **245,205** <R> and accepting other defaults.

8. Your drawing should now resemble Fig. 41.2 and consists of three inserted external references (all A:XREF1)

9. Save this drawing as **A:XREF2**.

10. Open the original A:XREF1 file, remembering that although it has been used as an external reference it was originally created as a WBLOCK, and as such it is also a drawing. The drawing consists of a hexagon, a circle and six small arrayed circles.

11. (a) Draw a circle, centre 100,100 and radius 35.

    (b) Draw a line from the point 100,100 to the point 100,155.

    (c) Using Change Properties, change the linetype of the circle and line to CENTRE linetype. You may have to load the different linetypes to achieve this.

    (d) Polar array the line about the point 100,100 for six items.

    (e) Refer to Fig. 41.3 for final result.

12. Select from the menu bar **File-Save** to automatically save and update A:XREF1.

13. Open drawing A:XREF2 and the three inserted external references should have been updated as Fig. 41.4.

14. Now exit AutoCAD LT.

Note

1. Figure 41.4. was updated without anything being done by the user. This was due to the external reference drawing A:XREF1. When this drawing was modified, all other drawings which contained A:XREF1 as an external reference were automatically updated. Think of the uses for such a powerful function.

2. This has only been an introduction to external references. The command is fairly straightforward to master, and the user should have no trouble with it, once they become proficient AutoCAD LT users.

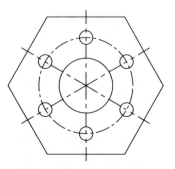

Fig. 41.3. Modified A:XREF1.

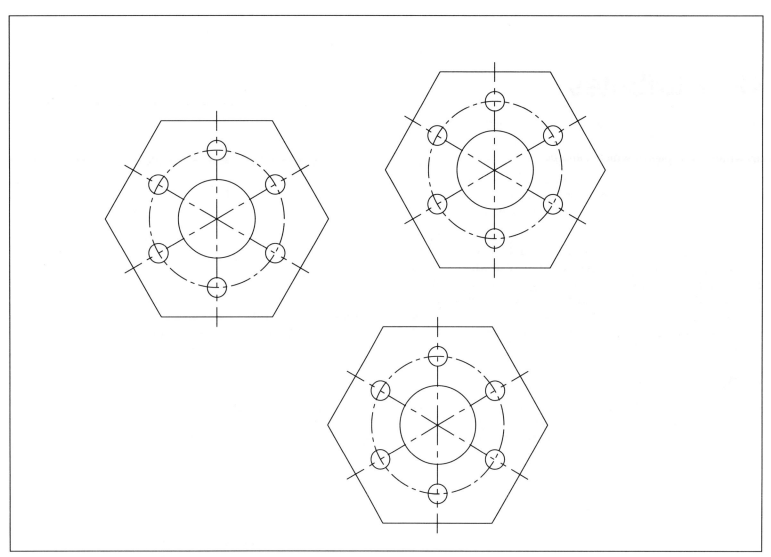

Fig. 41.4. Updated external references.

42. Attributes

An attribute is a text item which can be attached to a BLOCK or a WBLOCK. This allows the user to add repetitive type text to drawings, examples of which could be

(a) electrical circuits with all values added.
(b) weld symbols containing appropriate information.
(c) parts lists containing codes, numbers off, etc.

Attributes which are added to blocks can be edited, but their main advantage is that they can be **EXTRACTED** from the drawing and 'stored' in a special attribute extraction file. The extracted data can then be used as input to other computer packages, e.g. databases, spreadsheets, word-processors, CNC systems, etc. The editing and extraction facilities are really beyond the scope of this book, and I will concentrate on how attributes are attached to blocks and inserted into a drawing.

Getting started

Our attribute example will consist of a housing estate, each house being represented by a house symbol (a block). On each symbol we want to add the following information in the form of attributes

(a) the street number of the house.
(b) the name of the inhabitant.
(c) the number of rooms in the house.
(d) the value of the house.

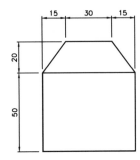

Fig. 42.1. House icons.

1. Open your A:STDA3 standard sheet.
2. Draw the house symbol as Fig.42.1 to the sizes given, but **do not add dimensions**. The lower left corner of the house is to be at the point (100,100) – this is important for text insertions.

Making the attributes

From the menu bar select **Construct**
                    Define Attribute...

prompt	Attribute Definition dialogue box (quite involved!)
respond	1. move the arrow to Tag box and it changes to an I bar
	2. left click at the left end of the Tag box
	3. I bar changes to a flashing cursor

4. enter: **NUMBER**
5. move cursor to Prompt box and left click at left end
6. enter: **What is house number?**
7. move cursor to Value box and left click at left end
8. enter: **999**
9. pick the Pick Point < at Insertion Point
10. prompt: Start point (with drawing screen)
    enter : **130,155<R>**
11. dialogue box with X:130, Y:155
12. pick arrow down at Left Justification box
13. pick **Center**
14. pick Height < and enter **10<R>**
15. dialogue box should resemble Fig.42.2
16. pick OK
17. the word NUMBER should be inserted on the 'roof' of the house symbol.

Repeat the **Define Attribute...** selection (three times) and enter the following information using the procedure described above (it may appear involved, but it is in fact relatively simple)

1. Tag INHABITANT
   Prompt Who stays in the house?
   Value ABCD
   Pick point enter 130,130**<R>**
   Justification Center
   Height enter 8**<R>**
   pick OK

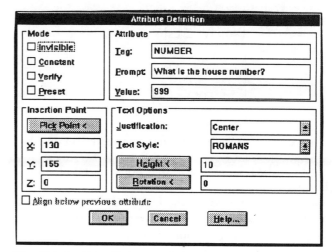

Fig. 42.2. Attribute Definition dialogue box.

2. Tag ROOMS
   Prompt Number of rooms?
   Value 9
   Pick point enter 105,105**<R>**
   Justification Left
   Height enter 6**<R>**
   Pick OK
3. Tag COST
   Prompt Price of house?
   Value 99999
   Pick point enter 130,115**<R>**
   Justification Center
   Height enter 5**<R>**
   Pick OK

Fig. 42.3. House icon after **Define Attribute** command (four times).

When all this data is entered, the house symbol should resemble Fig. 42.3.

When attributes are used for the first time, the three words Tag, Prompt and Value tend to cause confusion. The following should help to overcome this confusion

1. Tag is the actual attribute 'label' which is attached to the drawing at the insertion point selected. This tag can have any height and rotation angle as it is a text item.
2. Prompt is an aid to the user when the attribute data is being added to the inserted block.
3. Value is an artificial number or name for the attribute being added.

In our first attribute definition sequence, we were creating the house number, and as such entered the following in the dialogue box

1. Tag   NUMBER
2. Prompt   What is the house number?
3. Value   999

Making the block with the attributes

This is a normal block creation sequence, so select **Construct-Make Block...** and

prompt   Block Definition dialogue box
respond   (a) enter **HOUSE** as the Block name
                    (b) enter *X*: **100**, *Y*: **100** as the insertion point – obvious?
                    (c) Select object and window house and attributes then **<R>**
                    (d) Pick OK from dialogue box.

Now erase the house/attributes from the screen.

Attribute data

Our housing estate is to consist of six houses and the given in Table 42.1 are data is to be added as each house (block) is inserted into the drawing.

Table. 42.1. Attribute data

Tag						
NUMBER	1	2	3	4	5	6
INHABITANT	Smith	Brown	Green	Jones	Bloggs	McFarlane
ROOMS	5	6	5	4	7	8
COST	£60,000	£75,000	£55,000	£50,000	£100,000	£120,000

Attribute dialogue box

When a block with attributes is being inserted into a drawing, AutoCAD LT allows the user to enter the attributes

(a) from the keyboard
(b) using a dialogue box.

The dialogue box method is easier and is what we will use, but the dialogue box option must first be 'set' with the **ATTDIA** command. At the command line enter **ATTDIA<R>**

prompt	New value for ATTDIA<?>
and	(a) if <0> then keyboard entry is active
	(b) if <1> the dialogue box is active.
enter	**1<R>**

Inserting the attribute block

1. Insert your BORDER block at the point (0,0)
2. Insert your TITLE block at a suitable point
3. From the menu bar select **Draw-Insert Block...**

prompt	Insert dialogue box
respond	**pick File...**
prompt	Blocks Defined in this Drawing dialogue box
respond	**pick HOUSE then OK**
prompt	Insert dialogue box with HOUSE as block name
respond	**pick OK**
prompt	Insertion point
enter	**30,170**
prompt	X scale, Y scale, Rotation
enter	**3 <RETURNS>**

prompt	Enter Attributes dialogue box with all the prompts and default values displayed as originally entered.
respond	using the mouse, alter the defaults to

(a) Who stays in the – SMITH
(b) Number of rooms? – 5
(c) Price of house? – £60,000
(d) What is the house – 1
This results in Fig. 42.4.

respond	**pick OK**
and	the house symbol will be inserted at the point (30,170) with all the attribute values in place.

4. Repeat the Insert Block command and refer to Fig. 42.5 for the estate layout. The actual insertion point is at your discretion, but you should try and insert the houses in the correct number sequence and will need to watch the rotation angle? Add all the attribute data from Table 42.1 and complete your drawing with a road and any other text you think is relevant.

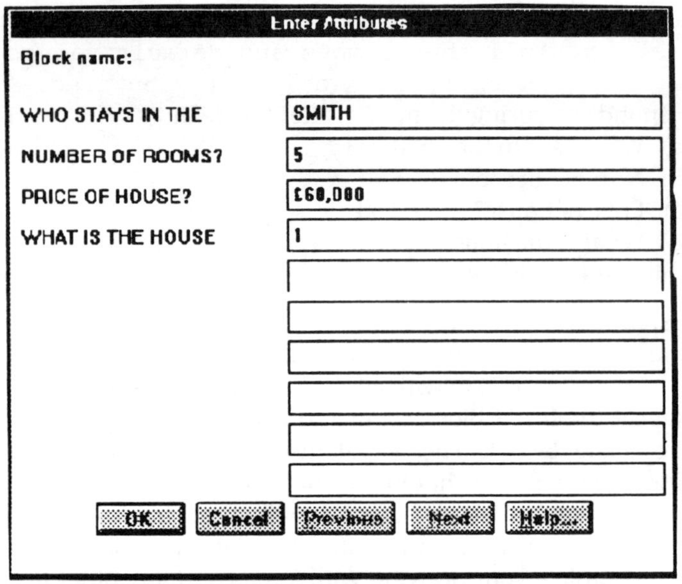

Fig. 42.4. Enter Attribute dialogue box.

❏ *Summary*

1. Attributes allow text to be added to BLOCKS and WBLOCKS.
2. Attributes are created using the Define Attribute command.
3. Attributes are inserted with the Insert command.
4. Attribute data can be inserted from the keyboard or by using a dialogue box. The ATTDIA variable determines what option is to be used.
5. Attributes can be edited and extracted from a drawing.

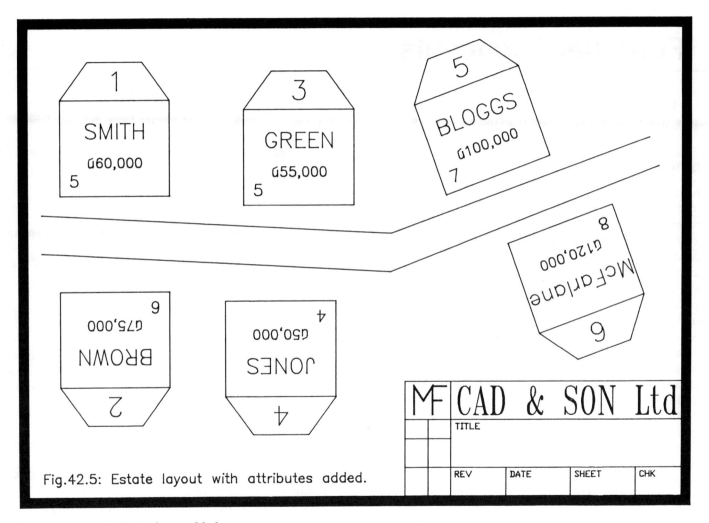

Fig.42.5: Estate layout with attributes added.

Fig. 42.5. Estate layout with attributes added.

43. Four 'new' concepts

In this chapter we will investigate certain options available with the **HATCH**, **MIRROR**, **STRETCH** and **EXPLODE** commands, which add some versatility to the user's skills.

Hatching text

Text which is placed in an area to be hatched can be displayed with a 'clear boundary' about that text item and was mentioned in an earlier activity. By selecting the text item as an 'object' the hatching will be added to the selected shape, leaving the text item unhatched.

1. Open your **A:STDA3** standard sheet and refer to Fig. 43.1.
2. Draw a 100×80 rectangle and multiple copy it to three other places on the screen.
3. Using the **TEXT** icon
   (a) enter a text item 'A' at a height of 30 as Fig. 43.1(a).
   (b) enter the phrase 'AutoCAD LT' at a height of 10 and rotation angle of 30 as Fig. 43.1(b).
4. Create a new text style using SANSSERIF BOLD and
   (a) add text items '1,2,3,4' at a height of 20 as Fig. 43.1(c).
   (b) add the phrase shown in Fig. 43.1(d) at a height of 10.
5. Select the HATCH icon and enter U, 45, 3, N in response to the prompts, then

prompt	Select objects and refer to Fig. 43.1(a).
respond	**pick the A text item then the four lines then right click**

The hatching will be added with a 'border' around the A.

6. Repeat the HATCH command and enter **U, 45, 4, Y,** then

prompt	Select objects and refer to Fig. 43.1(b).
respond	**pick the text phrase then the four lines and right click**

7. Select **Draw-Hatch...** from the menu bar, and select the **HONEY** hatch pattern, then pick OK

prompt	Scale for pattern and enter **1<R>**
prompt	Angle for pattern and enter **0<R>**
prompt	Select objects and refer to Fig. 43.1(c)
respond	**pick the four numbers, four lines then right click**

8. Select the STARS hatch pattern and with a scale of 1 and angle of 0, hatch the final shape – Fig. 43.1(d).
9. Your resultant drawing should be similar to Fig. 43.1.

Mirrored text

The **MIRROR** command will mirror all entities selected including text, but AutoCAD LT allows the user to have text items 'unmirrored' with the **MIRRTEXT** command. This must be entered from the keyboard.

1. Open **A:STDA3** and refer to Fig. 43.2.
2. Draw three shapes similar to those in the 'left-hand column' and add all text. Dimension one of the shapes.
3. Copy the three shapes (including text and dimensions) to another part of the screen.
4. Using the **MIRROR** command, window one complete set of shapes, and mirror them about a vertical line.

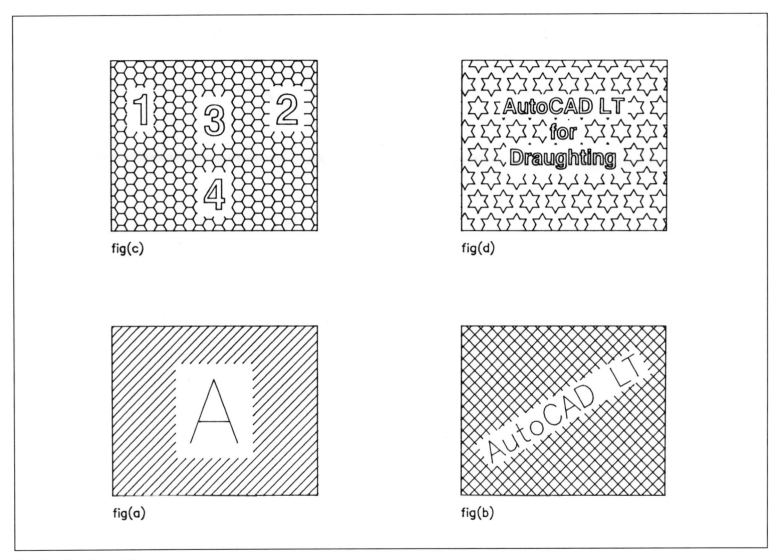

Fig. 43.1. Hatching with text.

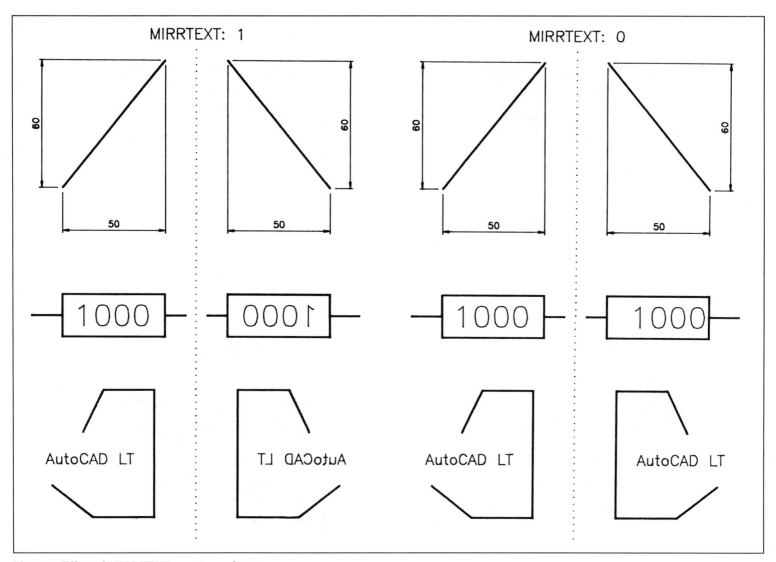

Fig. 43.2. Effect of **MIRRTEXT** on mirrored text.

5. At the command line enter **MIRRTEXT<R>**

    prompt   New value for **MIRRTEXT<1>**
    enter   **0<R>** or **1<R>** if **MIRRTEXT<0>**

6. With the MIRROR command, mirror the second set of shapes about a vertical line.
7. The resultant effect of MIRRTEXT<0> and MIRRTEXT<1> is displayed in Fig. 43.2.

Notes

1. MIRRTEXT is usually defaulted to 1, i.e. text is mirrored.
2. MIRRTEXT set to 0 does not mirror text.
3. All text is affected by MIRRTEXT.
4. Dimensions are *not* affected by **MIRRTEXT**, irrespective if they are default dimensions or entered from the keyboard.

Stretch

The **STRETCH** command does what it says – it stretches entities. Refer to Fig. 43.3 and

1. Open **A:STDA3**.
2. Draw a right-angled triangle of sides 30, 40, 50 and dimension the three lines, accepting the default dimensions.
3. Multiple copy the triangle and dimensions to two other places on the screen.
4. From the menu bar, select **Modify-Stretch** and

    prompt   Select objects to stretch by window or polygon...
                  Select objects_c
    respond   **window the bottom triangle** as shown
    prompt   6 found
    then   Select objects
    respond   **right click**
    prompt   Base point or displacement
    respond   **pick the base point indicated**
    prompt   Second point of displacement
    enter   **@–10,–10 <R>**

The triangle and dimensions will be stretched.

5. Repeat the **STRETCH** command on the other two triangles, selecting the window and base points indicated. Enter @–10,–10 as the second base point each time.
6. The result of these **STRETCH** commands is interesting. Certain lines and dimensions are altered (stretched). Can you work out the resultant dimensions based on the base point selected and the @–10,–10 entry?
7. Figure 43.3 also shows the same three triangles with the dimensions entered from the keyboard. The **STRETCH** command was used as before.

    Note that these dimensions remain unaltered with the **STRETCH** command.
8. Now try and stretch (a) a circle (b) a square with hatching.

Explode

The explode command was used with blocks and inserted a block as individual entities. The command can also be used with hatching, polylines and attributes.

Explode-hatching

1. Open **A:STDA3**, make layer OUT current and refer to Fig. 43.4.
2. Draw a rectangle and circle similar to Fig. 43.4(a).
3. Hatch the rectangle using U,45,3,N as entries to the prompts.
4. Select the EXPLODE icon and

    prompt   Select objects
    respond   **pick the hatching and right click**

5. The hatching should appear **black** as it is on layer 0. Check using the Layer Control dialogue box, freezing layer 0 — no hatching?. Thaw layer 0.

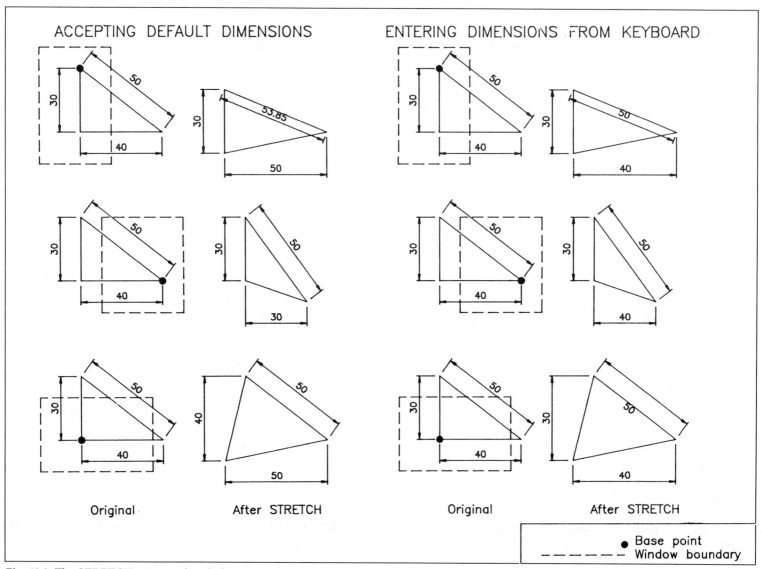

Fig. 43.3. The **STRETCH** command with dimensions.

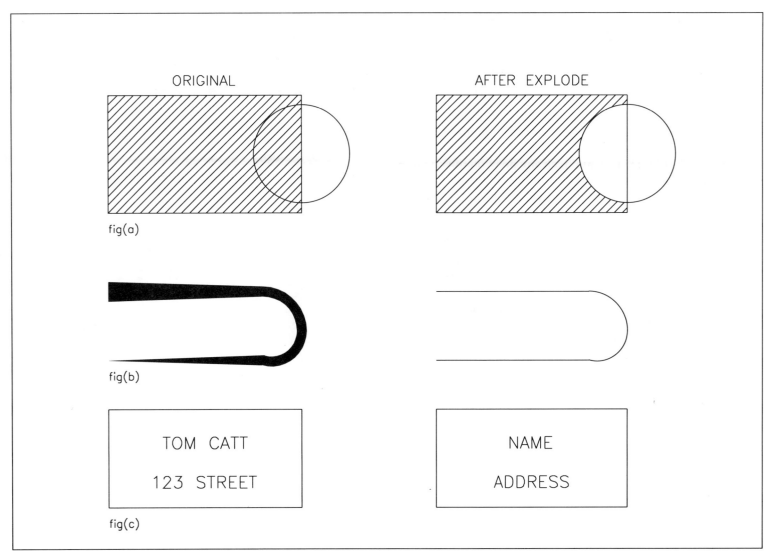

Fig. 43.4. The **EXPLODE** command with hatching, polylines and attributes.

6. Using the **TRIM** icon, pick the circle as the boundary, then pick the 'overlapping' lines to be trimmed – **ZOOM-window** may help.
7. The explode commands converts a hatch pattern into individual entities.

Explode-polyline

1. Draw a variable polyline/polyarc similar to fig(b). I used a start width of 10, then 5 and finally 0.
2. Select the EXPLODE icon and pick any point on the polyline then right click.
3. The polyline is converted into individual line/arc segments.
4. Use the ERASE command to prove this.

Explode-attributes

1. Make a simple block with two defined attributes as Fig. 43.4(c) – my attribute tags were NAME and ADDRESS, and the block name was ME.
2. Insert the block, and enter any values for the attributes.
3. Select EXPLODE and pick any point on the block.
4. The block is returned with the attribute tags displayed.
5. Blocks containing attributes are thus not 'automatically exploded' when they are inserted.

❏ Summary

1. Text can be included as objects when hatching. This leaves a clear area around the selected text.
2. Text can be 'unmirrored' with **MIRRTEXT**.
3. The stretch command returns updated dimensions, if the dimensions are default.
4. Explode can be used with hatching, polylines and attribute blocks.

44. Point filters

Orthographic projections in first/third angle are usually achieved using the construction line technique, i.e. from two views of a component, the third view is obtained using projection lines. By using a separate layer for the construction lines, the AutoCAD LT user can obtain the required view relatively easily. The third view can also be obtained from two drawn views by using point filters. As usual we will investigate with an example, so

1. Open your **A:STDA3** standard sheet with layer OUT current and refer to Fig. 44.1 which gives an isometric view of a 'shaped block'.
2. Using the sizes given, draw the plan and end elevation of the block but do not add dimensions.
3. We now want to construct the front view of the block using point filters. The sequence is rather long and repetitive, but persevere with it as the result is worth the effort.
4. Set the running object snap to INT.
5. Select the LINE icon and

prompt	From point
respond	**from the menu bar select Assist-XYZ Filters-.X**
prompt	X of
respond	**pick point (a)**
prompt	(need YZ)
respond	**Assist-XYZ Filters-.YZ**
prompt	YZ of
respond	**pick point (k)**

and cursor 'jumps' to the selected point on the screen.

Note its 'orientation' relative to points (a) and (k).

prompt	To point
respond	**Assist-XYZ Filters-.X**
prompt	X of
respond	**pick point (b)**
prompt	(need YZ)
respond	**Assist-XYZ Filters-.YZ**
prompt	.YZ of
respond	**pick point (k)**
and	line 1 is drawn
prompt	To point
respond	**Assist-XYZ Filters-.X and pick point (b)**
prompt	(need YZ)
respond	Assist-XYZ Filters-.YZ and pick point (l) – line 2 drawn
then	Assist-XYZ Filters-.X and pick point (c)
then	Assist-XYZ Filters-.YZ and pick point (m) – line 3 drawn
then	Assist-XYZ Filters-.X and pick point (a)
then	Assist-XYZ Filters-.YZ and pick point (m) – line 4 drawn
then	Assist-XYZ Filters-.X and pick point (a)
then	Assist-XYZ Filters-.YZ and pick point (k) – line 5 drawn
then	right click to end **LINE** sequence.

The front elevation outline of the shaped block should now be complete.

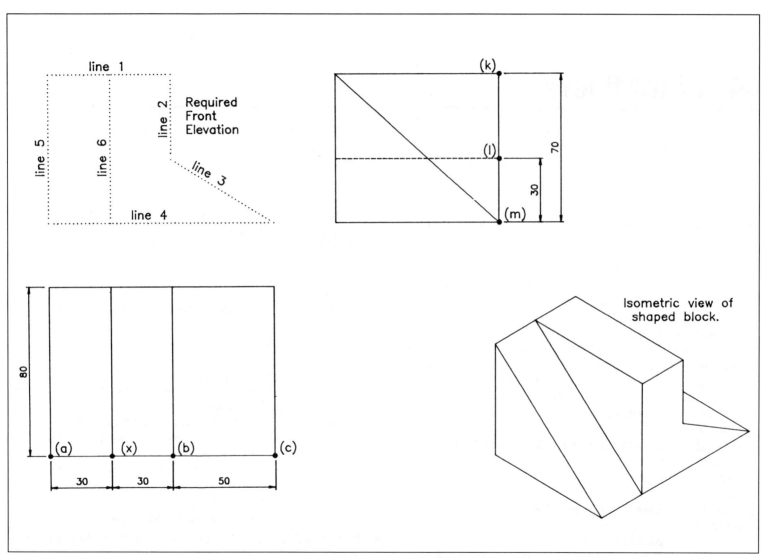

Fig. 44.1. Point filter example.

6. The vertical line can also be drawn using point filters, so select the line command again and L-

prompt	From point
respond	Assist-XYZ Filters-.Y and pick point (k)
then	Assist-XYZ Filters-.XZ and pick point (x)
then	Assist-XYZ Filters-.X and pick point (m)
then	Assist-XYZ Filters-.XZ and pick point (x)
then	right click to end sequence.

7. Your front elevation will now be complete.

❏ *Summary*

1. Point filters allow the user a method of accessing existing entities co-ordinates.
2. Point filters do not have to be used. They give the user an alternative method of constructing drawings.

Activity

I have not added any 'formal' activity with this chapter. The user should however think up a few 'shaped blocks' and roughly sketch out the three orthogonal views, i.e. plan. front elevation and end elevation. Draw any two views, then use point filters to complete the third view.

45. Isometric drawings

An isometric drawing is a 2D pictorial 'picture' of a 3D drawing and allows the user to visualise the component. AutoCAD LT allows isometric drawings to be constructed using two drawing aids, these being (a) an isometric grid and (b) isoplanes.

Setting the isometric grid

There are two methods which can be used to set the isometric grid.

1. Using the keyboard

At the command line enter **SNAP<R>** and

prompt	Snap spacing or ON/OFF/Rotate/Style<?>
enter	**S<R>** – for style
prompt	Standard/Isometric<S>
enter	**I<R>** – for isometric
prompt	Vertical spacing <?>
enter	**10<R>**

An isometric grid will be displayed.

2. Using the Drawing Aids dialogue box

From the screen menu select **Settings-Drawing Aids...** and

prompt	Drawing Aids dialogue box

Readers should by now be familiar with this dialogue box, and the area of interest to us is at the lower right hand corner. By activating the Snap/Grid box (i.e. an × in it) then picking OK, the isometric grid will be displayed.

Isoplanes

AutoCAD LT works with isoplanes when drawing isometrics. These planes are designated by two of the three X, Y, Z axes, and Fig. 45.1 illustrates the three isoplanes. The required isoplane can be 'set' by three different methods.

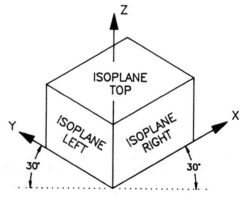

Fig. 45.1. ISOPLANE axes.

1. From the keyboard by entering **ISOPLANE<R>** and

    prompt   `Left/Top/Right<?>`
    enter   **T<R>** – for the top isoplane
    prompt   `Current isoplane is: Top`

2. Using the Drawing Aids dialogue box and picking the Left, Top or Right 'box' then OK.
3. Using the **TOGGLE** effect which is the **CTRL and E** keys. By holding down the CTRL key then pressing the E key, the user toggles the isoplanes until the required one is obtained.

Note

It is user preference as to what method is use to set the isometric grid and the isoplane setting. My personal preference is:
(a) isometric grid set from the keyboard and
(b) isoplane set with the toggle effect.

Isometric example

1. Open your **A:STDA3** standard sheet and refer to Fig. 45.2. This displays the isometric component we want to construct, as well as several stages in this construction.
2. Activate the isometric grid.
3. Set the grid spacing to 10 with **GRID<R>** then enter 10.
4. Set the isoplane to TOP. Toggle or dialogue box?
5. Select the **LINE** icon and pick a start point in the lower centre of the screen.
6. At the 'to point' prompts enter the following

@70<30<R>	for line 1
@40<90<R>	for line 2
@–70<30<R>	for line 3
close<R>	for line 4 and ends the LINE sequence.

    This gives Fig. 45.2(a), the first vertical face of the component.

7. Repeat the **LINE** command and select point A as the 'from point' then enter

@120<150<R>	for line 5
@90<90<R>	for line 6
@60<–30<R>	for line 7
@–50<90<R>	for line 8
INTersection point B	for line 9
<RETURN>	to end sequence.

    This gives Fig. 45.2(b) with the second vertical face drawn.

8. Select the **LINE** icon again and pick point C as the start point then

@70<30	for line 10
INTersection point D	for line 11
right click	to end sequence.

    The first horizontal surface is drawn as Fig. 45.2(c).

9. You should now be able to complete the other two faces as Fig. 45.2(d).
10. Circles in isometrics are drawn as ellipses, and the *correct isoplane must be set*. Set the ISOPLANE to TOP and then select the **ELLIPSE** icon and

prompt	<Axis endpoint 1>/Center/Isometric
enter	**I<R>**
prompt	Center of ellipse
respond	**pick a point in centre of a horizontal face**
prompt	<Circle radius>/Diameter
enter	**20<R>**

    The result should be Fig. 45.2(e).

11. Set isoplane-left and draw a circle (isometric ellipse) of radius 15 on the 'left vertical' face.
12. Set isoplane-right and draw two 10 radii circles(?) on the other vertical faces.
13. Your isometric drawing should now be complete.

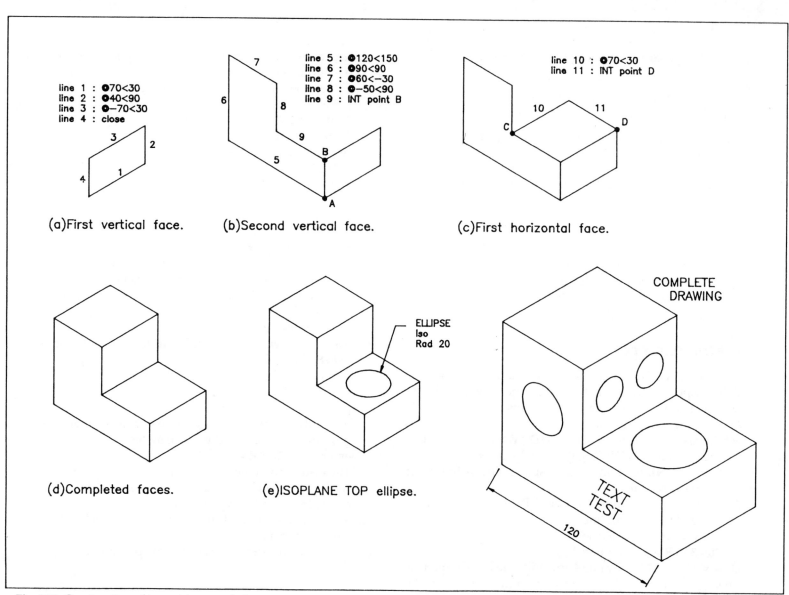

line 1 : ⊕70<30
line 2 : ⊕40<90
line 3 : ⊕−70<30
line 4 : close

(a)First vertical face.

line 5 : ⊕120<150
line 6 : ⊕90<90
line 7 : ⊕60<−30
line 8 : ⊕−50<90
line 9 : INT point B

(b)Second vertical face.

line 10 : ⊕70<30
line 11 : INT point D

(c)First horizontal face.

(d)Completed faces.

ELLIPSE
Iso
Rad 20

(e)ISOPLANE TOP ellipse.

COMPLETE
DRAWING

TEXT
TEST

120

Fig. 45.2. Construction of isometric example 1.

Task

Before leaving this worked example, try the following

1. Add a text item to one of the vertical faces. You will need to work out the text 'rotation angle'.
2. Dimension the long 'horizontal' side using the aligned option.

Both the text item and the dimension are not 'oriented' as expected. This is a major problem with isometrics.

Activity

One activity has been added for you to attempt. Tutorial 31 shows two traditional orthographic views of a component (first angle). Draw these two views and add the dimensions (if you can!). Complete the isometric of the component. It is fairly straightforward and should not give you too much trouble. I have added some hints on the drawing.

❏ Summary

1. An isometric drawing is a flat 2D drawing.
2. Relative polar co-ordinate entry is recommended.
3. The following co-ordinate entries are the same
   (a) @100<−30 and @100<330
   (b) @80<−20 and @−80<160.
4. Circles are drawn as isometric ellipses.
5. The correct isoplane must be set for isometric ellipses, but are not essential when drawing lines.
6. Adding text in isometric does not give the correct 'orientation'
7. Isometric drawings do not dimension as expected.

46. Extruded 3D drawings

Extruded 3D drawings are a good introduction to 3D for the user. They are not real 3D drawings, but introduce the user to some of the commands used in 3D. Extruded 3D drawings have been called 21/2D (two and a half) draughting.

Extruded terminology

An extruded drawing is drawn upwards or downwards from an elevation plane, this plane being set with the **ELEV**ation command. The actual extruded height (or depth) is called the **THICK**ness. The thickness is positive (+) if upwards and negative (−) if downwards and is *always perpendicular to the elevation plane*. The basic terminology is shown in Fig. 46.1.

Setting the elevation and thickness

Three methods are available to the user when setting the elevation and thickness for an extruded drawing, these being
  (a) using the Entity Creation Modes dialogue box – Fig. 46.2.
  (c) using the screen menu with SETTINGS – ELEV.
  (b) entering the ELEV<R> from the keyboard.

Worked example

Start a new drawing (not **A:STDA3**) accepting the default name given and refer to Fig. 46.3. We will construct the extruded drawing using a sequence of steps.

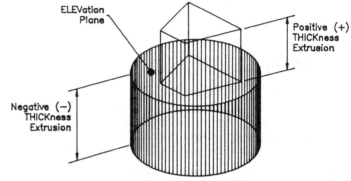

EXTRUDED TERMINOLOGY

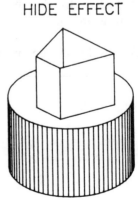

HIDE EFFECT

Fig. 46.1. Basic terminology.

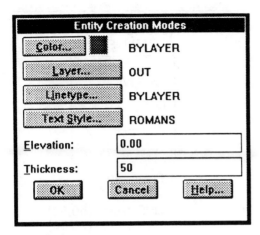

Fig. 46.2. Entity creation modes dialogue box.

Step 1 – the first elevation

1. From the menu bar select **Settings-Entity Modes...** and

prompt	Entity Creation Modes dialogue box
respond	**leave the Elevation at 0, and change the Thickness to 50**
then	**pick OK**

2. Select the **LINE** icon and draw a square
   from **20,20<R>**
   to **@100<0<R>**
   to **@100<90<R>**
   to **@–100<0<R>**
   to **close**
3. Use the Change Properties icon to change the colour of the square to red.

Step 2 – the second elevation

1. At the command line enter **ELEV<R>** and

prompt	New current elevation<0>
enter	**50<R>**
prompt	New current thickness<50>
enter	**30<R>**

2. Select the CIRCLE icon and draw a circle centre at (70,70) with a radius of 40.
3. Change the colour of this circle to green.

Step 3 – the third elevation

1. Set the ELEV to 80 and the thickness to 10 using the screen selection SETTINGS – ELEV.
2. Use the LINE command to draw a triangle
   from **50,50<R>**
   to **90,50<R>**
   to **70,100<R>**
   to **close**
3. Make this triangle blue.
4. You should now have a blue triangle inside a green circle inside a red square and appear to have an ordinary 2D drawing in plan view. To obtain a 3D drawing a new command is required.

Step 4 – the VIEWPOINT command

1. From the menu bar select **View**
   3D Viewpoint
   Rotate

prompt	Enter angle in XY plane.....
enter	**315<R>**
prompt	Enter angle from XY plane...
enter	**30<R>**

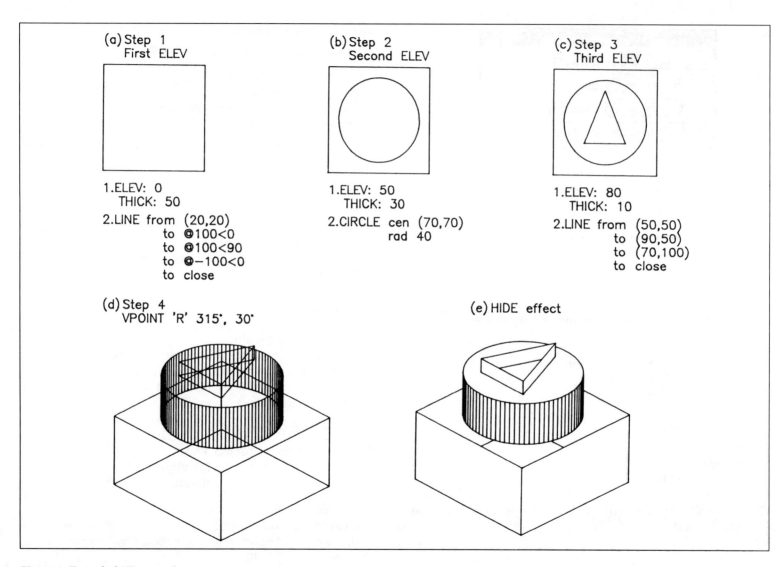

Fig. 46.3. Extruded 3D example.

2. Your drawing should now be viewed in 3D, but appear 'cluttered' due to the number of lines displayed. It is also difficult to tell if you are looking down on the object or looking up at it.

Step 5 – the HIDE command

1. From the menu bar select **View**
   Hide

prompt	Regenerating Drawing
then	Hide line: done 100%

2. Your drawing will be easier to 'see' and you will observe that you are looking down on it from an angle. This is due to the two angles entered with the Viewpoint command.

Step 6 – shading the component

1. From the menu bar select **View**
   Shade
   16 Color Filled
2. If you had changed the colours as indicated in the example, you will have obtained a very nice coloured component, which should impress not only yourself but anybody else.
3. To return to the original 3D extrusion, select **View-Regen**

Viewpoint

This is the command which allows the user to 'view' a component in 3D, and two angle values are entered from the keyboard. Use the command and enter different angles to observe the result. Also use the **HIDE** command after the viewpoint command. Figure 46.4 gives four different viewpoints of our worked example. Shade the component after each viewpoint entry, then REGEN.

❑ *Summary*

1. ELEVation and THICKness allow 3D extrusions from an *XY* plane.
2. The command is activated:
   (a) from a dialogue box
   (b) from the screen menu
   (c) from the keyboard entry.
3. The **VIEWPOINT** command is used to 'view' the component in 3D.
4. **HIDE** will remove hidden lines.
5. **SHADE** is a useful command for extrusions.
6. An extruded component has no top or bottom surfaces.

Activity

Extruded drawings invariably give a 'tower effect' and are relatively easy to construct. By setting the elevation and thickness the user can draw entities, then use the Viewpoint command to obtain the 3D drawing. I have included one activity for you to attempt, and if completed correctly, gives a very 'pleasing' drawing.

Tutorial 32: a sort of 'temple' drawn from lines and circles. Use the information given to construct the various levels and change the colours as each level is complete. The pillars are constructed by drawing a circle (level 3) then polar arraying this circle about the given point. When complete, use VIEWPOINT (315, 30) then **HIDE** then **SHADE**. Regen the drawing and try some viewpoints of your own.

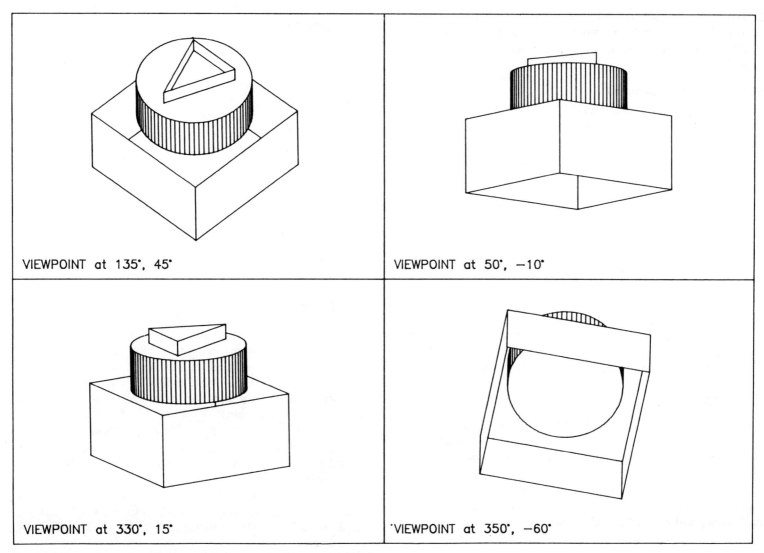

VIEWPOINT at 135°, 45°

VIEWPOINT at 50°, −10°

VIEWPOINT at 330°, 15°

'VIEWPOINT at 350°, −60°

Fig. 46.4. Four viewpoints of the extruded example, drawn with HIDE.

47. Introduction to 3D drawing

I had not intended to mention 3D drawings in this book, but with the chapters on isometric and extrude drawings, I realised that an introductory chapter on 3D would be of use to the reader. I must stress that this is a very abbreviated introduction to 3D, and does not fully cover the topic. When the user has completed the chapter, I hope that they will have an appreciation about how a 3D wire-frame model is constructed.

Getting started

Ideally 3D drawings require their own standard sheet, so begin a new drawing and set the following
  - (a) units – decimal (2 DP), decimal angles (0 DP)
  - (b) blips – off
  - (c) limits – (0,0) to (420,297)
  - (d) View-Zoom-All
  - (e) layers – 0 white continuous (given)
         OUT red continuous (current)
         OBJECTS blue continuous
         DIMEN blue continuous
         TEXT magenta continuous
  - (f) set text to ROMANS, accepting the 0 height default
  - (g) save as A:STD3D for any future 3D work.

The UCS icon

3D drawings are constructed using *X, Y, Z* co-ordinate input and absolute, relative and polar entry is permitted. To assist with 'orientation', AutoCAD LT is equipped with an icon which can be re-aligned by the user as required. This icon is usually turned off when working with 2D drawings, but can be activated by selecting from the menu bar **Assist-UCS icon** and

prompt `ON/OFF/All/Noorigin/ORigin<OFF>`
enter   **ON<R>**

An icon will be displayed in the lower left corner of the screen. This icon displays *X* and *Y* axes (normal 2D axes) with the letter W. UCS stands for 'User Co-ordinate System'.

Drawing a 3D wire-frame model

In this exercise we will construct a wire-frame model and investigate some of the options available when working in 3D. We will also investigate how text and dimensions are added to a 3D model and how to view a 3D model in multi-screen mode. The sequence is rather long, but well worth your time and effort.
1. Ensure OUT layer is current and refer to Fig. 47.1 which displays the wire-frame model in various stages of construction.

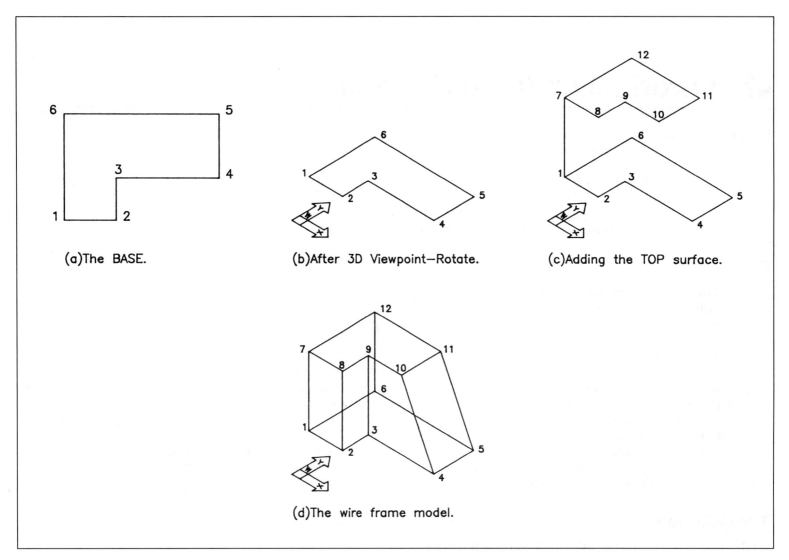

(a)The BASE.

(b)After 3D Viewpoint—Rotate.

(c)Adding the TOP surface.

(d)The wire frame model.

Fig. 47.1. Construction of 3D wire-frame mode..

2. Select the **LINE** icon, and draw a line sequence

   from **50,50<R>**   pt 1
   to **@50,0<R>**   pt 2
   to **@0,40<R>**   pt 3
   to **@100,0<R>**   pt 4
   to **@0,60<R>**   pt 5
   to **@150,0<R>**   pt 6
   to **close**   pt 1

   This gives the 'base' of the component – Fig. 47.1(a).
3. Change to 3D view with **View-3D Viewpoint-Rotate** and

   prompt   `Enter angle in XY.........`
   enter   **315<R>**
   prompt   `Enter angle from XY.........`
   enter   **30<R>**

   This command results in fig(b) and note
   (a) the base 'fills the screen'
   (b) the UCS icon has changed it's orientation.
4. Set a running object snap to ENDpoint and with the LINE icon, draw a line

   from   **ENDpoint point 1**
   to   **@0,0,100<R>** pt 7
   to   **right click**

   This is a vertical line from point 1 which is 100 units in the Z direction, i.e. vertically upwards. This line will probably have 'disappeared' off the screen, so select **View-Zoom-All** to 'see' all of it.
5. Repeat the **LINE** command and draw

   from   **ENDpoint point 7**
   to   **@50,0<R>**   pt 8
   to   **@0,40<R>**   pt 9
   to   **@50,0<R>**   pt 10
   to   **@0,60<R>**   pt 11
   to   **@–100,0<R>**   pt 12
   to   **@0,–90<R>**   pt 7
   to   **right click** to end **LINE** sequence.

You now have completed the 'top surface' of the component as Fig. 47.1(c).
6. Using the **LINE** command complete the component by drawing lines

   from   pt 2 to pt 8
   from   pt 3 to pt 9
   from   pt 4 to pt 10
   from   pt 5 to pt 11
   from   pt 6 to pt 12

   Your wire-frame model is now complete – Fig. 47.1(d).
7. Cancel the running object snap, and save your drawing as **A:3DEX1** in case of later problems – you will have a reasonable starting point.

Using the UCS icon – adding objects

We now want to add some objects (entities) to some of the surfaces of the model, and will use the 'power' of the UCS icon to assist us. Figure 47.2 shows the various stages in this sequence.
1. The wire-frame model is not 'centred' on the screen, so select the sequence **View-Zoom-Window** and

   enter   **120,-40** as the first corner
   enter   **40,400** as the other corner
2. Our first step is to 'move' the UCS icon and align it onto the top surface of the component, so select **Assist**
           Set UCS
           3 Point

   prompt   `Origin pt<0,0,0>`
   respond   **INTersection icon and pick point 7**
   prompt   `Point on positive portion of the X-axis`
   respond   **INTersection icon and pick point 8**
   prompt   `Point on positive Y portion of the UCS XY plane`
   respond   **INTersection icon and pick point 12**

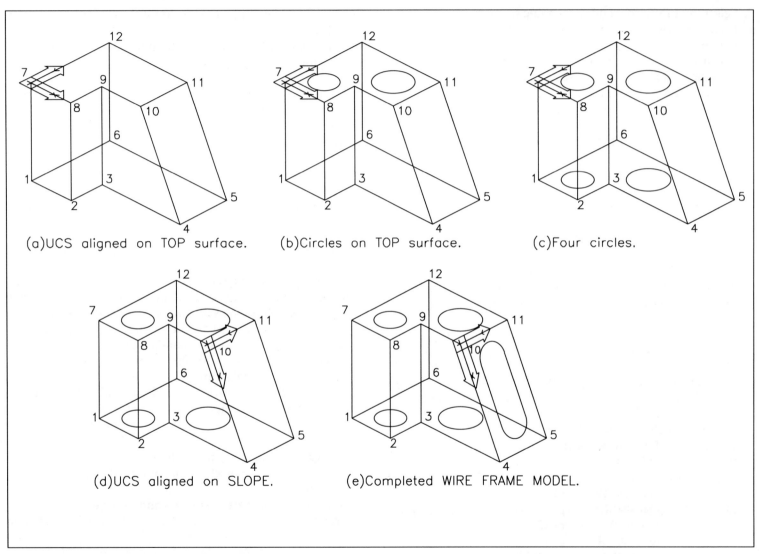

(a)UCS aligned on TOP surface.

(b)Circles on TOP surface.

(c)Four circles.

(d)UCS aligned on SLOPE.

(e)Completed WIRE FRAME MODEL.

Fig. 47.2. Aligning the UCS and adding objects.

3. The UCS icon should have moved. No?. If not, select the sequence **Assist-UCS icon** and enter **OR<R>** at the command line. The UCS icon should now be aligned on the top surface – Fig. 47.1(a). Move the mouse to point 7 and check the on-screen co-ordinates – they are (0,0), i.e. the origin is now at point 7 due to the UCS position.

4. This UCS position can be saved for future recall, so from the menu bar select **Assist**

Set UCS

Save

prompt   ?/Desired UCS name

enter   **TOP<R>**

5. Make **OBJECTS** the current layer.

6. Use the CIRCLE icon and draw a circle with centre at (25,25) and radius 15. The centre co-ordinates of this circle are relative to the origin which is at point 7. Draw another circle, centre at (70,70) and radius 20 – Fig. 47.1(b).

7. We now want two circles on the base similar to those on the top surface, and will achieve this by two different methods
   (a) use the CIRCLE icon, centre (25,25,–100) and radius 15.
   (b) COPY the larger circle on the top surface using its centre point as the base, by @0,0,–100.
   Can you work out these two sets of co-ordinate data? Remember that the wire frame model is 100 high/thick/deep.

8. You now have four blue circles as shown in Fig. 47.1(c).

9. The UCS icon has now to be aligned with the sloped surface, so select **Assist-Set UCS-3 Point** and
   (a) pick point 10 as the origin point (INT or END)
   (b) pick point 4 for the X-axis point
   (c) pick point 11 for the Y-axis point
   The UCS will be aligned along the slope as Fig. 47.1(d). The origin is now at point 10. Check that these co-ordinates are (0,0).

10. Save this UCS setting with **Assist-Set UCS-Save** and enter **SLOPE** as the UCS name.

11. Now draw the following
    (a) a circle, centre (25,30) with radius 15.
    (b) a circle, centre (85,30) with radius 15.
    (c) a line from (25,15) to (85,15)
    (d) a line form (25,45) to (85,45)
    These co-ordinates are absolute for the origin at point 10.

12. **TRIM** the unwanted parts of the circle to give Fig. 47.1(e).

13. Your wire frame model is now complete. Save at this stage.

Adding text and dimensions

Text and dimensions can be added to a 3D model, but the position of the UCS is critical to ensure correct orientation. We want to add text and dimensions to three of the model surfaces, so

1. Refer to Fig. 47.3.

2. Select **Assist-Set UCS-3·Point** and
   (a) pick point 1 as the origin
   (b) pick point 2 as the X-axis point
   (c) pick point 7 as the Y-axis point

3. The UCS aligns itself with the front face of the model – Fig. 47.1(a).

4. Save this UCS position as FRONT.

5. Make TEXT the current layer.

6. With the TEXT icon
   (a) use the (C)entre option
   (b) enter a start position of (25,80)
   (c) enter a height of 6 and rotation angle of 0
   (d) enter the following text   **F<R>**

                                         R<R>

                                         O<R>

                                         N<R>

                                         T<R><R> – two returns.

7. Make DIMEN the current layer.

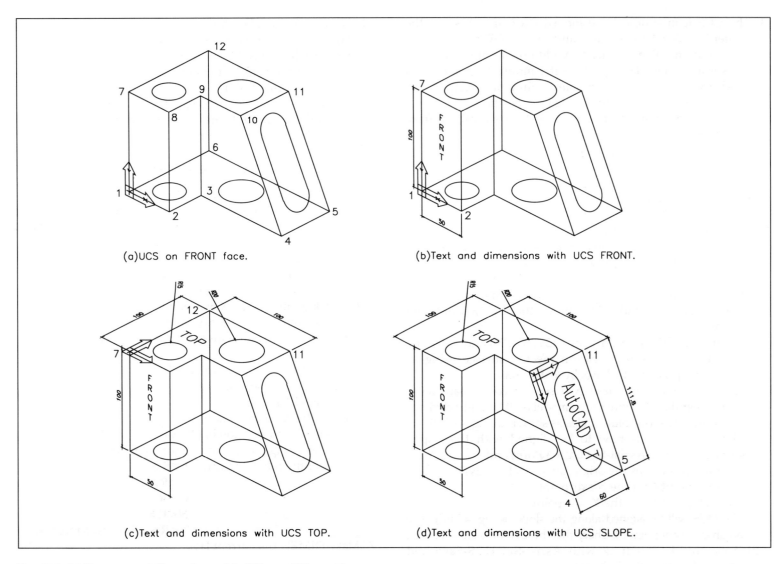

Fig. 47.3. Adding text and dimensions with different UCs positions.

8. Using linear dimensions
   (a) horizontally dimension between points 1 and 2.
   (b) vertically dimension between points 1 and 7
   Note that you may have to alter some of the dimension settings, but I'll leave that to you!
9. The resultant model should be fig(b).
10. Text and dimensions have now to be added to the top surface, and the UCS position must be restored, so **Assist-Set UCS-Restore** and

    prompt   `?/Name of UCS to restore`
    enter   **TOP<R>**
11. The UCS icon is on the top surface.
12. Add the following text and dimensions (using correct layers)
    (a) **TEXT:** start point at (10,50), height 10, rotation 0, text TOP
    (b) horizontally dimension from point 12 to point 11
    (c) vertically dimension between points 7 and 12
    (d) radial dimension the two circles on the top.
13. The result should now be Fig. 47.1(c).
14. Restore UCS SLOPE and add
    (a) TEXT, fitted between points (20,25) and (90,25) with a height of 15. The text is AutoCAD LT.
    (b) horizontal dimension from point 5 to point 11
    (c) vertical dimension between points 4 and 5.
15. The result is Fig. 47.1(d).

Note on text and dimensions

1. Text is aligned relative to the UCS position.
2. Dimensions are dependent on the UCS position and
   (a) horizontal is *always* in the X direction
   (b) vertical is *always* in the Y direction.

Multi-views of the model

Now that we have added text and dimensions to our model, we want to view it in multi-screen mode, so
1. Restore UCS FRONT.
2. Select **Assist-Set UCS-X axis Rotate** and

   prompt   `Rotation angle about X axis<0>`
   enter   **−90<R>**
3. The UCS icon now 'lies' on the base of the model.
4. Save this UCS position as BASE.
5. Select from the menu bar   **View**
                                      Viewports
                                      4 Viewports
   The screen will be divided into four individual viewports, each displaying the 3D wire-frame model.
6. Only one viewport can be 'active' at a time and this is indicated by the on-screen cursor cross hairs. Moving the mouse to another viewport displays an arrow, and a left click will make that viewport active.
7. Make the lower left viewport active and select
                                  View
                                  3D Viewpoint Presets
                                  Top
   A top view of the model will be displayed (note the text)
8. With the top left viewport active, select
                                  View
                                  3D Viewpoint Presets
                                  Front
   The viewport will display a front view. Again note the text.
9. In the top right viewport, select **View-3D Viewpoint Presets-Right** to give a view from the right.

10. We have displayed a top, front, right and 3D view of the wire frame model, but the three new views may be slightly 'off the screen' and we will now 'centre' them.
11. With layer 0 current, freeze layer DIMEN.
12. With the lower left viewport active, enter **ZOOM<R>** and

prompt	All/Center/...............
enter	**C<R>** – the center option
prompt	Center point
enter	**75,50,50<R>** – this being the model 'centre'
prompt	Magnification or Height<?>
enter	**150<R>**

The top view of the model should now be centred in the viewport.
13. Repeat step 12 in the top left and top right viewports, entering 75,50,50 as the center point and 150 as the magnification.
14. Leave the lower right viewport as it is.
15. The three views of the model are centred in each viewport, and 'line up' with one another as orthogonal views. Fig. 47.4 displays the result.
16. Save your multi-screen view.
17. Exit AutoCAD LT – your work is now completed.

Note

For those readers who know about 3D drawing, this chapter will be a bit of an anti-climax. I have deliberately not introduced several of the options available and have not mentioned Paper Space. I feel that as this is an introductory book on AutoCAD LT, such a subject is not required.

❏ **Summary**

1. 3D wire-frame models are constructed form X, Y, Z co-ordinate input.
2. The user has control over the UCS icon.
3. The position of the UCS icon is important when adding text and dimensions.
4. Wire-frame models can be viewed in different multi-screen modes.
5. Top, front, right views of the model are easily obtained.
6. Views can be 'centred' in an individual viewport.

Activity

As this was an introduction to 3D drawing I have not added any activities. If you have managed to work your way through the example given, you have achieved quite a lot.

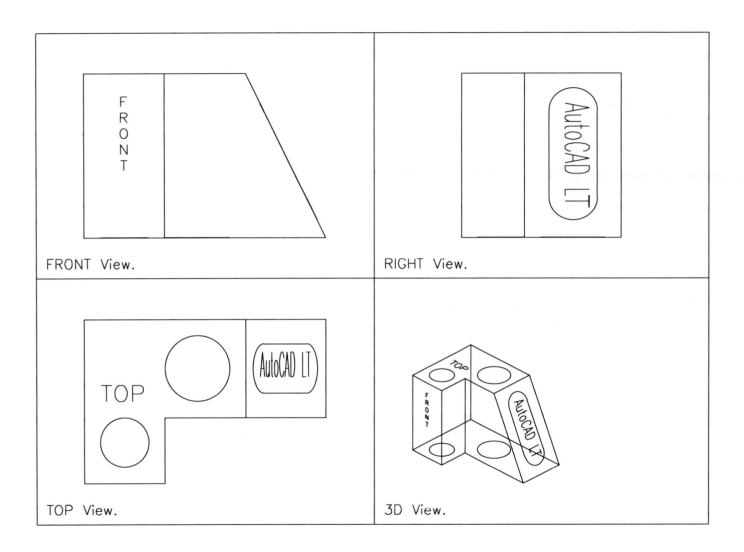

Fig. 47.4. Multi-screen viewports of the wire-frame model.

Conclusion

This book has been written to help those who require guidance in using AutoCAD LT. If you have worked your way through the various chapters, you should now know the package reasonably well. I have not managed to cover every topic but I hope that you now have the confidence to investigate subjects not covered in this book. You certainly have the ability if you are reading this section.

AutoCAD LT becomes easier the more it is used, and I would recommend that you spend as much time as possible on it. Simple or complex drawings will increase your speed and improve your skill.

I hope that you have enjoyed working through the examples and any comments (constructive or otherwise) would be more than welcome. As I write this, I have been thinking about a followup book covering the more advanced topics in the AutoCAD LT package.

Good luck with your drawings!!

Bob McFarlane

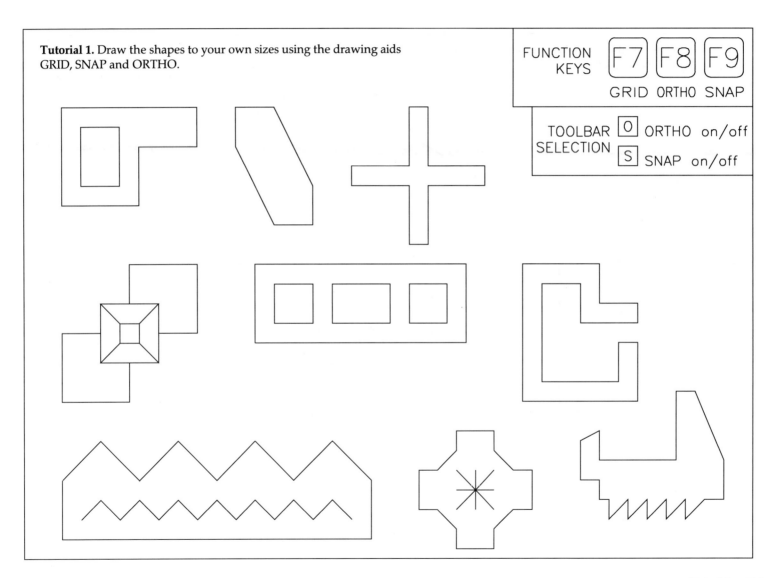

Tutorial 1. Draw the shapes to your own sizes using the drawing aids GRID, SNAP and ORTHO.

FUNCTION KEYS

F7 F8 F9

GRID ORTHO SNAP

TOOLBAR SELECTION

O ORTHO on/off

S SNAP on/off

Tutorial 2. Draw the three templates to the sizes given. The start points are A(30,30), B(165,190), C(300,135).

HINTS
Use RELATIVE/POLAR
co—ordinate input as
required ie @

COMMANDS
LINE
ERASE??

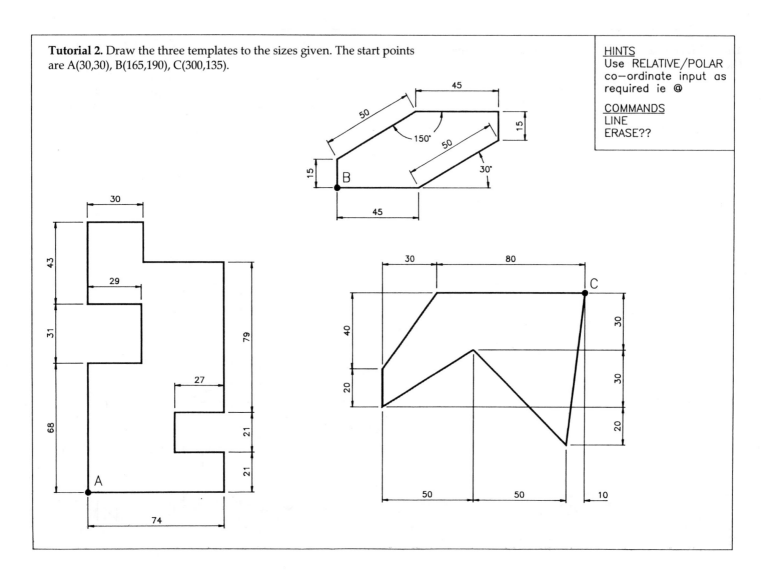

Tutorial 3. Draw the three shapes to the sizes given. The start points are A (30,30), B(185,140), C(165,20).

HINTS 1.Use absolute co—ords for the start point.
2.Use relative co—ords for outline.

COMMANDS
LINE
CIRCLE — CEN,RAD
CIRCLE — TTR
ERASE?

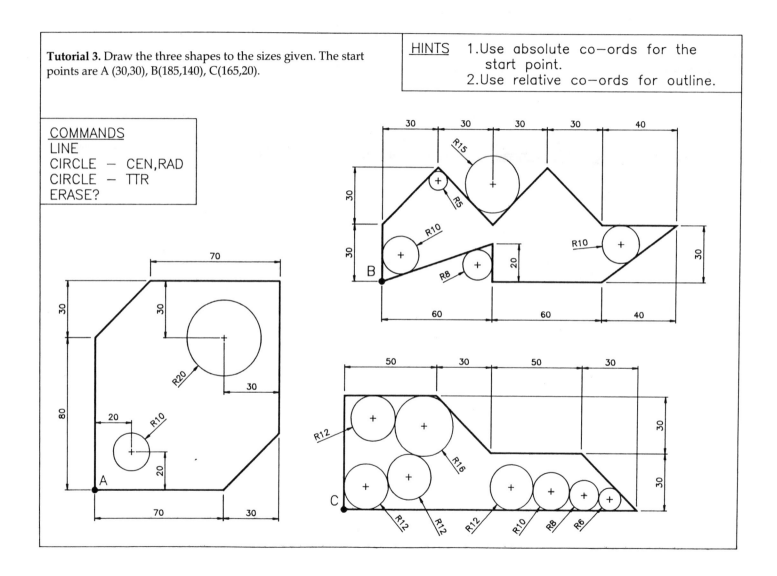

Tutorial 4. Draw the four shapes using the OSNAP modes given.
The start points are A(50,165), B (20,45), C (225,180), D(255,60).

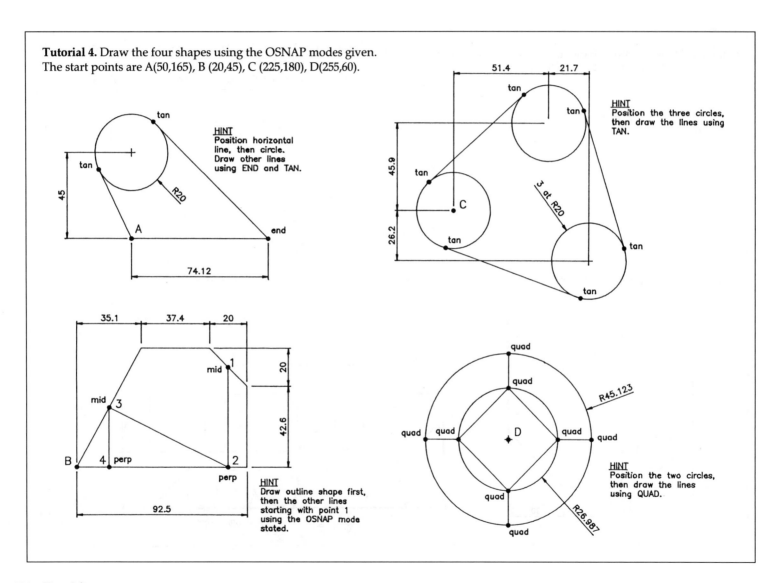

HINT
Position horizontal
line, then circle.
Draw other lines
using END and TAN.

tan

R20

A

end

45

74.12

HINT
Position the three circles,
then draw the lines using
TAN.

51.4   21.7

tan

tan

45.9

tan

C

3 at R20

tan

26.2

tan

tan

tan

35.1   37.4   20

mid
1

mid
3

20

42.6

B

4 perp

2

perp

92.5

HINT
Draw outline shape first,
then the other lines
starting with point 1
using the OSNAP mode
stated.

quad

quad

R45.123

quad   quad   D   quad   quad

quad

R26.987

quad

HINT
Position the two circles,
then draw the lines
using QUAD.

Tutorial 5. Draw the two templates full size.

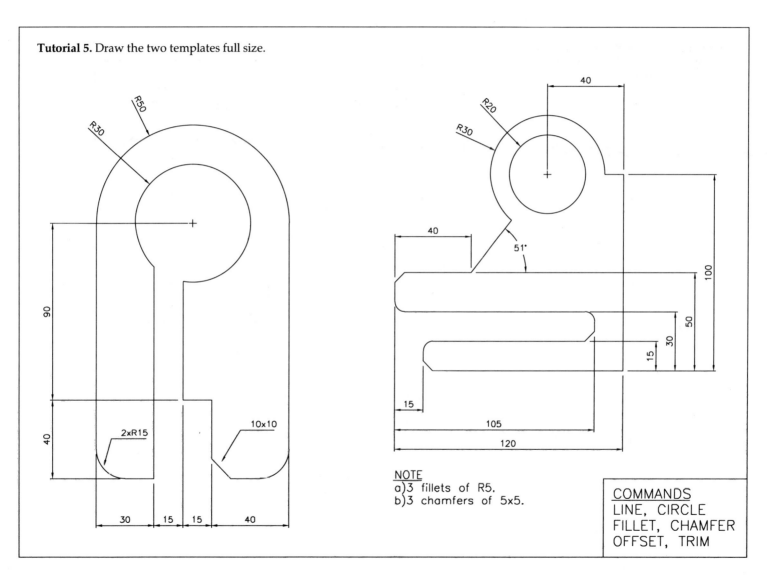

NOTE
a)3 fillets of R5.
b)3 chamfers of 5x5.

COMMANDS
LINE, CIRCLE
FILLET, CHAMFER
OFFSET, TRIM

Tutorial 6. Draw the three shapes as shown, making use of the OFFSET and TRIM commands as much as possible.

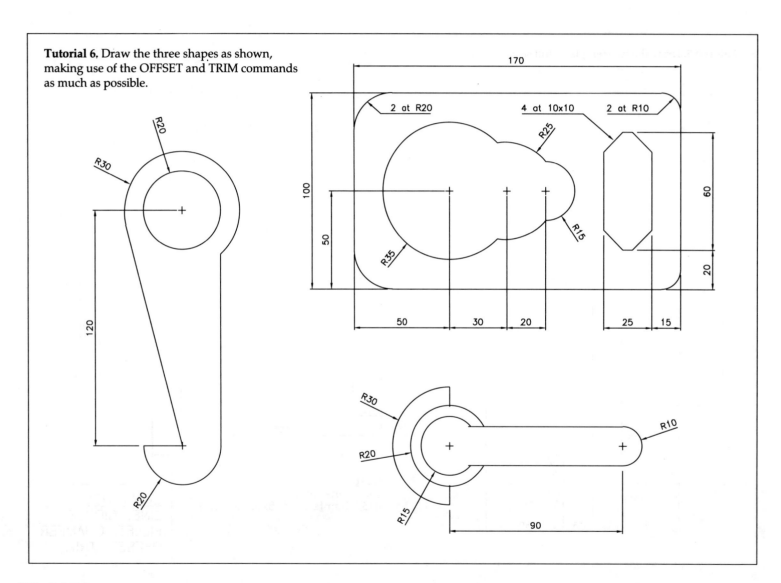

Tutorial 7. Draw the two components adding all text (use layers)

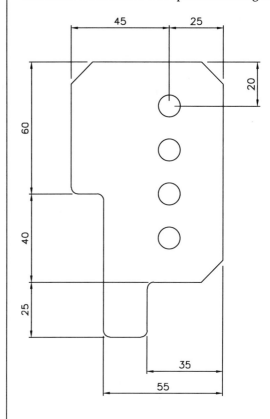

COPPER SHIM

0.15mm thick

NOTE: 1.All chamfers are 10x10
2.All fillets are R3

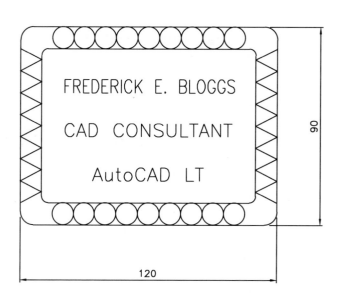

FREDERICK E. BLOGGS

CAD CONSULTANT

AutoCAD LT

NAME CARD
(PLASTIC)

NOTE: 1.10mm offset distance
2.Fillet radii are 3 and 6 respectively
3.Design is your own.

Tutorial 8. Draw the two components full size using layers. Add all text and dimensions.

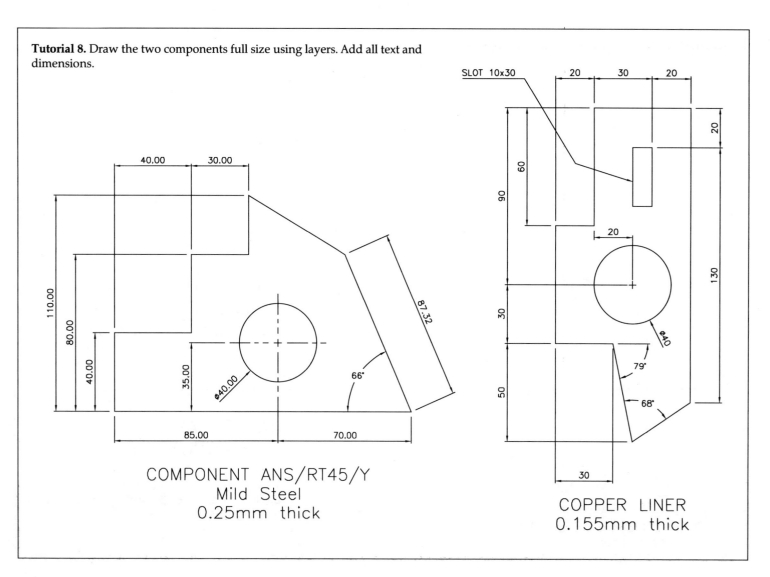

SLOT 10x30

COMPONENT ANS/RT45/Y
Mild Steel
0.25mm thick

COPPER LINER
0.155mm thick

Tutorial 9. Draw the three shapes and add all text and dimensions. Use layers.

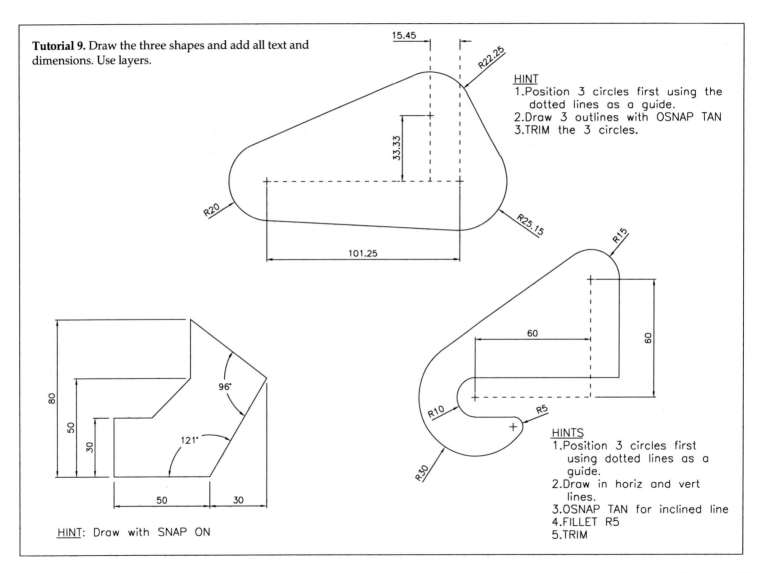

15.45

R22.25

33.33

R20

R25.15

101.25

HINT
1. Position 3 circles first using the dotted lines as a guide.
2. Draw 3 outlines with OSNAP TAN
3. TRIM the 3 circles.

R15

60

60

R10

R5

R30

HINTS
1. Position 3 circles first using dotted lines as a guide.
2. Draw in horiz and vert lines.
3. OSNAP TAN for inclined line
4. FILLET R5
5. TRIM

80

50

30

96°

121°

50

30

HINT: Draw with SNAP ON

Tutorial 10. Draw and fully dimension, adding all text. Use layers

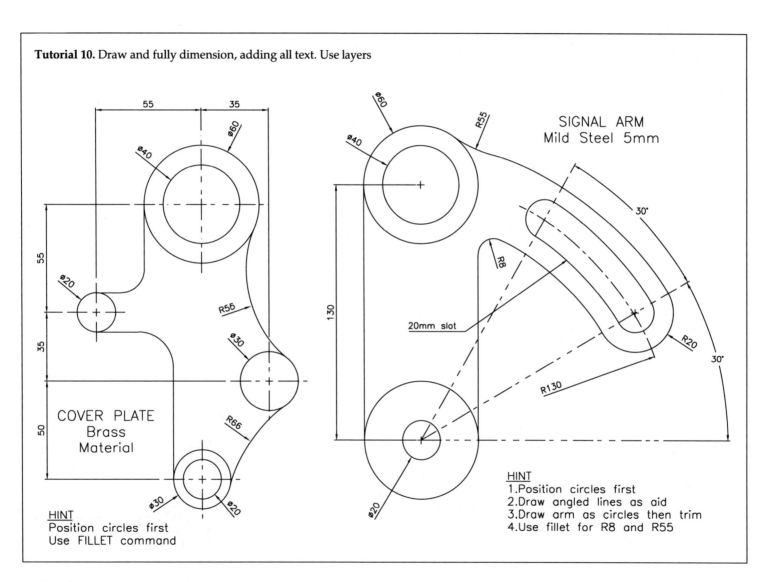

55   35

Ø40
Ø60

55

Ø20

35

R55

Ø30

COVER PLATE
Brass
Material

50

R66

Ø30   Ø20

HINT
Position circles first
Use FILLET command

Ø60
R55

SIGNAL ARM
Mild Steel 5mm

Ø40

30°

130

R8

20mm slot

R20

30°

R130

R8 and R55

Ø20

HINT
1.Position circles first
2.Draw angled lines as aid
3.Draw arm as circles then trim
4.Use fillet for R8 and R55

Tutorial 11. Draw full size adding all text and dimensions.

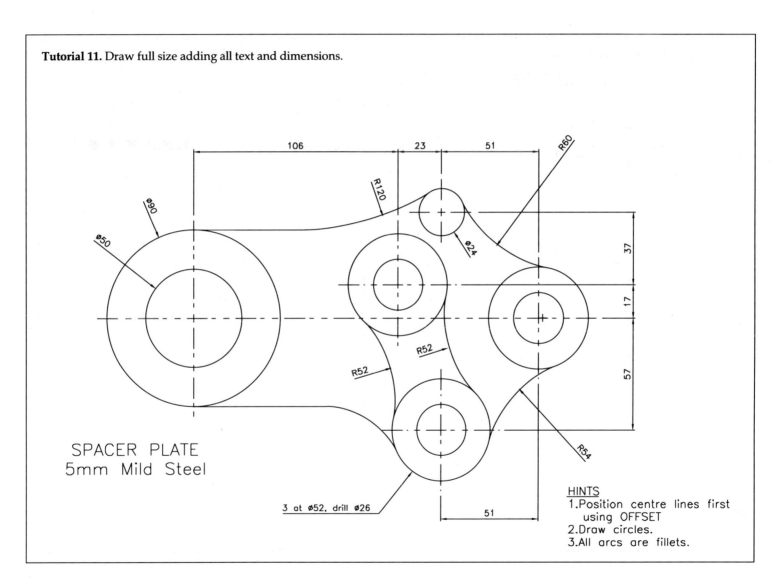

SPACER PLATE
5mm Mild Steel

3 at ⌀52, drill ⌀26

HINTS
1. Position centre lines first
   using OFFSET
2. Draw circles.
3. All arcs are fillets.

Tutorial 12. Draw the circuit as shown.

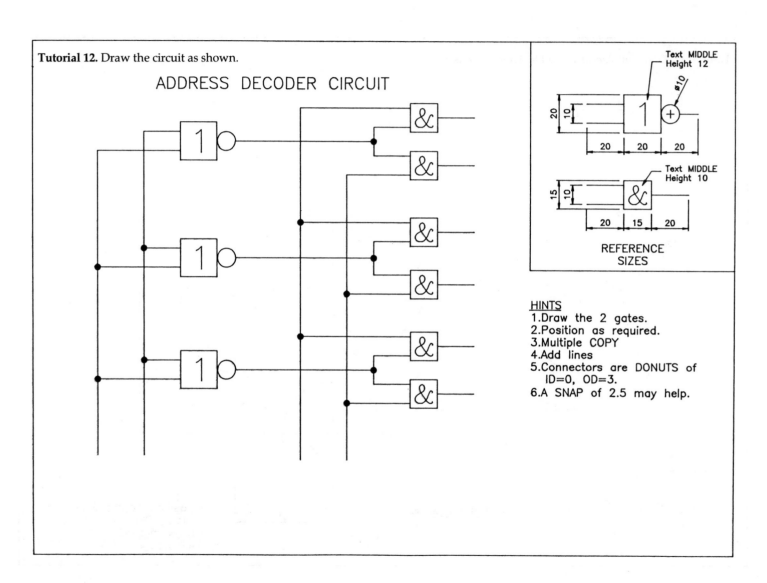

ADDRESS DECODER CIRCUIT

REFERENCE
SIZES

HINTS
1. Draw the 2 gates.
2. Position as required.
3. Multiple COPY
4. Add lines
5. Connectors are DONUTS of ID=0, OD=3.
6. A SNAP of 2.5 may help.

Tutorial 13. Draw the template full size as shown.

RUBBER TEMPLATE

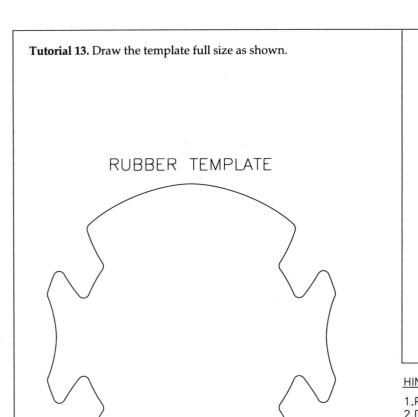

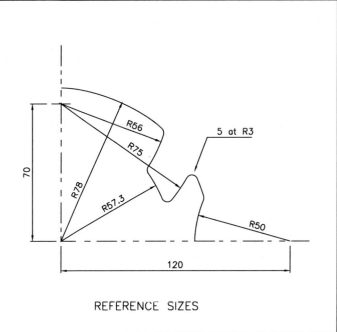

REFERENCE SIZES

HINTS

1. Position 2 centre lines first.
2. Draw 5 full circles.
3. TRIM circles to centre lines and to each other as required.
4. Add the fillet radii.
5. MIRROR command twice.

Tutorial 14. Draw the given part memory cell using MIRROR and copy.

PART MEMORY CELL
(drawn at 0.69 full size)

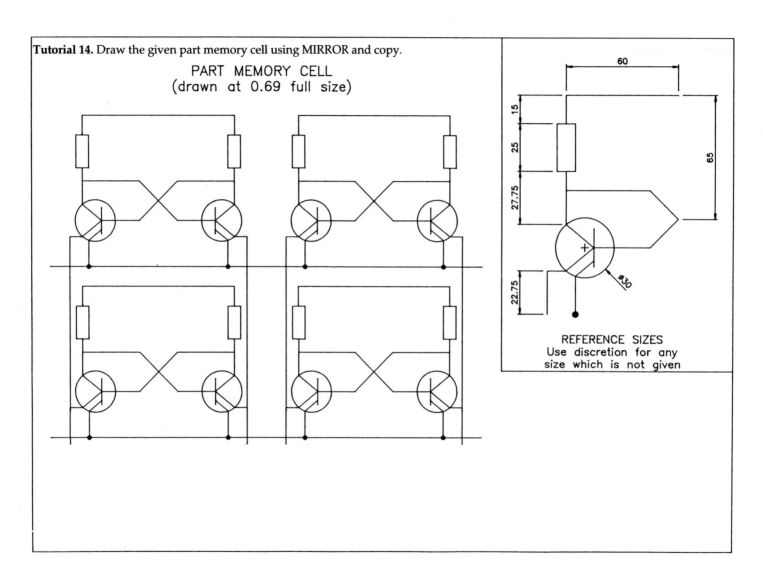

REFERENCE SIZES
Use discretion for any
size which is not given

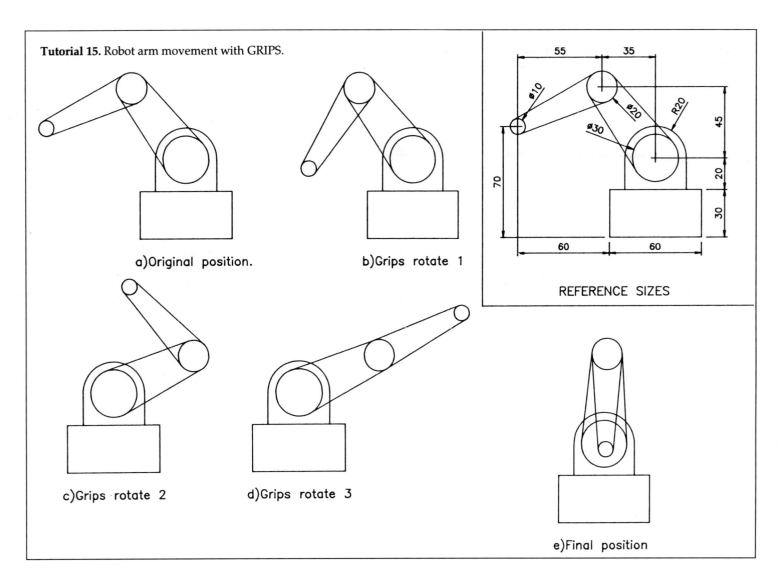

Tutorial 15. Robot arm movement with GRIPS.

a)Original position.

b)Grips rotate 1

c)Grips rotate 2

d)Grips rotate 3

REFERENCE SIZES

e)Final position

Tutorial 16. Draw the cover plate full size as shown. Add the hatching. Also add the text and all dimentions. Use layers appropriately.

HINTS
1.MIRROR command
2.Hatch with :
   U,45,3,N
3.TRACE layer method

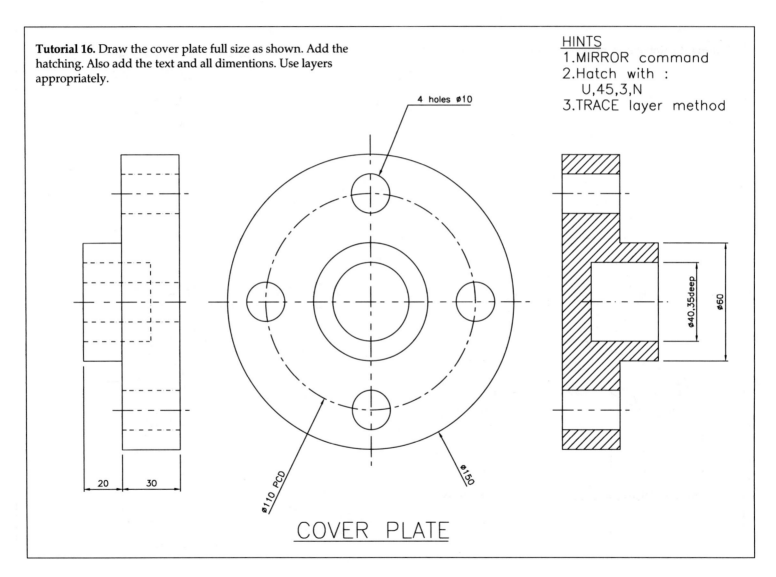

4 holes ⌀10

⌀40,35deep

⌀60

20   30

⌀110 PCD

⌀150

COVER PLATE

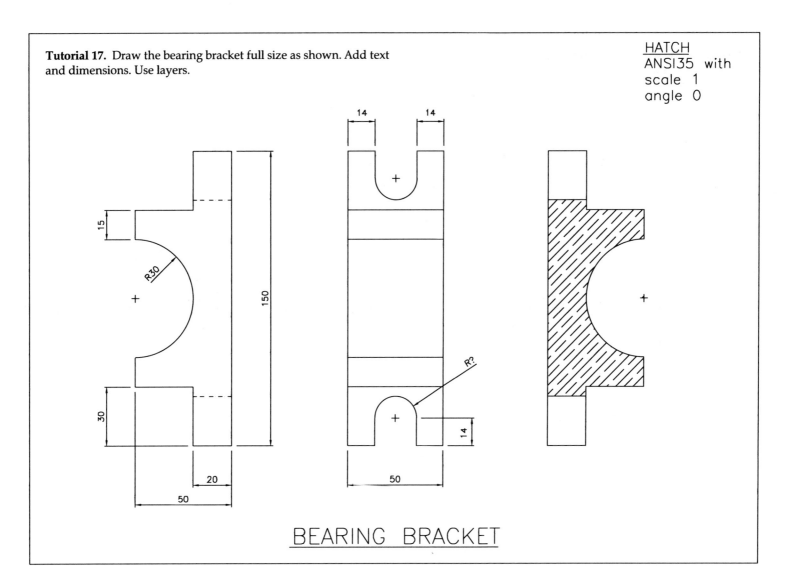

Tutorial 17. Draw the bearing bracket full size as shown. Add text and dimensions. Use layers.

BEARING BRACKET

Tutorial 18. Draw full size, adding all hatching, text and dimensions.

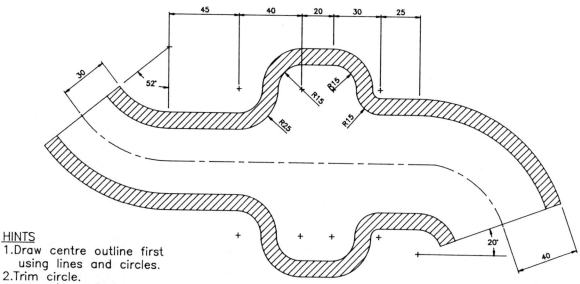

HINTS
1.Draw centre outline first
   using lines and circles.
2.Trim circle.
3.Offset 'inward' by 10.
4.Mirror central section.
5.Add the arcs.
6,Hatch can be achieved
   by selecting the lines
   and arcs.
7.Dimensioning takes some thought?

STEAM EXPANSION BOX
Material : Mild Steel
Thickness : 10mm

Tutorial 19. Draw full size adding all text and dimensions. Use layers.

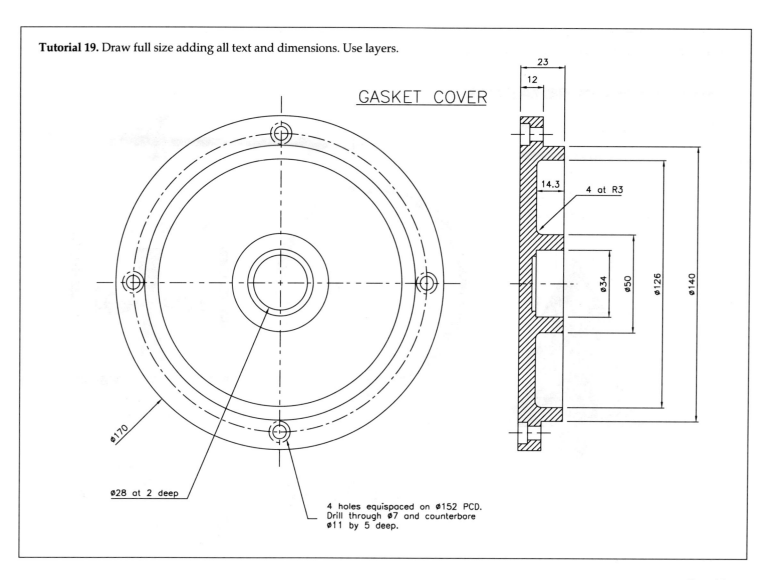

GASKET COVER

23

12

14.3

4 at R3

Ø34

Ø50

Ø126

Ø140

Ø170

Ø28 at 2 deep

4 holes equispaced on Ø152 PCD.
Drill through Ø7 and counterbore
Ø11 by 5 deep.

Tutorial 20. Draw the shapes using the polyline command.

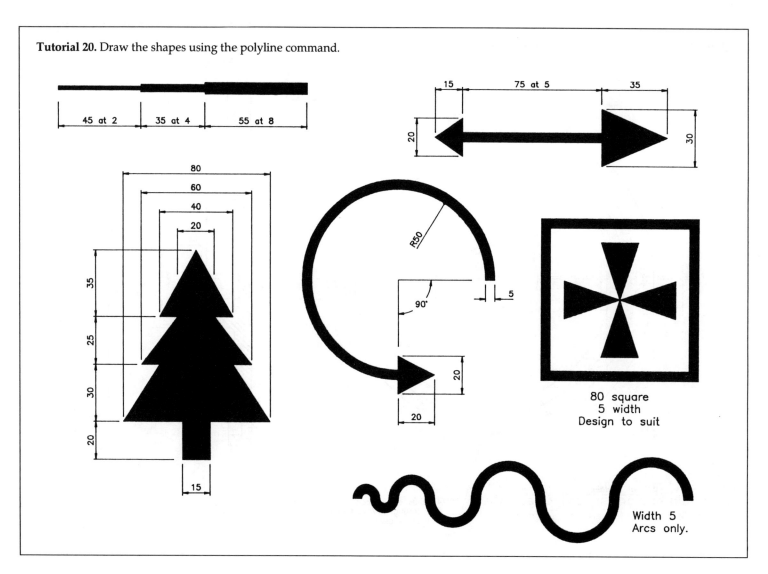

45 at 2   35 at 4   55 at 8

15   75 at 5   35

20   30

80
60
40
20

35

25

30

20

15

R50

90°

5

20

20

80 square
5 width
Design to suit

Width 5
Arcs only.

Tutorial 21. Draw and dimension the component as shown.

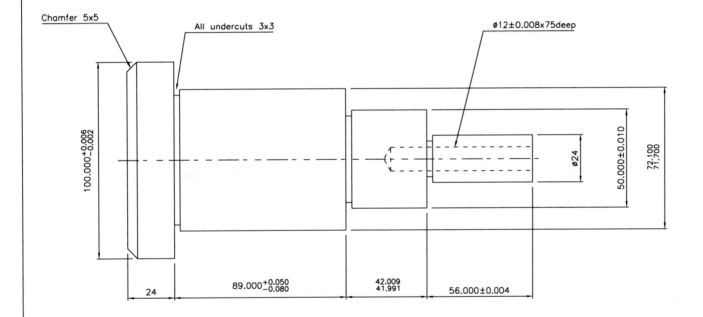

HINTS
<u>HINTS</u>
1. OFFSET and TRIM will assist with the outline
2. Use dimension styles to set the variance
   and limits — I used 7 styles?
3. Use LEADER with CONTROL CODES for the ø12 dimension.

Tutorial 22. Draw full size and add all text and dimensions.
Use layers correctly.
Set dimension styles.

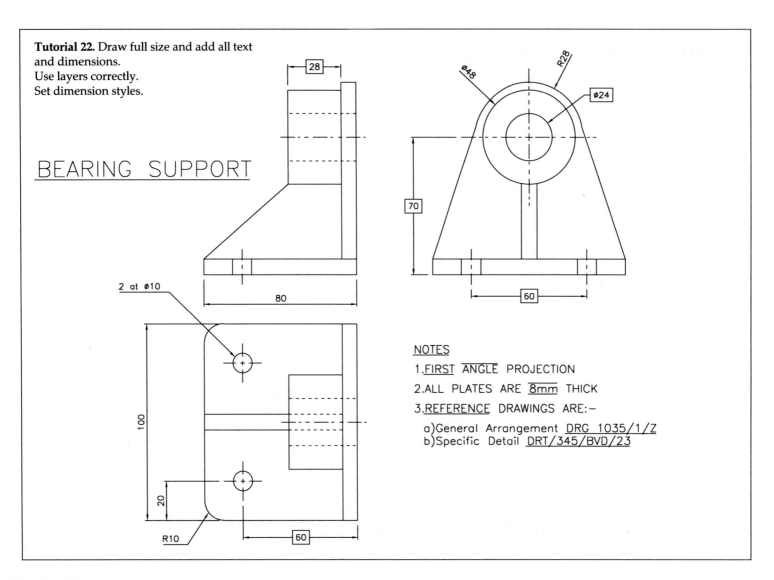

BEARING SUPPORT

28

Ø48

R28

Ø24

70

60

2 at Ø10

80

100

20

R10

60

NOTES

1.<u>FIRST</u> <u>ANGLE</u> PROJECTION

2.ALL PLATES ARE <u>8mm</u> THICK

3.<u>REFERENCE</u> DRAWINGS ARE:-

a)General Arrangement <u>DRG 1035/1/Z</u>
b)Specific Detail <u>DRT/345/BVD/23</u>

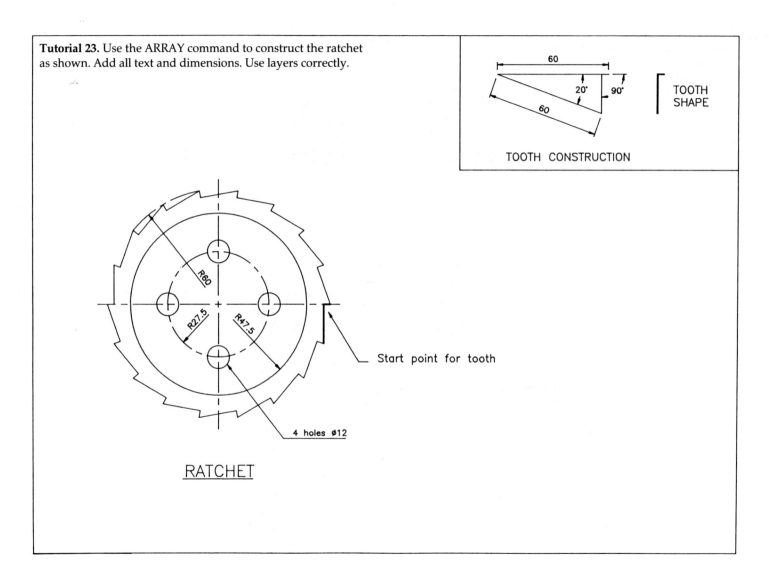

Tutorial 23. Use the ARRAY command to construct the ratchet as shown. Add all text and dimensions. Use layers correctly.

60

20° 90°

60

TOOTH SHAPE

TOOTH CONSTRUCTION

R80

R27.5

R47.5

Start point for tooth

4 holes ⌀12

RATCHET

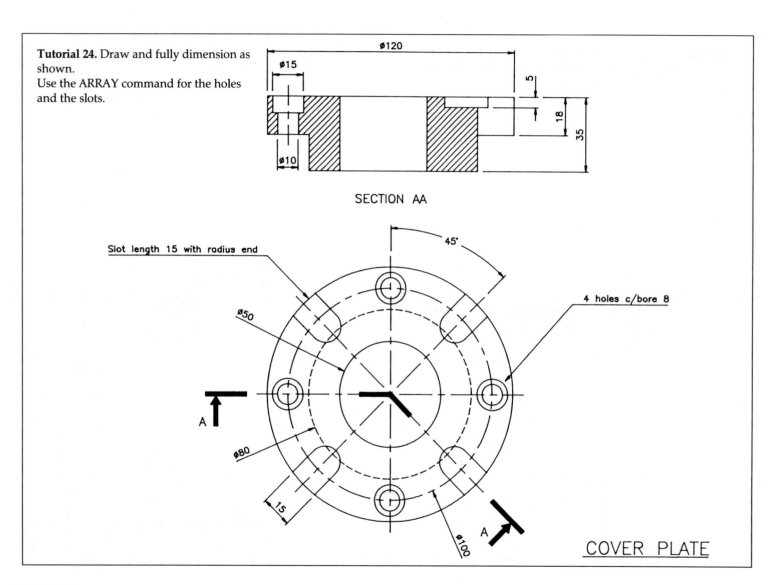

Tutorial 24. Draw and fully dimension as shown.

Use the ARRAY command for the holes and the slots.

ø120

ø15

5

18

35

ø10

SECTION AA

Slot length 15 with radius end

45°

4 holes c/bore 8

ø50

A

ø80

15

A

ø100

COVER PLATE

Tutorial 25. Draw the bulb to the sizes given and then copy it to another point on the screen. Scale the copied bulb by 0.5 and add the text. Try and dimension the original bulb.

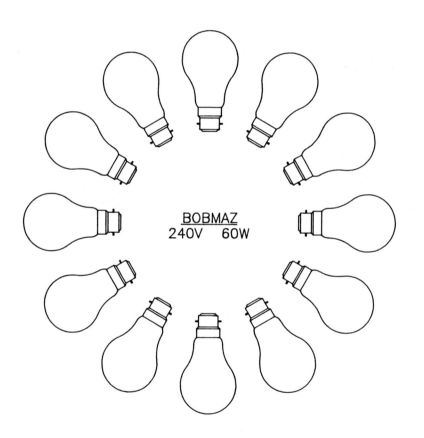

BOBMAZ
240V   60W

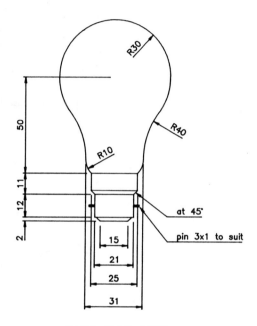

BASIC BULB SIZES

HINTS

1. Draw the straight line part first.
2. OFFSET will help with this.
3. Position the R30 radius centre. — OFFSET again?
4. Draw the R40 arcs as TTR circles then TRIM.
5. The R10 arcs are tricky!!!
6. Array centre is at your discretion.

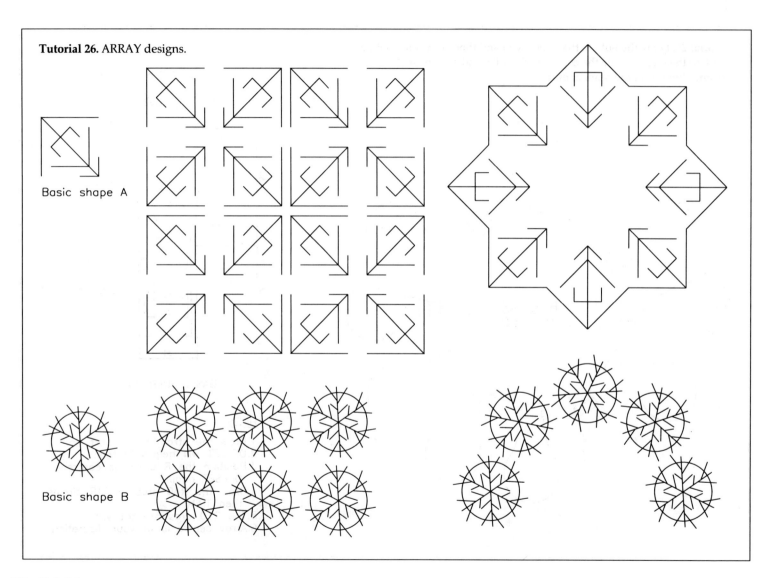

Tutorial 26. ARRAY designs.

Basic shape A

Basic shape B

Tutorial 27. Use the ARRAY/CHANGE method to draw the clock face and speedometer shown.
Sizes not given are at your discretion.

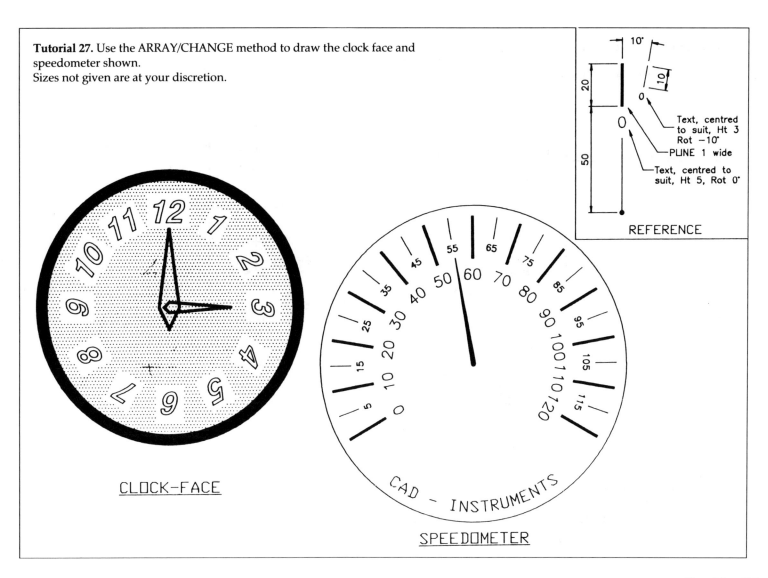

CLOCK-FACE

SPEEDOMETER

REFERENCE

Text, centred to suit, Ht 3 Rot −10°

PLINE 1 wide

Text, centred to suit, Ht 5, Rot 0°

CAD - INSTRUMENTS

Tutorial 28a. 1. Draw the shapes to the sizes given.
2. Make blocks of each size with the suggested names.
3. Proceed to Tutorial 28b.

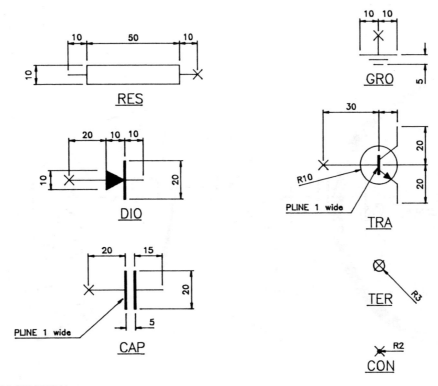

NOTES
1. DO NOT DIMENSION
2. The insertion point (X) is a suggestion only.
3. Use your discretion for sizes not given.

Tutorial 28b. Using the blocks created from Tutorial 28a, construct the given circuit. Add all text.

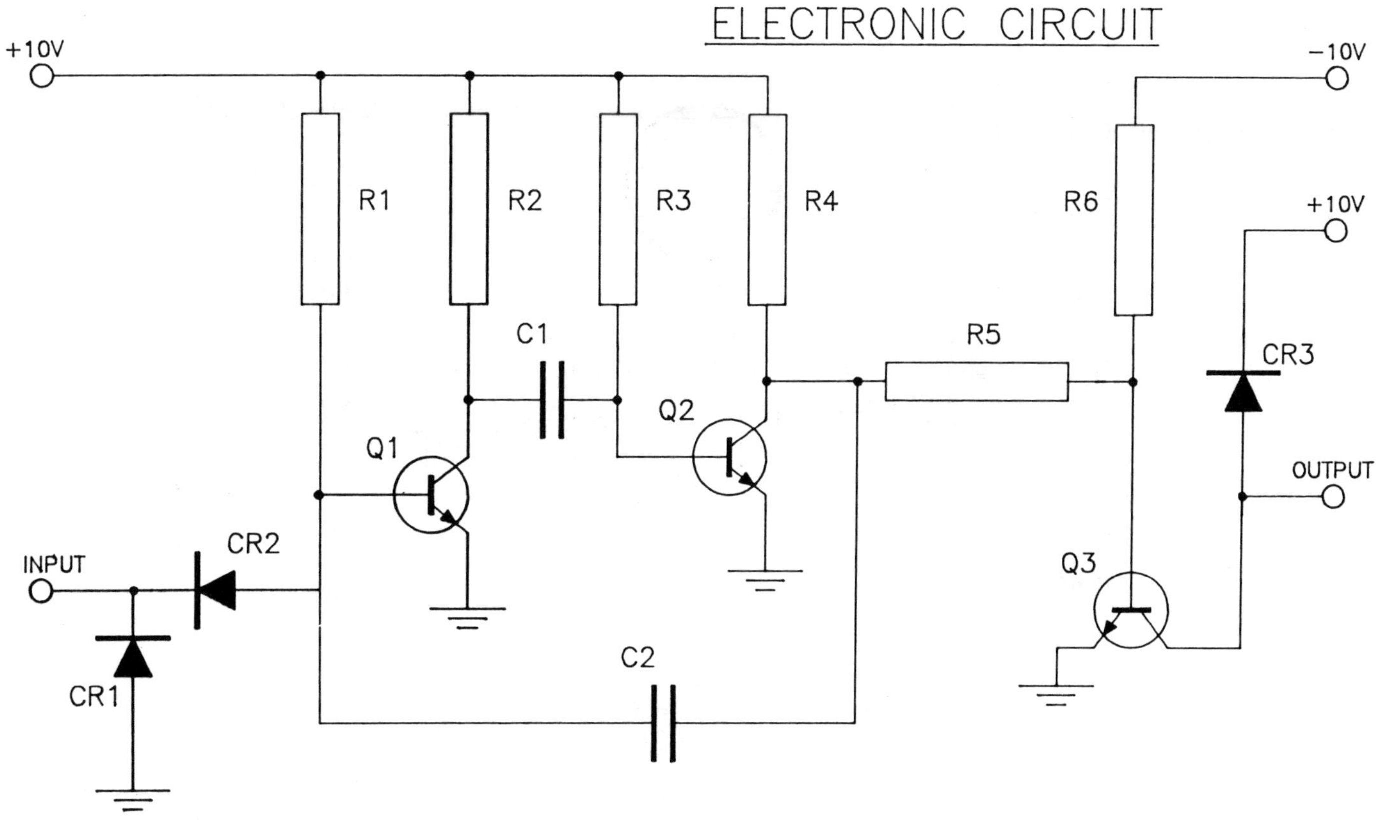

ELECTRONIC CIRCUIT

+10V
−10V
R1   R2   R3   R4   R6   +10V
C1   R5   CR3
Q2
Q1   OUTPUT
CR2   Q3
INPUT   C2
CR1

NOTE: All blocks are inserted full size, but the rotation angle has to be determined.

Tutorial 29a. Using the sizes as reference draw the given shapes and make blocks of each. The names are suggestions only. Proceed to Tutorial 31b.

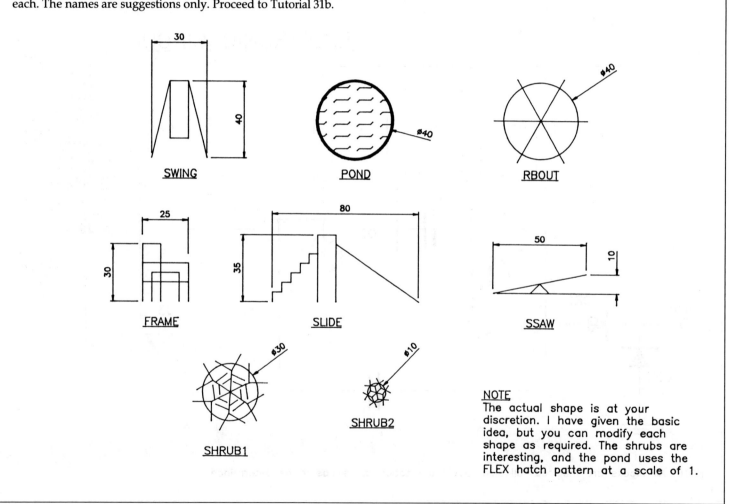

NOTE
The actual shape is at your discretion. I have given the basic idea, but you can modify each shape as required. The shrubs are interesting, and the pond uses the FLEX hatch pattern at a scale of 1.

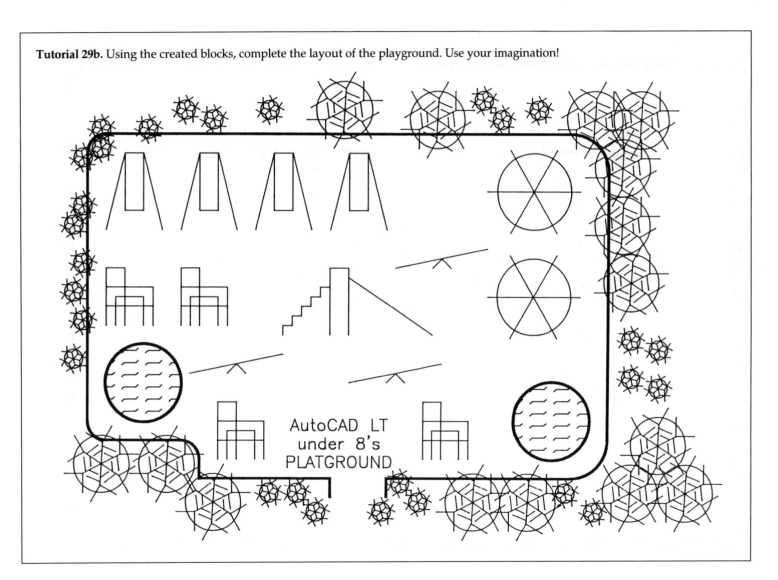

Tutorial 29b. Using the created blocks, complete the layout of the playground. Use your imagination!

AutoCAD LT
under 8's
PLATGROUND

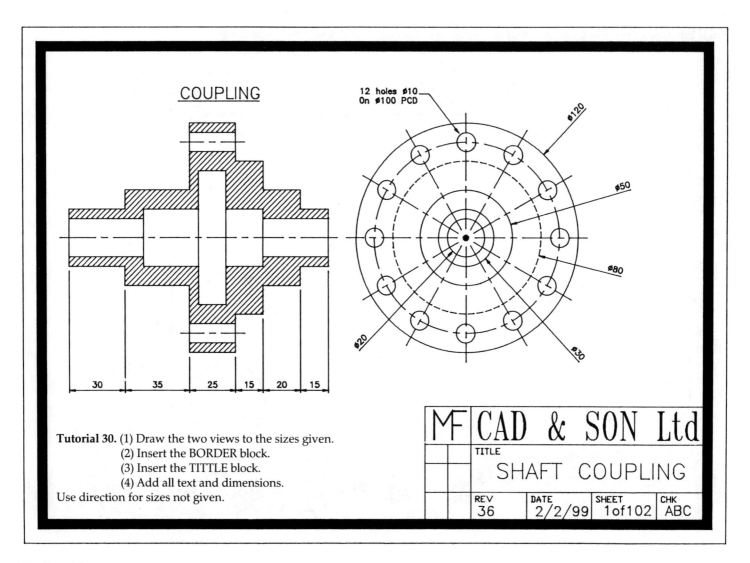

COUPLING

12 holes ⌀10
On ⌀100 PCD

⌀120

⌀50

⌀80

⌀20

⌀30

30 | 35 | 25 | 15 | 20 | 15

Tutorial 30. (1) Draw the two views to the sizes given.
        (2) Insert the BORDER block.
        (3) Insert the TITTLE block.
        (4) Add all text and dimensions.
Use direction for sizes not given.

MF CAD & SON Ltd

TITLE
SHAFT COUPLING

REV	DATE	SHEET	CHK
36	2/2/99	1of102	ABC

Tutorial 31. Isometric activity.

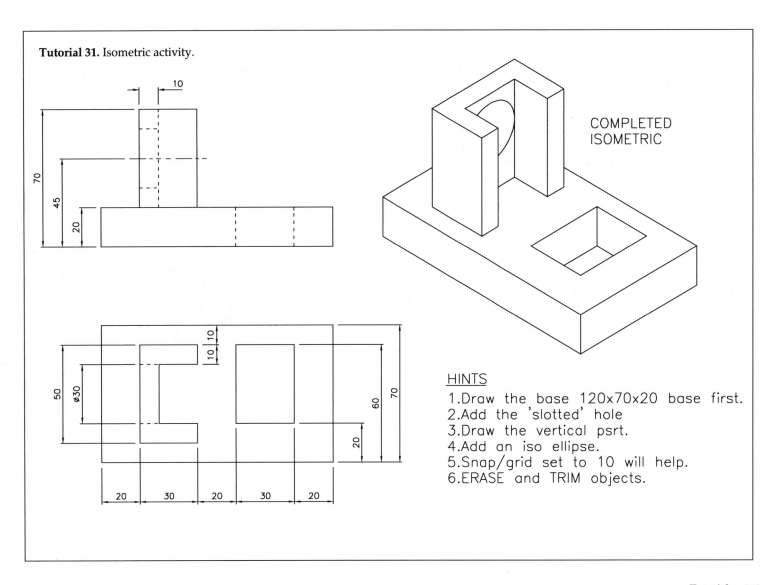

COMPLETED
ISOMETRIC

10

70

45

20

50

ø30

10 10

60

70

20

20   30   20   30   20

HINTS
1.Draw the base 120x70x20 base first.
2.Add the 'slotted' hole
3.Draw the vertical psrt.
4.Add an iso ellipse.
5.Snap/grid set to 10 will help.
6.ERASE and TRIM objects.

		ELEV	THICK	COLOUR
Level 1	Circle	0	40	RED
Level 2	Square	40	20	BLUE
Level 3	Circle	60	100	YELLOW
Level 4	Square	160	20	GREEN

Viewpoint at 280°, 30° drawn with HIDE.

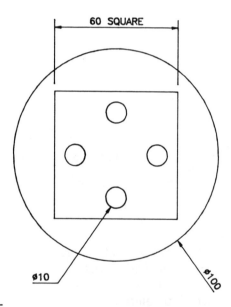

60 SQUARE

ø10

ø100

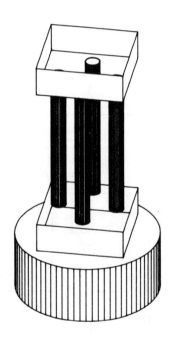

NOTE

1. Circle centre at point (130,130)
2. Lower LH corner of square at point (100,100)
3. Lowest ø10 circle, centre at point (130,110)
4. ø10 circle polar arrayed about (130,130) for four items.

Tutorial 32. Extruded component.

Index